COMMON SECURITY
AND CIVIL SOCIETY IN AFRICA

Edited by

Lennart Wohlgemuth
Samantha Gibson
Stephan Klasen
Emma Rothschild

NORDISKA AFRIKAINSTITUTET 1999

The papers in this volume were presented at a conference, *Beyond the War of Images: Towards Common Security and New Partnership with Africa*, held in Stockholm in November 1997. The conference was organised by the Nordic Africa Institute and the Common Security Forum, with the support of the Swedish Ministry for Foreign Affairs and the John D. and Catherine C. MacArthur Foundation.

This book is published with support from the Swedish Ministry for Foreign Affairs.

Cover: Alicja Grenberger

© the authors and Nordiska Afrikainstitutet, 1999

ISBN 91-7106-450-8

Printed in Sweden by Elanders Gotab, Stockholm 1999

Contents

Preface

Emma Rothschild and Lennart Wohlgemuth

This book is the outcome of a conference on common security and civil society in Africa, held in Stockholm in November 1997, and organised jointly by the Nordic Africa Institute in Uppsala and the Common Security Forum, based at the Centre for History and Economics, King's College, Cambridge, and the Harvard Center for Population and Development Studies. The Common Security Forum is an international network of academics and policy-makers, which developed out of the work of the Palme Commission on Disarmament and Security Issues, and which has been concerned with political, economic and social conceptions of security. The two African members of the Palme Commission, Olusegun Obasanjo—who was imprisoned in Nigeria at the time of the November 1997 conference—and Salim A. Salim, played a major role in the initial development of the concept of common security, as applied both to Europe and to Africa. Thabo Mbeki, who participated in the work of the Palme Commission in the mid-1980s, outlined a future of common security in southern Africa. Like these three statesmen, the papers presented here seek to go 'beyond the war of images', to imagine a different and more secure future.

The idea that security is to be achieved by cooperation more than by confrontation, and that it is an economic and social as well as a military condition, has been a commonplace of international politics for some 20 years. The geometry of common or extended security is complex. But it usually involves an extension of the domain of security (to the security of individuals and groups as well as of nations), of the sources of security (international, local and non-governmental organisations, as well as national governments), and of the characteristics of security (economic, social, political, environmental, and human, as well as military). Among these diverse kinds of security, it is political security which has come into particular prominence at the end of the 1990s, most strikingly in Africa.

Political security, in the sense of legal and political institutions such that individuals feel secure both in their individual rights and in the development of political culture, has come to be seen as the foundation of all other kinds of security. Democratic institutions, together with education and the social market economy, are at the centre of the Partnership Africa programme, which was discussed extensively at the November 1997 conference, and which has formed the basis for subsequent Swedish development co-operation in Africa. The concept of a partnership for development has indeed become a continuing theme of international development policies. Legal institutions and capacities are seen as the condition for economic growth and economic security. Effective government institutions are seen as essential to the improvement in public health, which is a condition for human security. Effective local, national and international cooperation is seen as essential for environmental security. Political institutions are seen, in Africa as in other regions, as the only effective means of preventing violent conflict, both within and between nations. A political culture which makes possible the non-violent conduct of conflicts is seen, even more than conventional 'conflict prevention', as the source of lasting security. The establishment (or re-establishment) of the rule of law is seen as the best security that violent conflicts, once 'resolved', do not recur.

The papers presented in this volume are concerned with five major themes. They pose many questions; some of the answers suggested in the course of the conference are summarised in the introductory chapter by Samantha Gibson. The first theme is *economic and social change*. Has economic development—especially in the rapidly growing cities of West and Southern Africa—led to changes in political culture and organisation? Does such political change in turn make violent conflict less likely? What are the linkages between economic and political reform, and how are these reflected in multilateral and bilateral policies? How has urbanisation influenced economic diversification and political organisation? What is the pattern of economic and social inequality, including inequality in health, both within and across African countries? To what extent do differing patterns of demographic change influence inequality and development?

The second theme is *the prevention of violent conflict*. Common security is about political cooperation to prevent conflict (or to make it likely, at least, that conflicts will take a peaceful form). What does such cooperation involve in Africa? Can the incipient organisations for conflict prevention, especially in eastern and southern Africa, contribute to a new international politics? How should regional and local mediation groups be supported by international policies? What is the role of non-African countries and international organisations in peace-keeping and conflict prevention? Should post-conflict reconstruction be seen as an integral part of conflict prevention? Is there a role for international organisations in domestic and local policies to prevent violent conflict, including constitutional reform, support for the police and judiciary, and efforts to reduce urban violence?

The third theme is *the causes of conflict*. The rhetoric of the post Cold War period suggests that the causes of war and violence are to be found not in international politics but in such supposedly new tendencies as environmental stress, rapid population growth, or ethnic enmity. How is this rhetoric to be evaluated in relation to Africa? There are large concentrations of refugees in several parts of Africa. Is it reasonable to see this as a source of future conflict, and if so, what policies might be appropriate? Can future environmental conflicts be anticipated, for example over major investment projects, or over competition for land and water, and if so, what might be done to make it likely that such conflicts will be relatively peaceful? Can the introduction of more innovative ways of managing boundaries contribute to political stability? How important, as causes of conflict, are arms transfers to African countries, trade in the existing stock of arms, and the production and distribution of major and minor weapons?

The fourth theme is *political security*. Governance and civil society are now seen as central to political culture. How does violent conflict, or daily political violence, influence politics? How important is a relatively free press, and a culture of government and opposition? Are new information technologies likely to have a major influence on politics in poor rural communities? How much has the decline in university education affected politics in several African countries? Does the growth of NGOs strengthen or weaken political culture? Is there a role for new judicial institutions, on an African but supra-national basis, for example in relation to human rights? What are the relationships—which Kwame Anthony Appiah explores in an essay in the present volume—between different strands in African political thought and the supposedly universal politics of cosmopolitan liberal democracy?

The fifth theme is *the international politics of development partnership*. The prospects for common security in Africa pose difficult questions for international, as well as for African politics. The continuing discussion of relations between 'humanitarian'/ 'emergency' and 'long-term' policies shows how overwhelming and inconsistent are the demands now made on international institutions in Africa. Does the pronounced recent tendency towards 'new' conditionalities (for example in relation to governance, the environment, women's rights, policies against corruption) serve to weaken domestic political processes? Are such conditionalities consistent with a dialogue-centred programme? Have they had the effect of reducing African political 'capacities', including civil service institutions? How does the tendency to emphasise civil society and NGOs in development programmes affect African states? To what extent have international policies for imposing reductions in government expenditure also harmed African states, and thus African politics? Is public expenditure, for example on education, public health, social security and the civil service, simply too low? Is a more 'equal' Africa one which should expect a continuing reduction in resource flows for 'development cooperation' or 'partnership'? If there is more equal dialogue between Africans and bilateral or multilateral partners, does that mean that the opinions of Africans will have more influence on other countries' policies? Is there—to return to one of the central questions for the Common Security Forum—an international political society?

The organisers of the conference are most grateful to the Swedish Ministry for Foreign Affairs for their generous support, and to Mats Karlsson, Jan Cedergren and Anders Bjurner for their substantive contributions throughout the project. We would also like to thank Adebayo Olukoshi and Kajsa Övergaard in Uppsala, Michaela Wilhelmsson in Stockholm, and Stephan Klasen, Asha Patel and Noala Skinner in Cambridge, for their help in arranging the meeting, and Samantha Gibson, Pratik Kanjilal, and Inga Huld Markan for editorial help. We are grateful to all the participants in the meeting, and to all the contributors to this volume.

Beyond the War of Images: Towards Common Security and New Partnership with Africa

Samantha Gibson

Summary of the Common Security Forum Annual Policy Forum Meeting on Africa

The Common Security Forum held its annual meeting in Stockholm 17–18 November. The meeting was jointly organised with the Nordic Africa Institute of Uppsala, with the support of the Swedish Foreign Ministry. The Common Security Forum is an international network of researchers and policy makers concerned with security broadly defined, including its environmental, military, economic and political dimensions. The Forum is co-ordinated at the University of Cambridge and Harvard University, with affiliated centres in Russia, Japan, India, Norway, and South Africa.

This year's Forum focused on common security and civil society in Africa. Participants were researchers and policy makers from Africa, Asia, Europe and North America, and included Pierre Schori, Mats Karlsson and Gun-Britt Andersson from the Swedish Ministry for Foreign Affairs, Carl Tham of the Swedish Ministry of Education and Research, Adebayo Adekanye from the University of Ibadan, Kwame Anthony Appiah of Harvard University, Catherine Cissé of the War Crimes Tribunal in the Hague, Yusuke Dan from Tokai University, John Grimond from *The Economist*, Ruth Iyob from the University of Missouri, Mary Kaldor from the University of Sussex, Anthony Lewis from *The New York Times*, Patrick Molutsi from the University of Botswana, Kirsti Lintonen from the Finnish Foreign Ministry, Callisto Madavo from the World Bank, Thandika Mkandawire of the Centre for Development Research in Copenhagen, Ahmedou Ould-Abdallah from the Global Coalition for Africa, Olara Otunnu from the International Peace Academy, Alassane Ouattara of the International Monetary Fund, Lisbeth Palme of UNICEF Sweden, and Bengt Säve-Söderbergh from IDEA.

The first day of the meeting focused on economic and political security in Africa. In contrast to common media images of a continent ravaged by violent conflict and economic crisis, a picture of a rapidly changing and diverse continent emerged. Some participants spoke of an 'African Renaissance', referring to recent progress many countries have made on economic, political, and social fronts. They pointed out that even in those countries still plagued by war, 'islands of civility' persisted. Most Forum participants agreed that the prospects for achieving political and economic security in Africa are more promising today than they were ten years ago.

Despite the general sense of 'Afro-optimism' that characterised most Forum discussions over the two days, the sessions dedicated to economic and political security identified several serious threats to the extension of security in these realms. Lingering debt burdens, deterioration of many national health care systems, AIDS, relatively new health problems like road fatalities and alcoholism, and high levels of inequality were all cited as threats to economic growth and human development. Potential threats to recent gains made in democratic consolidation and greater respect for human rights include high illiteracy rates, military forces independent of civilian control, weak opposition parties, unaccountable government institutions, low levels of human rights awareness, and an unequal distribution of arable land.

Discussions about how those threats might be addressed returned consistently to the importance of country- and community-specific *African* solutions, drawing from the positive experiences of the years since independence, as well as the recognition of the mistakes of the past. Forum participants argued forcefully that involvement on the part of the international community in the form of support for these 'home grown' solutions is welcome—often necessary—but 'one size fits all' remedies prescribed from outside are not. It was agreed that indigenous capacity for research and for analysis of African political, social and economic questions should be nurtured, and more efforts to support local scholarship that contributes to 'home grown' solutions should be undertaken. The overwhelming majority of international research activity today is the result of agendas set by the North. The 'enlightened self-interest' of both North and South would be served by tackling this 'scientific apartheid', expanding research agendas that include greater emphasis on analysis of African problems, and building the capacity for development of African solutions unique to African conditions.

Improvement of political security was seen to have greatest promise in support and development of strong, accountable institutions in both government and civil society, as well as in providing for constitutional and statutory laws that establish mechanisms for majority rule and protection of minority rights. If political security is ensured, and society's inevitable conflicts are to avoid violence as a primary means of resolving disputes, the resilience and responsiveness of local, national, and international political institutions is critical. A good deal of the discussion focused on the role of new political parties formed since the end of the Cold War, and the importance of African democrats providing their publics with a forum for lively national debate and meaningful political and economic choices. It was agreed that, whenever possible, Northern donors should contribute to democratic consolidation in those countries undergoing transitions from authoritarian rule. Strategic support to both civil society and the state were considered appropriate interventions for those international actors interested in supporting transitions to more democratic societies.

There was lively discussion about the potential value of cultural and political practices that are 'indigenous' or 'traditional' in many African societies, and how these practices might be built upon in order to strengthen democracies and foster democratic political cultures on the continent. Several participants cautioned against uncritical romanticisation of 'traditional African values', since this approach could potentially be used to undermine rights, including of women.

While most participants were quick to agree on general principles that underlie political security (including respect for human rights, accountable government, and relatively equitable distribution of wealth), there was less agreement on the extent to which there is a discrete set of 'good policies' that are fundamental to political and economic security in any country. The policies and principles embodied in structural adjustment programmes were a primary focus of this debate, with many participants objecting to the often autocratic manner in which African economic policies appeared to have been determined, particularly in the 1980s.

The second part of the day was dedicated to consideration of Sweden's new Partnership Africa policy. The new approach is based on an expanded definition of 'enlightened self-interest', shared goals and values, transparency of interests, explicit codes of conduct, mutual respect, and greater equality. The Partnership Africa policy advocates moving away from the aid-focused relationships of the past, to a more comprehensive approach to Swedish-African cooperation that would include stronger alliances in areas as diverse as the arts, trade, media, research, and the environment. The Partnership approach takes a long-term view of Swedish-African partnership, and pledges to 'listen to Africa', recognising that meaningful relationships and useful responses to complex issues can require commitments of as much as 20–30 years. The perception of Africans as *subjects*, not objects of development, is at the core of Partnership Africa.

Participants responded to Sweden's new approach to partnership with Africa with enthusiasm, and saw the Foreign Ministry's year-long consultation with African leaders in government, civil society, and academia as an important step towards improving the quality of North-South cooperation. Participants were interested in how the Partnership would proceed, stressing the importance of involving trade, military, and other policy components in order to ensure a consistent and unified approach to African development. Several discussants argued that the conception of equality underpinning the Partnership Africa project is a fundamental departure from much of the aid rhetoric of the past, and the move toward greater mutual respect and equality will be dependent in part upon improving Swedish people's perceptions of Africa. Participants challenged the 'disaster/disease/war/famine' image projected by much of the mainstream media, and considered how better coverage of African arts and culture might make Swedish perceptions of African life more accurate—thus helping to make the partnership more equal.

The session included animated discussion surrounding how Partnership Africa might be implemented: What new programmes and activities will be a part of strengthened African-Swedish relations? On what grounds will Sweden choose partnership countries, if they are to be selective, but at the same time not abandon needy people? What type of countries might be excluded from a Partnership approach? As Sweden looks to further develop relationships with Africa beyond the official aid programme, what dimensions of society will be prioritised in partnership activities? Participants were greatly encouraged by Sweden's commitment to 'listen to Africa', but then asked: Who is 'Africa'? They debated whether African views are most accurately expressed through the government, the legislature, or various civil society groups.

Discussions on the second day focused on the changing nature of war and violence in Africa, with particular emphasis on conflict prevention and post-conflict reconstruction. In the post-Cold War period, conflict in the context of decreasing state legitimacy is increasingly common. (This is in contrast to wartime scenarios of the past, when states mobilised people, resources, and strategies.) A strategy common to many of the new wars is reliance upon cheap, small arms; and control of territory through forced migration or genocide of minority populations. Today's conflicts claim more women and children as a proportion of total casualties than in any previous conflicts, and combatants tend to fund their efforts through looting and roadblocks, taxing humanitarian relief, and collecting remittances from sympathisers abroad. Variants of these new wars have posed threats to the political, economic, and social security of Africans in 20 out of 48 countries in sub-Saharan Africa since 1990.

Among the practical issues considered during the war and violence session were the need for greater coherence among international actors in African conflicts (including governments, international organisations, diplomats, the OAU, the media, and international NGOs), and the importance of a code of conduct governing these interventions. In related discussions, several participants raised the question of the international community's lack of accountability in complex emergencies, and argued that each of the United Nations humanitarian interventions should be independently investigated and evaluated. Other issues addressed during the session were the inherent difficulties in administering international justice after genocide—including protection of witnesses participating in UN trials, ensuring the cooperation of countries hosting fugitives from international law, and the tendency towards short-termism in international commitments to post-conflict situations. There was widespread agreement that both the underlying structural causes and the 'triggers' of violent conflict are not well understood, and that effective local and national political institutions are the cornerstone of lasting peace in any country.

The last session of the Forum focused on governance and civil society. Most discussants agreed that (contrary to the arguments of many leaders who violated human rights in the name of 'nation-building' or 'development') the most fundamental African values are rooted in tolerance, respect, and recognition of the inherent dignity of human beings. While participants recognised that African cultures are diverse, it was agreed that many 'village values' are consistent with the notion of universal human rights. They argued that the strength of community-centred values in many African cultures need not preclude respect for the rights of individuals in those societies.

Enlightenment-based principles that include provision for freedom of expression and the independent media, protection of individual rights, and universal access to basic health and education were widely acknowledged to be fundamental components of strong civil societies *and* states, and ultimately, common security. A better informed, mobilised citizenry will be a critical component to building 'developmentalist' democracies, and an alternative to what one participant termed 'choiceless' democracies. Forum participants agreed that defending and empowering vulnerable people, building a culture of tolerance and patience, and enhancing the legitimacy of political systems are pressing issues in the North, as well as in the emerging democracies of Africa.

A good deal of discussion centred on what role the international community should play in governance and state-civil society relations in Africa. Several participants noted that international actors tend to have influence only at the margins of complex processes like post-conflict reconstruction and transitions to democracy. While discussants agreed that donors and other outsiders cannot control domestic political processes in Africa, they observed the recent dramatic increase in development aid directed to the political sector. They debated the circumstances under which outside resources should be directed to organisations with explicitly political agendas, and cautioned against the sometimes indiscriminate manner in which donors supported so-called 'democracy promotion' groups without considering the extent to which some of these groups are or are not internally democratic or non-violent. At the same time, participants noted that even development aid that does *not* directly engage with the democracy and governance sector affects internal political dynamics in aid-recipient countries.

A theme recurring throughout the two days was the dynamic interaction between African states, civil society, and international actors in economic and political development. While there were different views and conflicting opinions, participants agreed that Africa can draw on its own rich history, cultures, experiences, and values—many of which are African expressions of universal norms—when resolving conflicts and promoting common security throughout the region.

Shifting Commitments and National Cohesion in African Countries*

Thandika Mkandawire

The relationship between the economy and security is complex. This is particularly the case in Africa, where many processes simultaneously impinge on security. The matter is rendered even more complex by the fact that the economy's impact on security is mediated by state-societal relations; identical economic conditions can engender totally different social and political consequences. It is also difficult to relate the economy to security without being overly deterministic. Given the high correlation between conflict and poor economic performance, it is tempting to assert a simple causal relationship by falling back on a reductionist position where one variable bears the full explanatory burden even when the evidence points to other permissive conditions for conflict. With all these caveats in mind, I will proceed to highlight economic matters that influence common security in Africa. I therefore run the risk of falling victim to an economic determinism that reduces all current crises to an economic crisis.

For a paper on economic matters, I may seem to unduly stress the ideological context of policy-making. This is deliberate for a number of reasons:

a) policy-making is inherently a political affair, despite attempts by international technocracies to 'depoliticise' it;

b) every nation needs an ideological as well as material underpinning to ensure social connectedness and a collective sense of purpose;

c) it is probably the case that post-colonial situations are more demanding with regard to national ideology than the situation faced by the emerging nation-states in Western Europe in the eighteenth and nineteenth centuries;

d) the policy-making emphasis connects economic policy to civil society, the arena where ideological debates and struggles over the definition of strategies and trajectories of national development and social transformation take place; and finally and most significantly,

---

* The author would like to thank Yusuf Bangura, Peter Gibbon and Ebrima Sall for comments on the paper. The usual caveats about responsibility hold.

e) policy commitments signal ideological inclinations.

The point is that when we consider what economic policy contributes to national and regional security, we have to bear in mind that those ideas that seek to bind people to some semblance of a shared project, or that constitute what Hirschman calls 'developmental conspiracies', will be decisive in mapping the course of events in Africa. Any discourse on the economy and security must, therefore, factor them into the national purpose that the economy and security are supposed to serve. It is part of the argument of this paper that the erosion of nationalist ideals and their being rendered incoherent by both their mischievous use in power games and the recalcitrant demands of the global economy are creating an ideological-moral vacuum that is leaving African politics unanchored and therefore potentially flammable.

The economy impacts on security through two channels: through its own 'spontaneous' workings and through the actions of those who shape it. To the extent that no society today practises *laissez faire*, it is the latter channel that shapes the interaction between the economy and problems of security. In the case of Africa in the last 30 years, three central preoccupations have profoundly shaped the behaviour of key actors and their perceived imperatives with respect to the economy and society. The first was the nationalist preoccupation with the definition and constitution of a nation through a process of what was commonly known as 'nation-building'. The second was achieving 'development', understood as economic growth, structural change and social progress. The third and the more recent preoccupation, lasting close to two decades now, has been 'structural adjustment'. I shall argue that shifting commitments by the African governments are part of the African security problem today. More specifically, displacement of the first two preoccupations by adjustment has led to a shift in commitments and has produced a discursive and policy framework that has left policy-making rudderless. This lack of consistency is contributing to the erosion of national cohesion and increasing conflict. I further argue that we have to bring back to centre stage the concerns of nation-building and development if discussions on peace and security are to have any meaning for the majority of Africans. In this second round, democracy must be the guiding principle.

Nationalism, nation-building and the national economy

Despite the many years of predictions of its demise, nationalism has profoundly affected debates on development policy. And even today in its beleaguered state it continues to influence perceptions of the 'national interest', the sense of national cohesion and the measure of acceptable or non-acceptable foreign interventions in African economic policy-making and economies. Nationalism is, of course, never the same everywhere and is never driven by the same forces. However, for post-colonial Africa, a central pre-occupation of nationalism, not rarely bordering on an obsession, was 'nation-building'. To appreciate the intensity of this preoccupation we have to think of the colonial legacy and the reflexive responses of nationalism to that legacy. I am aware that within and outside Africa reference to the colonial period when discussing current African problems is increasingly considered scapegoating. It is asserted that Africa's problems predate colonialism which, in terms of the *longue durée,* was a brief episode in African history and, therefore, cannot be made to bear so much of the burden of history. The primordial ties around which Africa's murderous conflicts are played out predate colonial rule, which may indeed have tamed such conflicts only for them to emerge again after its departure (Bayart, 1993). Besides, colonial rule has been dead for more than 30 years now and it surely must be up to Africans to deal with these conflicts.[1] I understand both positions. It is indeed true that some conflicts in Africa have a much longer history than colonial rule and are based on identities not 'invented' by the colonialists.[2] And there can be no doubt that African governments and elites have behaved in a manner that has made certain conflicts inevitable or have given new life to certain dormant conflicts.

This said, the colonial nexus matters if only because it defined the primary spatial markers within which the drama of nation-building is taking place, within which conflicts have been lived and within which solutions are now sought (see for instance Mamdani, 1996; Young, 1988). 'Decolonisation', with all the idiosyncratic interpretations given to it, has taken up considerable time and resources in much of Africa. This is because there were always at least two understandings of the process. There were the colonisers' deliberate 'last-stand' hegemonic strategies to give the 'natives' nothing more than 'flag independence'. On the other hand, there was the quest by the new elites not only for 'true independence' but also for hegemony in the emerging nation-states, a quest that accounts for the top-down notion of the 'nation-building' enterprise in Africa. In the economic sphere, the erstwhile

---

[1] For an excellent account of the attempts to disassociate the post-colonial crisis from the deficiencies of decolonisation see *Sovereigns, Quasi-Sovereigns and African* by the Guinean scholar Siba N'zatioula Grovogui (N'zatioula Grovogui, 1996).

'The related authoritative discourse considers post-colonial institutional deficiencies to be intrinsic to the constitution of the new states. This means that the organic shortcomings of the former colonies are independent of deliberate pre-independence strategies and tactics adopted by protagonists of decolonisation. The discourse also reflects the contention that the structures of the present international order limit the capacity of African nations to achieve self-determination and full sovereignty. It effectively minimises the stifling effects of the subjection of Third World entities to a global political, cultural, scientific and technological apparatus that guarantees Western hegemony within a hierarchical international order' (N'zatioula Grovogui, 1996).

[2] I have always thought that the literature that suggests that all our conflicting identities are merely colonial 'inventions' is demeaning of African people's sense of themselves. It has given colonial rule an omnipotence it never achieved in real life. This is, of course, not to deny that it manipulated certain differences and gave greater salience to certain hierarchies or conflicts.

colonialists sought to maintain all the economic structures that have normally been associated with 'neo-colonialism' while the nationalists sought to 'decolonise' the economy through nationalisation, indigenisation, diversification of external economic contacts (non-alliance), etc. These contradictory strategies have contributed to some of the problems that have doggedly stalked African policy-making since independence.

Perhaps the single most important legacy of colonial rule was the 'divide and rule' policies it practised up to the very end and even afterwards. Its importance lies not so much in the fact that it sowed disunity where unity had hitherto prevailed (which it did not) but that it conditioned the nationalist movements against anything that smacked of ethnic identities. The struggle for independence called for a unification of the diverse indigenous groups within the colony against the colonial master. While in many cases the first anti-colonial movements had clear ethnic identities, these were gradually submerged into single-issue nationalist movements that sought political independence. The creation of such movements was a testimony to the political acumen of the new elites that led them. It was, however, also a response to the colonialist machinations of 'divide and rule' and to the explicit insistence by the colonialists that they would not transfer power to divided societies. And so, while fomenting and exploiting division on the one hand, the colonialists demanded on the other that the nationalists demonstrate that they indeed represented one nation. The result was a conception by the nationalists of unity that abjured cultural and ethnic identities. The 'tribalist' became one of the most abhorred political figures in the African nationalist bestiary.

The post-colonial task of 'nation-building' and the continued imperialist exploitation of ethnic identities further reinforced the nationalist quest for unity. We should not forget the tremendous implications of the 'Katanga secessionist' movement on African nationalist understanding of ethnic claims and their relationships with imperialism. Katanga, more than anything else, convinced Africans that the erstwhile colonial masters, now in the guise of neo-colonialists, would manipulate ethnic identities to secure resource enclaves or to simply weaken the new nations. One consequence of all this was that the new governments mistook any manifestation of ethnic identity or articulation of ethnic claims as divisive and consequently treasonable. The thin line between unity and uniformity was erased as new governments moved towards one-party rule for fear that multi-party rule would simply degenerate into 'ethnic politics'. Authoritarian rule saw itself as the guardian of the nation against the divisive demons of tribalism. Here we see the source of a major blind spot in African politics that was to make even manageable conflicts so devastating. Africa, a continent of more than a thousand ethnic groups, was to adopt political postures and institutional arrangements that simply denied the existence of such diversity.

Politics being what it is, the public denial of ethnic pluralism did not prevent politicians from mobilising and manipulating ethnicity. The result was a schizophrenic polity in which the politics of 'ethnic balance' was the rule of the day, practised by people who denied ethnicity. Politicians were nationalist by day and tribalist by night.[3]

In terms of economic policy, such a quest for national unity gave further stimulus to centralising tendencies in making and implementing policy. The post-colonial governments were suspicious of decentralisation, which they feared might escalate into 'secessionism'—the *bête noire* of nationalist politics. Efforts by regions or ethnic groups towards self-improvement were either frowned upon as regionalist or tribalist, or were simply suppressed. One consequence of this centralising posture was that central authority was often weighed down by issues that could otherwise have been dealt with at local levels but which assumed a menacing character once elevated to national levels. It is probably the same fear of the centrifugal forces of the market that gave impetus to the much-bemoaned 'dirigiste' policies.

One issue that haunted the nationalist was the fissiparous and divisive implications of regional imbalance spawned by the development process. And so one of their obsession was to bring isolated or hitherto neglected areas into the national economy. Several instruments were used. These included regional distribution of development projects, pan-territorial pricing policies, quota-systems in the allocation of education, extensive rural health and education expansion, etc. Often, these policies made little economic sense and the subsequent fiscal and economic crises were to expose their high costs to society. They are now fashionably condemned as examples of wasteful patron-clientelism or rent-seeking. However, to judge them exclusively in economic terms is to completely miss the point, which was essentially political. In the context of new nations and extreme unevenness of development, spatial redistributive policies were absolutely essential. The abandonment of these projects has in many ways made certain groups or regions feel marginalised and has provided ground for the seeds of discontent that may be contributing to current conflicts in some countries.

In retrospect, regional imbalances could have partly been addressed through local initiatives. Decentralisation could not only have been a more efficacious way of dealing with some local-level problems, but would also have unburdened the state of a number of problems which, when handled at the central level, usually became a menace to national unity. It is of course easy to see all this now with the advantage of hindsight, especially given the

---

[3] This denial of ethnic identities was made worse by ideological positions that simply denied ethnicity as a social category. Thus in the more 'radical' African state 'class analysis' was to act as a prism that filtered away other social categories with devastating results. Frelimo's 'Kill the tribe to build the Nation' was in many ways to contribute to the success of RENAMO in mobilising large sections of Mozambique against the state or at least rendering them passive.

success of the nationalists themselves in creating a strong sense of nation-hood in their respective countries.

Another common feature of the nationalists' policy was 'national own-ership' of 'strategic sectors'. Colonialism in Africa effectively blocked the emergence of an indigenous capitalist class worthy of the name. One conse-quence of this was that national ownership invariably meant state owner-ship, irrespective of the ideological proclivities of the leadership. Nyerere stated the problem most clearly in the following terms:

> The question is not whether nationals control their economy but how they do so. The real ideological choice is between controlling through domestic private enterprise, or doing so through some state or other collective institution.

> But although this is an ideological choice it is extremely doubtful whether it is a practical choice for African nationalists. The pragmatist in Africa ... will find that the real choice is a different one. He will find that the choice is between foreign ownership on the one hand and local collective ownership on the other. For I do not think there is a free state in Africa where there is sufficient local capital, or a sufficient number of entrepreneurs for locally based capitalism to dominate the economy. Private investment in Africa means overwhelmingly foreign private investment (cited in Saul, 1973).

A second preoccupation of the nationalists with respect to ownership was that even within the nation itself property might fall into the 'wrong hands' or into the hands of one ethnic group, and thereby produce property rela-tions that could not be politically sustainable because they intensified re-gional, ethnic or racial imbalances. The current wave of privatisation seems totally insensitive to these concerns (Mkandawire, 1994b).

Developmentalism

A second legacy from colonialism was underdevelopment. On the eve of in-dependence, Africans found themselves with extremely underdeveloped economies. Political independence was therefore seen as a major instrument against the scourge of the 'unholy trinity of poverty, ignorance and disease', to use a phrase of the era. It was in this sense that Nkrumah used the 'Seek Political Freedom First and the Rest Shall Follow' call, not in the vulgar sense that political independence would solve everything. Consequently, after gaining independence, 'development' leading to industrialisation be-came the corollary and the material concomitant of national sovereignty.[4] It

---

[4] As in many other cases, it was characteristically Kwame Nkrumah who was to articulate the nationalist quest for development and industrialisation in its most uncompromising form when he wrote:

'Industry rather than agriculture is the means by which rapid improvement in Africa's living standards is possible. There are, however, imperial specialists and apologists who urge devel-oping countries to concentrate on agriculture and to leave industrialisation for some later time when their population is well-fed. The world's economic development, however, shows that it

became the rallying-cry of the new states. Indeed, 'development' became one of the sources of legitimacy for the new states. As formulated by Partha Chatterjee:

> Self-government consequently was legitimate because it represented the histori-cally necessary form of national development. The economic critique of colonial-ism, then, was the foundation from which a positive content was supplied to the independent national state: the new state represented the only legitimate form of exercise of power because it was a necessary condition for the development of the nation (1993:203).

It should be underscored that 'development' was quintessentially a nation-alist project. Different schools of thought have related to it differently. Seers (Seers, 1983) had a neat scheme for classifying attitudes towards and the content of nationalism that I reproduce below. While most nationalist movements could be placed in the lower left-hand quadrangle (holding their nations together by doses of populist rhetoric and policies), over the years other variants have emerged in the fascist direction (relying on brute force and xenophobia). It is also my view that what we are witnessing today is a shift from the various quadrangles to the upper right-hand quadrangle in which markets play a leading role and nationalist preoccupations are dis-missed. Consequently, I will only deal with the neoclassical view because of the importance of that perspective to current policy-making.

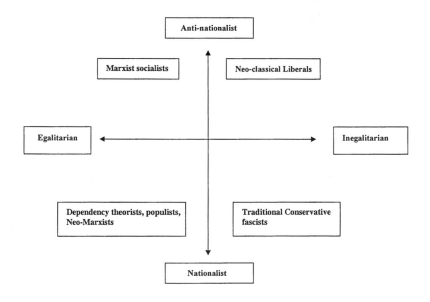

---

is only with advanced industrialisation that it has been possible to raise the nutritional level of the people by raising their levels of income' (Nkrumah, 1965).

Nationalism being from the realm of 'passions', to use Hirschman's word (1982), it has never fitted in well with the rational discourse of orthodox economics, which has usually been blamed for the poor performance of African economies, more specifically for interference with markets and property rights through nationalisation and indigenisation policies and through forced industrialisation.[5] Thus, for Harry Johnson, a leading neo-liberal economist who wrote extensively on nationalism, while nationalism appears as a 'driving force' responsible for efforts by less developed countries to accelerate their economic development by economic planning, it is also the 'major political influence responsible for the fact that many features of the policies, concept, and methods of economic development planning in such countries either do not make economic sense or would make economic sense only in certain specific and rather exceptional economic circumstances the actual presence of which no one has felt it necessary to establish by empirical economic research' (1967).[6] There is, of course, some irony in the fact that those who pose as value-free scientists should decry the interpersonal and intertemporal distributional preferences that nationalism may suggest.[7] A more empathetic and often paternalistic view is that given Africa's experience with capitalism under both slavery and colonial rule, Africans could not be expected to look favourably at capitalism and foreign domination. They were therefore likely to adopt nationalistic policies that sought alternatives to capitalism. As the colonial era receded in time, Africans would be less tied to nationalist projects and would, as they seem to be doing now, be less hostile to capitalism and to the presence of foreign capital.

This view of the relationship between nationalism and economic growth is too simplistic and one-sided. To be sure, there are many cases where scoundrels, seeking a last refuge in nationalism, have devastated economies through racial discrimination or the xenophobic expulsion of non-nationals.

---

[5] The most strident critics of nationalism and economic policy have been Bauer and Johnson (Bauer, 1981; Bauer, 1984; Johnson, 1967; Johnson, 1971).

[6] Johnson here tendentiously ignores the many economic arguments (economics of scale, 'infant industry', imperfect information) that justified on theoretical grounds a whole range of state interventionist policies (Krugman, 1992; Stiglitz, 1989; Taylor, 1983,) However even more tendentious is his assumption that while import substitution policies are nationalistic, export promotions ones, being market friendly, are driven by economic reason and not by such putatively irrational 'passions' as nationalism. This of course goes against the obvious association between nationalism and export-driven development strategies of the high performing Asian economies. The linchpin of the ideologies of these 'developmental states' was everywhere nationalism. (See Amsden, 1985; Fukui, 1992; Hawes and Liu, 1993; Jomo, 1996; Koo and Kim, 1992; Wade, 1991). The galvanising role of nationalism in economic development is, of course, not a new one. The argument by Alexander Hamilton and Frederick List for protectionist policies for USA and Germany respectively were informed by unbridled nationalism.

[7] Or as Penrose states:
'It is, of course, irrational of economists to label other people's preferences 'irrational' provided that these preferences are consistent and that their implications are appreciated by those expressing them. 'Psychic disutility of dominant foreign control should, of course, be a legitimate concern in any theory where the notion of 'community preferences' is respectable' (Penrose, 1974).

Nationalism may have encouraged economically costly Pharaonic projects that the leadership claimed to have enhanced the stature of the nation. Nationalism may also have contributed to senseless searches for autarkic 'self-sufficiency' in all kinds of activities, to adventuristic militarism, etc. But all this is only one side of the story. The other is that in the processes of development, nationalism can serve as a means of promoting and coping with development (Breuilly, 1982). History is replete with cases where nationalism has propelled economies towards high levels of accumulation. Nationalism has been used to impose enormous sacrifices on the citizenry to raise savings to attain 'self-sufficiency' in all kinds of things considered essential to national sovereignty (armaments, food, industry etc.). The 'irrationality' of nationalism has given utility to investments of great risk or long gestation that the market would be hard put to justify, given its 'myopic' vision. Indeed, as Felix notes, because of the 'leaps' that a late industrialiser must make, their investments will tend to violate market wisdom and so they 'must find some of their rationale and political support in prophetic, ideological visions of the long-run national interest' (Felix, 1977).

Nationalism provides an ideological rationale to the indigenous classes in their competition with foreign rivals. It guides policy choice by giving 'weights' to arguments in the nation's 'social welfare function' both in terms of interpersonal (national versus foreign) and intertemporal distribution (between generations) of costs and benefits. It often spawns new elites who may regard nationalism as a cohesive force 'providing identity and purpose' to the modernisers (Breuilly, 1982). The ruling class needs 'nationalism' for its own internal cohesion and discipline. And to the extent that the absence of elite consensus and the prevalence of elite conflicts have been the source of so much suffering, anything that brings about a modicum of discipline among the elites is worth considering.[8]

In the light of the dismal failure in the African countries, it is difficult to imagine that development was ever a serious item on the agenda of the post-colonial state. Thus Claude Ake states: 'The ideology of development was exploited as a means for reproducing political hegemony; it got limited attention and served hardly any purpose as a framework for economic transformation' (Ake, 1996). However, it is my view that for most of the first generation of African leaders 'development' was indeed a central preoccupation. By political ideology and social origins, most of the leaders were deeply committed to the eradication of poverty, as the parlance of the time put it. Indeed, in many countries the manifestos of nationalist movements explicitly identified poverty as one of the main scourges that the attainment of independence would address. The other two were ignorance and disease.

---

[8] African elites have spent considerable time trying to discipline other social classes and very little to discipline themselves. This applies to both political and economic affairs. They have sought privileges from governments or other classes with no reciprocal act on their behalf.

Together, they formed an 'unholy trinity' against which nationalist swords were drawn in the post-colonial era. And many policies and schemes such as community development, rural credit systems, adult literacy, health and education were instituted. As Lipton and Ravallion caution us, ' One should not confuse a belief in what were to become (with the benefit of hindsight) failed theories and policies with a lack of poverty-orientation in policy design' (1995:2359). Referring to the many schemes set up to address poverty, Lipton observes: 'Many such schemes were ill-conceived or ill-implemented; most, perhaps, were not incentive-compatible. But the post independence intellectual climate was explicitly sympathetic to the poor' (Lipton and Ravallion, 1995:2560). It is necessary to remind ourselves of these commitments at a time when cynicism and the triumphalism of ideologies of selfishness and greed would suggest that poverty alleviation is best left to competition and individual effort, and the devil take the hindmost.

The centrality of 'development' was such that it acquired the status of an ideology—which I call 'developmentalism'—that transcended or subsumed everything else. More pertinent for our paper, it held that human rights and democracy had to be sacrificed until African countries were developed. 'Democracy is a luxury we cannot afford,' was one of the many inanities uttered in the name of development. Academic treatises were written to provide a veneer of scientific respectability to such statements. The fear of the 'revolution of rising expectations' called for authoritarian governments that would steer the nation towards the difficult task of development unencumbered by the demands for instant gratification by myopic populations.

And so the prevalent understanding of the exigencies of both nationalism and developmentalism pushed African countries to forms of government that made the continent singularly incapable of dealing with its diversity. More significantly, the top-down and authoritarian manner of responding to the two imperatives led to a failure to devise political arrangements and institutions that could accommodate the diversity of African countries. Both the intellectual understanding of development at the time and the nationalist totalising tendencies produced statist policies that in many ways led to a failure to harness markets and added to the structural rigidities of African economies and polities.

We should also note that in states in which nationalism and developmentalism are central pillars of the dominant ideology, policy formulation usually has to walk the tightrope of the conflicting imperatives of accumulation and legitimation. It entails the avoidance of both legitimation and fiscal crises and reflects the different ways in which governments can maintain the consent of the people who are subjects of state power (through legitimacy enhancing 'social expenditures') while fostering the expansion of material production, through private or state accumulation. In societies torn by conflict or of high social mobilisation, pressures on the state to spend on public consumption will be unrelenting. This will inevitably lead to fiscal crisis as the state is forced into deficit spending and as it adopts policies that are not compatible with the stimulation of private capital.[9] Solutions to the fiscal crisis may lead not only to the abandonment of certain commitments but may force the nation-state to yield to foreign-imposed conditionalities, as has happened to many a state in Africa. Such policies may lead to the erosion of national sovereignty and to the public perception of the national government as merely an agent of foreign powers. We return to this point below.

Performance: A chequered record

In most cases, the nationalists were successful in kneading together the various ethnic groups into citizens of one country and in de-legitimising secessionist tendencies. Two positive consequences of this: there are hardly any interstate wars in Africa, nor are secessionist movements a major factor—at least not yet. The nationalists were also successful in launching African economies on some path of economic growth. The strategies of development adopted by most African countries have been labelled 'import-substitution industrialisation'. It basically involved state interventionist measures to encourage the establishment of industries to progressively substitute for certain manufactures. The conventional view is that such strategies were a complete failure and accounted for the inflexibility of African economies in the face of global changes. The record is different. As Figure 1 clearly shows, the much maligned and (misinterpreted) 'dirigiste' policies pursued by African states were associated with fairly rapid rates of growth. This growth took place across a whole range of countries with varying ideologies. It was also during this phase that many African countries witnessed the first attempts at industrialisation.

On the social front, they expanded social services dramatically, raising levels of school enrolment and lowering mortality rates considerably. Some of the most dramatic changes in school enrolment ratios in human history took place in Africa during this period.

There were, of course, problems with this path of growth. It remained heavily dependent on a limited range of exports for fuelling its industrialisation processes. Since revenue from trade played such an important role in the fiscus, the strategy left states with very narrow and unstable revenue bases and thus made African governments prone to fiscal crises that in turn led to the reversal of some of the post-colonial social gains. Contrary to comments by some of its strident critics, the strategies adopted by African countries were not autarkic as they were premised on 'inviting' foreign in-

---

[9] Note that some of the redistributive policies may result in investment in human capital that should benefit accumulation in the long-run. However, private investors may not consider such long-term externalities in their investment decisions and may simply see increased public expenditure as inflationary and therefore a threat to the future returns of their investment.

Figure 1. *Per capita income 1962–1994*

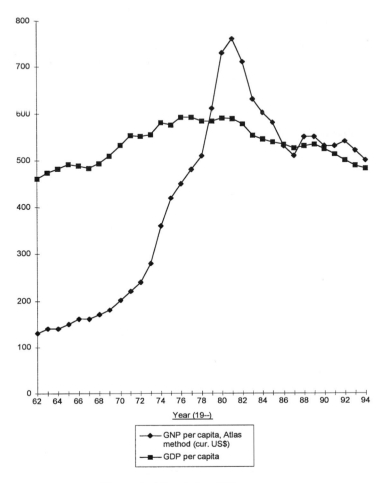

Source: Calculated from World Bank data diskettes.

vestment and on continued exports of raw materials to finance the imports of the necessary equipment and intermediate goods for capital accumulation and production. Few mechanisms for the mobilisation of domestic savings were put in place and savings in African nations remained far below those of Asian counterparts. The weakness of such strategies was to be dramatically exposed by the crisis of the mid-1970s, from which the continent has yet to recover. Such a narrow and unstable fiscal base did not provide the state with the wherewithal to provide for a minimum of its commitments even in normal times.[10]

---

[10] It is perhaps worth pointing out parenthetically that even for those countries whose revenues were secured by access to 'rents', such a structure of revenue had implications on the behaviour

The growth path generated high levels of inequality both socially and spatially, which was worsened by widespread corruption. Where social inequality overlapped with spatial and ethnic inequality, the seeds were sown for some of the conflicts that ravage Africa today.

These changes in the economy shaped the contours of modern-day civil societies. First, they led to accelerated urbanisation without matching employment creation, largely because of its relative capital intensity. The result was substantial increases in the informal sector. Thanks to the low levels of urbanisation during colonial rule, Africa remains the least urbanised continent even today, despite accelerated post-independence rates of urbanisation. Both urbanisation and relatively high levels of education produced 'civil societies' that are today the key political factors. There had always been controversy over the political colouring of this new civil society. The earlier literature on urbanisation and employment creation held the view that the process was leading to labour-market segmentation that would produce a 'labour aristocracy' and 'working poor' in the informal sector (Arrighi, 1973; ILO, 1972). Such a 'labour aristocracy' would tend to be part of the 'coalition' that pursued policies that excluded large sections of the population and would probably be uninterested in democracy, having entered into exclusionary corporatist arrangements with the state and capital. A more recent variant of the same argument, but of right-wing provenance, argues that the rent-seeking 'urban coalition' would seek to defend the policies that had led to the present crisis and would be opposed to democratisation, which would empower the rural masses. Although much has been written about the 'urban bias' of African politics, urban-rural conflict is not as salient as this literature suggests. The smallness of the urban population and the relatively low levels of urbanisation also meant that urban populations straddle the two geographical spaces, urban and rural, with the result that the politics of one easily spills over into that of the other. The point here is that the rural plight has much greater political salience in African urban politics than is allowed for by theories based on 'urban bias'. Such politics often take on a regionalist colouring.

Remarkably, for much of Africa, these pre-crisis years were relatively peaceful, at least when viewed from the vantage point of our bloodstained present. One should recall that the 'security' discourse of the time always contained the fear that rapid economic growth would unleash 'the revolu-

---

of the state that was inimical to the pursuit of national cohesion. In cases when the revenue accruing to the state is independent of domestic producers and the state does not have to negotiate with many and dispersed producers for its access to economic surplus, it is perfectly possible for the state to have all the necessary revenue even when the infrastructure outside the revenue producing enclave is falling apart due to conflict. This may partly explain the kind of state responses to conflict in Angola, Congo, Nigeria and the former Zaire. It is unimaginable that the plantation or estate classes in Côte d'Ivoire or Malawi could tolerate such a degradation of rural infrastructure for so long without urgently calling for peace. Things are more complicated when the adversaries of the state—the so-called 'warlords'—also have their own enclaves for revenue extraction, as UNITA's Savimbi has.

tions of rising expectations', which would trigger revolutionary action driven by the inequities associated with such growth.[11] As it turned out, the 'revolutionary pressures' did not bring down the walls of the national project. The Maoist vision of peasants marching on the beleaguered cities never materialised anywhere in Africa. It may be that this economic growth underpinned the tolerance of growing inequalities as a result of what Hirschman refers to as the 'tunnel effect', which produces gratification over advances by others on the expectation that one's turn is in the offing (1981). I would add that visible material and social progress, the lustre of nationalism and the persuasiveness of its argument that one was 'indigenising' hitherto exclusively foreign privileges blunted the divisive impact of growing inequity. The converse was that the economic slowdown would intensify conflicts over a diminishing national pie.

Crisis and adjustment years

African economies have been adjusting for close to 15 years now. Opinions differ as to whether the packages introduced by the Bretton Woods Institutions (BWI)[12] were indeed the only solutions for Africa. I have my own doubts (Mkandawire and Soludo, 1999).

There is, however, an emerging consensus, namely that whatever other problems structural adjustment programmes (SAPs) may have solved (inflation, balance of payments crises, disequilibria, and market distortions), they have not placed Africa on a sustainable path of development. First, they have failed to stimulate investment and even the most touted 'economic miracles' have produced anaemic growth rates in per capita income (Elbadawi et al., 1992; Engberg-Pedersen et al., 1996; Helleiner, 1994; Mkandawire and Soludo, 1999; Mosley et al., 1995; Mosley and Weeks, 1993; Ndulu and Elbadawi, 1996). Per capita income has declined steadily for most African countries during the last two decades. Africa is the only continent in which labour productivity in agriculture has declined, with the result that the continent is the only one whose per capita food availability has declined.

African economies are recovering somewhat. The IMF's estimates of GDP growth for 1996 and 1997–98 are 4.5 and 4–5 per cent respectively (IMF, 1997). As with all good news, many have rushed to proclaim paternity for these improved rates of growth. The BWIs are already claiming that the growth is the result of their policies. However, a closer look shows that

---

[11] The work of Huntington (Huntington, 1968) is the most cited in this respect but as Gendzier demonstrates these concerns were a major pillar of political development studies at least in the USA (Gendzier, 1985).

[12] The World Bank and the International Monetary Fund were established at an international conference in Bretton Woods, New Hampshire; thus, they are known as the 'Bretton Woods Institutions' or the 'Bretton Woods twins'.

growth can largely be attributed to buoyant external demand, higher commodity prices and improved terms of trade (an increase of 7.4 percentage
points during 1994–1996). Note, however, that investment rates remain per-
ilously low and 'lag well behind those in the more successful developing
countries' (IMF, 1997).

It should also be noted that, given the continent's levels of poverty and
demographics, these improvements in growth are still miserly and barely
cover population growth (IMF, 1997). Obviously, if these gains from 'commodity booms' are to lead to a sustainable rate of growth, economic policy
must move away from stabilisation and adjustment and take on once again
the issues of nation-building and economic development and all the tensions
and tough choices the pursuit of these dual objectives entails. 'Leaving to the
market' such portentous issues is plainly suicidal in the African context.

There has been an increase in the flow of foreign capital into Africa.
However, much of this is going into mining enclaves or speculative portfolio
investments. What we are witnessing is a revival of the monocultural primary export economies of yesteryear. Ghana is going back to the days of
gold and cocoa and Zambia back to copper. SAPs have failed to achieve
much export diversification of African economies. Instead, what we are
likely to see are new export enclaves, protected in the extreme by private
'security' companies like South Africa's Executive Outcomes.

Second, economic policy programmes have thus far failed to address
one major source of conflict in Africa—poverty and inequality—partly because, as BWIs themselves now readily admit, poverty alleviation was not a
central item on the adjustment agenda.[13] Even assuming, as the BWIs now
claim, that 'real adjustment only began in 1987',[14] Africa was the only continent in which the number of people whose income fell below the poverty
line of US$ 1 per person per day increased between 1987 and 1993—from 38
per cent to 39 per cent. Some 220 million people are income poor. It should
be recalled that, although the World Bank at times tries to argue on the basis
of first principles that adjustment has benefited the poor, it was a central
tenet of adjustment that adjusting countries could go through a 'vale of
tears' before reaching the promised land. What may not have been foreseen,
perhaps, was the breadth of the vale and the extent of the tears.

As for the urban working class, their living standards fell victim to the
process of making African industries competitive, as labour markets became
more 'flexible'. Social indicators such as education and health have declined.
Income distribution is today among the worst in the world, worse in some
cases than the notorious Latin American examples. Both the crisis and ad-

---

[13] In the 1994 report on Africa, the World Bank conceded that its programmes had not really
addressed the issue of poverty (World Bank, 1994).

[14] One problem in evaluating adjustment is that it involves arbitrary time dimensions giving
them the character of a moving target. For Africans who thought they had been adjusting all
along, it may come as a surprise that the BWIs actual claim adjustment is new.

justment have led to the marginalisation of large sections of the population. The withdrawal of the state and their detachment from the national economy due to the collapse of physical infrastructure has compelled them to seek ways of survival that may not always be contributive to national cohesion. This worsening of income distribution is taking place at a time when liberalisation and the easing of liquidity constraints has led to 'consumption booms', as witnessed by the proliferation of luxury cars and other premium imports. It is probably this juxtaposition of conspicuous opulence and squalor that is making African cities so insecure.

Although significant numbers of Africa's poor are found in urban areas, most of them still live in the countryside. What happens there will be crucial to the prospects of peace and security in Africa. Perhaps the most worrisome feature of new developments in the African countryside is the institution of processes that might unleash communal and class violence over land rights. Although colonialism produced new elites or selectively incorporated old ones, it basically had a levelling effect on native populations. This is most evident in rural areas where colonialism blocked the emergence of a native agrarian capitalist class for fear that it would eventually demand independence. So, except in areas of colonial settlement, peasant access to land was not seriously challenged and extraction of surplus was largely through exchange—poll taxes, marketing boards, terms of trade effects, etc. Today, we witness an acceleration of the processes of land alienation sanctioned by the new market ideology which argues that land 'titling' and the creation of land markets are the key to the African agrarian malaise, on the dubious grounds that the lack of 'well-defined property rights' has slowed down growth in African agriculture.[15]

The new policies, premised as they are on private property, have sought to introduce 'land markets' and title deeds to communal lands.[16] The resultant land alienation will therefore be the first major challenge to the African peasantry's access to land at a time when population pressures are eroding Africa's 'land surplus' status. Such alienation can only provoke new social movements that can easily dismember some African states if they are not properly managed. Except in such countries as Ethiopia or those of Euro-

---

[15] There is a political and sociological side to all this that may be worth mentioning *en passant*. A new phenomenon is the growing gap between the new intelligentsia and rural populations. If the first generation of African leaders had decidedly rural backgrounds, the new leadership is entirely urban. Its political antennae are much less likely to be sensitive to rural voices. It is also more likely to be impatient with the slow pace of rural transformation and may thus condone levels of land alienation that have hitherto been rare. One should note that a whole generation of urban-based bureaucrats are retiring and for them land acquisition may be the only way of ensuring a decent life in old age.

[16] In recent years, the World Bank has adopted a more cautious policy position on land reform. Rather than direct 'titling' of communal land, rights, under the impulse of market policies, are changing and a land market is emerging. The role of the state in this case is to facilitate formalisation and consolidation of the newly emerging system of private property (World Bank, 1989). For an excellent critical review of this position see Platteau, 1996.

pean settlement, Africa has thus far been spared 'peasant revolts'. We have had some foretaste of violence relating to conflicts over land rights in Ghana, Nigeria, etc.

Table 1. *Trends in income poverty in developing countries*
(Poverty line at $1 a day per person, 1985 PPP$)

Region or country groups	People below poverty line (%)		Share of all poor people (%)		No. of poor people (millions)
	1987	1993	1987	1987	1993
Arab states	5	4	1	1	11
East Asia, South East Asia and the Pacific	30	26	38	34	446
East Asia, South East Asia and the Pacific (excl. China)	23	14	10	7	94
Latin America and the Caribbean	22	24	7	9	110
South Asia	45	43	39	39	515
Sub-Saharan Africa	38	39	15	17	219
Developing countries	34	32	100	100	1,301

Source: UNDP, 1997

And finally the new economic policies, while perhaps 'getting the prices right' have invariably 'got the politics wrong' and thus contributed to the crisis of governance in many Africa countries (Hutchful, 1995a; Mkandawire, 1994a; Mkandawire and Olukoshi, 1995; Sandbrook, 1993). Political analysis informing the BWIs on policy-making in Africa has essentially consisted of a combination of public choice thinking and neo-Weberian views about the neo-patrimonial nature of African states.[17] The argument is that both rent-seeking and neo-patrimonial activities have led to essentially 'redistributive' policy regimes that benefited the organised urban interests. These in turn had pushed or defended policies that hurt the rural sector— food subsidies, overvalued exchange rates, taxation of agricultural exports, etc. Given the absence of democracy and the 'collective action' problems of organising rural interests, policy could only change if policy-makers were 'freed from capture' by essentially urban interests. This analysis accounted for the poorly-veiled preference for authoritarian regimes that had the 'political will' to ride roughshod over urban interests (Hutchful, 1995a; Hutchful, 1995b; Mkandawire, 1994a; Mkandawire and Adebayo, 1995; Olukoshi, 1996). As the clamour for democracy grew loud, open espousal of authoritarian rule was dropped and a more daring (some might say foolhardy) strategy was adopted. This would involve restructuring society itself 'to minimise (the) vulnerability (of adjustment programmes) to derailment by those who stand to lose from the reforms' and to encourage 'an increase

---

[17] See for instance Gulhati, 1990; Summers, 1994; World Bank, 1989.

in power of interest groups that will benefit from the reforms in the course of adjustment' (World Bank, 1994:217–218).[18]

It should be stressed that the civil society to which these appeals were to be made was precisely the one that had been demonised in the dominant political analysis. It was also precisely these groups that have led the struggles for democratisation. This partly explains the nervousness of the BWIs with respect to the new democratic dispensations as they ponder the 'paradox' that political parties elected by the 'rent-seeking' urban coalitions are pursuing far-reaching economic liberalisation polices. Pleasantly surprised by the compliance of the new democracies to the SAP conditionalities, the BWIs have intensified their pressures on these democracies without any further thought about the implication of these policies on democratic transitions and consolidations.

The dominant political analysis of African society, having relegated the 'national project' to the realm of rent-seeking and self-aggrandisement, simply ceased to take ideological expressions and nationalist sensibilities seriously and gave moral support to foreign interventions that were to take place in Africa. After all, one was battling the 'rent-seekers' on behalf of the poor. The presence of foreign advisers and experts reached levels that were unthinkable in other parts of the world.[19] Soon such interventions were to be a source of embarrassment even to the donors themselves, as evidenced by the *cri de coeur* of a former World Bank Vice President, Edward Jaycox:

> After 30 years of technical assistance, and so much money spent, Africa's weak institutions, lack of expertise, and current need for more—rather than less— assistance tells us we have failed badly in our efforts ... The donors have done a disservice to Africa, and many African governments have participated blindly (Edward Jaycox, 1993).[20]

The issue here is not merely whether 'ownership' of policy would or would not have helped Africa. Rather, it is that whatever the problematic nature of the nation/developmentalist project, it constituted a basis upon which were built social coalitions that have thus far guaranteed Africa a modicum of peace. Adjustment has eroded that political basis. The restructuring it has entailed has led to the dismantling of the post-colonial social compact

---

[18] One instrument was the so-called 'safety net' programmes which were explicitly given the additional objective of drumming up political support for SAP. Consequently, the donors insisted on the high 'visibility' of such programmes to counter the political opposition to SAP.

[19] In discussion with Asian colleagues, Africans are always at great pains to explain this foreign presence to the Asians who are absolutely astonished by what they think is our lack of 'national pride'. When the Malaysian Prime Minister, Mahathir Mohammed, visited African countries in 1997, the main message was that Africans must cultivate national pride and assume control of their national policies.

[20] Similar sentiments were echoed by the United Nations. 'One thing that Africa is not short of, however, is external advice. Africa has perhaps received more advice per capita than any other continent.' (UNDP, 1992).

between state and society and between the rulers and the ruled.[21] It has definitely undercut the ideological and fiscal basis of redistributive policies, which have been strongly vilified as simply aspects of cronyism, clientelism or rent-seeking.

The 'adjustment' imperative has so overwhelmed both the legitimation and accumulation imperatives on state policies that nationalist restatements of commitments to national building and development usually have a hollow ring. Key aspects of policy are no longer 'national' in character. Instead, they are policies sought by foreign institutions with national governments serving as reluctant and unreliable 'agents'. Hence the escalation of 'conditionalities' to reduce recidivism and moral hazards.[22] This has led to a paradox: precisely when the genuineness of its commitments is in most doubt, the ruling elite may suddenly discover a greater political value in nationalism to counter particularistic demands intensified by the crisis. The ruling class must lean heavily on the crutch of the myth of a homogeneous nationalist cause and movement to conceal the profound division engendered by the adopted model of crisis management. It must portray itself as the sole arbiter of 'national interest' if only to obfuscate other divisions in society. Under such stress, nationalism loses its emancipatory aspects and becomes an apologetic and mystifying state ideology. And at this point it easily assumes terrifying forms of xenophobia and genocide.

The strength (and one might say, the discreet charm) of African nationalism has actually been its vagueness with respect to the identity of the political community it embraced while being quite certain about the boundaries of its territory. Where nationalism has sought more definite and fixed identities, it has only fanned ethnic cleansing, irredentist expansionism or genocidal exclusion of the Other. In these crisis years, we see an increased abuse of nationalism that leads to political behaviour among the new breed of leaders that is simply incomprehensible in old nationalist terms. We saw it earlier in the expulsion of Ghanaians from Nigeria and people of Asian origin from Idi Amin's Uganda. Chiluba's declaration of nationals as non-nationals on the basis of the birth of their parents and the similar action against Quattara by Bedie in Côte d'Ivoire would be incomprehensible to the founding fathers of these nations. This search for exclusionary national identities induced by crises of legitimacy poses a new threat to African societies and common security. The historian Hobsbawm reminds us that the shift from the conception of a nation as an entity whose inhabitants were heterogeneous and whose citizenship had nothing to do with ethnic origin, religious

---

[21] This problem is not peculiarly African. On Asia see Pasha, 1996.

[22] That this principal-agent perspective of the relationship between donors and African governments has become a central one in policy-making is suggested by the growing literature on the subject. (See for instance Collier, 1996; Dhonte, 1997; Killick, 1996; Mosley, 1996). This perspective and the policy instruments it is spawning go hand in hand with calls for transferring the 'ownership' of policies to Africans.

belief, spoken language or other personal characteristics towards a conception of a citizenry based on a 'community' whose members were united by a supposed common origin (ethnicity) and history, by common language and culture, by symbols, mores and beliefs has led to much suffering:

> Systematic attempts to form such homogenous ethnic-linguistic states have been made from time to time since the First World War. They implied (and imply) the break up of all larger pluri-ethnic and pluri-lingual states, and since humanity is not divided into neatly separable pieces of homogenous territory, the forcible homogenisation of ethnic-linguistic nation-states. The methods of achieving this have, since 1915, ranged from mass population transfers to genocide (1996:271).

Reining in the state

The state is central to the discourse on security because everywhere it is a political institution for upholding a given social order. Its imperatives include: a) the search for hegemony in the territory over which it rules, b) responses to perceived threats whether external or internal, c) the pursuit of autonomy from societal forces, d) the enhancement of its legitimacy for the effective exercise of power and e) the drive to assure its revenue (Young, 1988). At the same time, the state is the institutional locus for contest and collaboration among different classes and social groups. Consequently, even the most predatory state must pursue societal projects that make the reproduction of that society possible. In a capitalist economy, the facilitation of accumulation by private individuals is a central imperative. Indeed, it can be argued that success in responding to the other imperatives will depend to a considerable extent on the levels and rates of accumulation, which in turn depend upon the efficacy of the state with respect to the other goals.

The African state, once the apex of the edifice of development and modernisation, today stands vilified for its bureaucracy, for its inefficiency, for being the source of the most iniquitous forms of self-aggrandisement, for fomenting conflict, for stifling individual and societal creativity and initiative. It is an institution whose relevance and reach are being eroded by the ineluctable forces of globalisation on the one hand and the growth of civil society and local interest groups on the other hand. The African state is being pulled in two directions. It is being forced to shed power on the local scene by reducing itself. And yet it is required to embark on some of the most far-reaching restructuring of the economy through measures that quite obviously require a strong state, both in terms of political acumen and technical capacity. It is also required to provide physical and social infrastructure to make it a worthy member of global governance. What is sought is a state beholden to outside forces but autonomous of local actors and operating in the global arena unencumbered by the clamour of domestic politics.

One policy that has been held with a tenacity that can only be attributed to ideological fervour has been the 'reining in of the state'. This has taken two forms. One has involved simply cutting down state expenditure. The

other has involved assumption by international organisations of key functions of the state by literally hijacking the critical instruments of policy-
making or by reducing the state to the status of an agent for the execution of
policies developed elsewhere. Both these sets of policies have severely com-
promised the integrity of the state in the eyes of its people and have denied
it the means of managing conflicts and contradictions within society. The
imposition of conditionalities and cross-conditionalities has tied the hands
of African states, disabling them from carrying out their functions as
national governments.

To protect policy from 'capture' by domestic interest groups, attempts
have been made to insulate aspects of the state from domestic politics. In
addition, there is the multiplication of institutions enjoying autonomy from
democratically elected compromises or purportedly shielded from the 'rent-
seeking' activities of lobbyists. This is done in the name of autonomy. However, the usual situation is that while such authorities are autonomous of
local institutions they are totally beholden to international bureaucracies
and foreign governments who provide munificent patronage in the form of
consultancy fees, trips, etc. The hiving-off of chunks of government in this
way dilutes the reach of democratic rule and introduces within society what
has been appropriately referred to as 'authoritarian enclaves'. This not only
undermines the credibility of democratically elected institutions but also
blunts the effectiveness of democratic governance to deal with the many
problems of nation-building and conflict-resolution.

Nation-building and regional co-operation

In the current conceptualisation of security, the establishment of regional
mechanisms for ensuring common security is on the agenda. However, if
these mechanisms are to have a political anchoring and material base, they
must be related to the larger political issue of regional integration. It has always been an article of faith in African politics that regional co-operation
would reduce some of the conflicts in Africa by reducing interstate conflicts
and by producing political spaces that took into account the ethnic strad-
dling that one sees in Africa. It would also promote common mechanisms
for resolving conflicts and for mutual protection.

It is often asserted that African regional integration has been blocked by
the multiplicity of ethnicities and nationalities and the artificiality of
borders.[23] On the contrary, partly because of the artificiality of colonial bor-

---

[23] Much has been said about the 'artificiality' of African borders as a source of conflict. I per-
sonally do not attach much importance to it. All borders are after all 'artificial'. And in any case
few conflicts in Africa are interstate or across borders. And we should not forget that the identities acquired as Ghanaians, Nigerians, Zambians, Malawians do not date only since independence but go as far back as the colonial delineation of those territories as Gold Coast, Northern
Rhodesia, Nyasaland etc. In other words being a 'Ghanaian' or 'Nigerian' is almost a century-
old concept now, a fact that explains why secessionist movements play such a minor role in

ders and partly because of the multiplicity of identities of Africans, African nationalism was both inward- and outward-looking—both national and continental. Indeed, in its most sophisticated self-expression it took the form of continental ideologies—pan-Africanism, African Personality, Negritude, etc. The failure to show any achievement in the form of integration or establishing a *pax Africana* may have persuaded some to dismiss these continental ideologies. While the fear of war within the country or with neighbouring countries can be a useful basis for concentrating the mind and for thinking of mechanisms for ensuring regional peace, it seems to me that positive incentives for regional co-operation are a more reliable driving force. Hence the age-old pan-African dream of regional co-operation and unity is still a valid point of departure in thinking about common security in Africa. Pan-Africanism's ideological appeal remains a potent force and is much more deeply etched in African self-perception than is often recognised, if the testimony of our artists is to be taken seriously. No continent is celebrated by its artists as much as Africa. No continent is as sung about, as portrayed in painting and sculpture, as the African continent. Africans do take their identity quite seriously, as simply one important identity among many they wear—national, ethnic, etc. And so if Africa is not uniting it is not because of some deep-seated primordial identities that block such schemes. The paradox in Africa is that such identities may prove more of a nuisance to creating national identities than pan-African identities.

Regional co-operation failed in Africa partly because of the absence of a national constituency, petty nationalism and jealousy over newly-acquired sovereignty. These factors blocked the institutionalisation of regional mechanisms for conflict management and resolution. African states were content to reduce the OAU to an organisation that guaranteed non-interference with the affairs of member states, who were allowed to do virtually as they pleased with their citizens. Even when such conflicts spilled across borders, the OAU was simply not capable of doing much. It was perhaps naïve to have imagined that the tinpot dictators that emerged in Africa would have agreed to share their absolute political authority over their citizens with a higher authority. It is not usual for dictators to enter into federal arrangements with anyone.

In 1980, partly in response to the crisis, African heads of state met in Lagos and adopted the Lagos Plan of Action (LPA) as a guide to Africa's continental co-operation. Almost simultaneously, the World Bank released the Berg Report (World Bank, 1981). Although the LPA continues to dominate the official discourse on regional co-operation, it was the Berg Report which, by adjusting the economic orientation of member states, set the stage

---

old concept now, a fact that explains why secessionist movements play such a minor role in African conflicts. Those who talk about redrawing African borders are simply playing Russian roulette with African countries; they would tamper with national identities that most Africans have learnt to live within, albeit not always happily.

for the subsequent trajectory of efforts at regional integration. The positions implicit in these documents were diametrically opposed, although the Berg Report claimed that its proposals were the short- to medium-term counterpart of the LPA. The Berg Report was based on the assumption of the unilateral freeing of trade on a non-preferential basis, and adjusting countries have had to follow these conditionalities. The LPA was based on the creation of a central decision-making authority with a structure for co-ordinated and reciprocally preferential policies (Oyejide et al., 1997). Virtually every successful integration scheme has followed the latter path. For those who strictly hold to the notion of unilateral freeing of trade, regional schemes such as those that featured in pan-African discourse would be superfluous. As for the BWIs, they have suspected that since they implied trade restriction on extra-regional countries, regional integration schemes would dilute and compromise the strength of SAPs. Consequently, they have only perfunctorily given them official recognition while proceeding to impose unilateral liberalisation of trade on individual African countries. It should be obvious that when individual countries are outwardly oriented towards global markets, they are unlikely to constitute a firm base for regional schemes.

Regional integration will require a rethinking at the national level of national objectives, relating them to regional schemes. No responsible government can knowingly adhere to regional schemes that have unfavourable consequences for its people, especially if they happen to be voters. These remarks suggest a new premise for regional co-operation. Such a premise must be built on the full recognition of existing national states and their aspiration and must be precise about the costs and benefits to each nation of entering into a regional arrangement. Pronouncements about the benefits of regional co-operation to the region as a whole, which international bureaucrats are wont to tout as bait for adhesion by individual states to regional arrangements, will simply not do.

Concluding remarks

For all the Thatcherite assertion that 'there is no alternative', we need to continue to think of macroeconomic policies and global economic arrangements that assume that peace and security matter. In concluding, then, I shall list some of the elements of such policy thinking.

New order once again

One recurring theme in the nationalist discourse was the need to reshape the international economic order. Non-alignment and, later, the more explicit articulation of demands for a New International Economic Order were expressions of this quest for global change. With the loss of the moral stature of the nationalists, the collapse of the bipolar world and the triumphalism of the West, calls for such an order sound terribly passé. It is now simply assumed that the world order (often conflated with world markets) is basically sound and that every country must 'adjust or perish'. Africa, on the brink of the precipice of total marginalisation, is under particularly heavy pressure to change and stop whining about past injustice and foreign domination. In this perspective, Africa enters the discourse of 'common security' as an embarrassment to the human conscience or simply as a real or potential nuisance, because of the effects that the collapse of African states and societies would have —the resultant disorder would make the continent a haven for drug-traffickers and a source of disease. There is no room here for the view that Africa's integration into the world system may have started on the wrong foot and that some global adjustment may be necessary. At the risk of sounding old-fashioned, I will insist that a 'common security' that is worthy of its name must seriously recognise the need for change in the world order partly by re-examining both the direction and levels of resource flows and partly by reshaping institutions of global governance. Issues of debt, access to markets, investment and aid should be covered under this rubric.

Democratisation

It is necessary to make democratisation a central aspect of thinking about common security in Africa if we are to avoid the dominance of a militaristic and diplomatic view of security. We noted how nation-building and development were used to rationalise authoritarian institutions and practices. We now run the danger of having 'security' play the same role. Nigeria's attempt to buy back international respectability by acting as the guarantor of security and even 'democracy' is symptomatic of this trend. The accolades showered on Uganda, Rwanda and Ethiopia point to its danger.

Part of the problem of common security relates to the failure to devise appropriate institutions to manage our diversity, especially under conditions of crisis. The many democracies that exist are characterised by a whole range of different features that do not compromise their essential democratic characteristics and that are reflective of their political histories—presidential versus parliamentary democracy, majoritarian versus proportional, etc. In many cases in Africa, we have simply adopted the constitutional arrangements of our erstwhile constitutional masters, often with disastrous results. Africa is quintessentially a continent of many ethnic groups and many languages. For some, this is the source of all our problems. Simplistic journalistic accounts have etched this vision of a murderous pluralism in the minds of many. And yet the fact is that most Africans live in peace within nations with many ethnic entities and nationalities. The problem in Africa has been the failure to realise that, given such diversity and the possibilities of 'exit' due to the porousness of our borders, we can only govern ourselves democratically if we are to avoid conflicts. The historical construction of our nation-states, their ethnic mixture and their agrarian structures literally condemn us either to democratic rule or to ethnic violence and military rule. And so as we look at issues of common security we have to pay special attention to the struggles for democratisation and to problems of democratic transition and consolidation.

Obviously, if democracy is to be a credible instrument of conflict resolution and if the different social actors are to take democracy seriously, the institutions of democracy must be seen to enjoy powers that are universally applicable and over issues that really matter. We have elsewhere cautioned against the making of 'choiceless democracies' through styles of policy-making by international aid organisations in which conditionalities leave no room for choice by elected bodies (Mkandawire and Soludo, 1999). The ponderous interference by BWIs short-circuits the process of social interaction at the national level.

Bringing nation-building and development back in

The building of ethnically pluralistic nations and economic development remain on the agenda in African countries despite the Machiavellian and xenophobic use to which they have been put over the years. As we have all learnt, such nation-building must not be conflated or limited to state-building, as has been the case in Africa, but must involve the self-construction of a strong civil society on the basis of the continent's rich cultural, national and racial diversity. Both of these processes—the strengthening of state capacity and the emergence of a vibrant civil society—require a democratic order. Not only is a state that is firmly embedded in its society *necessary* for development, it shall in turn benefit from prosperity. The founding fathers of African nations obviously failed to edify self-sustaining sovereign nations. However, if the central preoccupations of their platforms—national sovereignty and dignity, equality, elimination of the 'unholy trinity of poverty, hunger and disease'—are not addressed, then talk of common security will sound hollow. In many ways, the many threats to individual and common security stem from the abortion of the nationalist project and not from its inherent flaws, as is at times suggested.[24] The current crisis may have lowered our visions so that common security is reduced to the absence of conflicts and guarantees of merely sustainable livelihoods. I believe that we ought to reject this minimalist view if we are to address Africa's many problems.

---

[24] Even Davidson as an astute observer of the African condition and history has reached the conclusion that it is this nation building and development project, or what he pejoratively calls 'nation-statism' that constitutes the 'Black Man's Burden'—burden because not only did it build on the problematic map produced by the 'Scramble for Africa' but because it detached from any historical and cultural moorings that a truly African project would have had. The implicit solution proposed by Davidson is surprising in its ahistorical voluntarism, especially coming from a historian (Davidson, 1992).

We need to place nation-building and development, including rapid economic growth, back on the agenda. In its current form, economic policy-making is too bogged down in matters of stabilisation and debt-payment to be of much use. The 'fundamentals' it insists on getting right are too narrow to encompass the 'fundamentals' for development, peace and security. The content and meaning of development and nation-building have changed since the sixties. They will both be more democratically anchored and less 'dirigible'. The specific contours will, of course, differ from country to country but clearly, both will succeed only if they are truly national initiatives and are linked to a large project of pan-African co-operation and common security.

References

Ake, Claude. 1996. *Democracy and Development in Africa.* Washington, DC: Brookings.

Amsden, A.H. 1985. "The State and Taiwan's Economic Development", in P. Evans, D. Rueschemeyer and T. Skocpol (eds), *Bringing the State Back.* Cambridge: Cambridge University Press.

Arrighi, Giovanni. 1973. "International Corporations, Labour Aristocracies, and Economic Development", in G. Arrighi and J. Saul (eds), *Tropical Africa. Essays on the Political Economy of Africa.* New York: Monthly Press Review.

Bauer, Peter. 1981. *Dissent on Development.* London: Weidenfeld and Nicolson.

Bauer, Peter. 1984. *Reality and Rhetoric: Studies in the Economics of Development.* London: Weidenfeld and Nicolson.

Bayart, Jean-Francois. 1993. *The State in Africa: The Politics of the Belly.* London: Longman.

Breuilly, J. 1982. *Nationalism and the State.* Manchester University Press.

Chatterjee, Partha. 1993. *Fragments of the Nation.* Princeton, NJ: Princeton University Press.

Collier, Paul. 1996. "The Role of the African State in Building Agencies of Restraint", in M. Lundhal and B. Ndulu (eds), *New Directions in Development Economics: Growth, Environmental Concerns and Governments in the 1990s.* London: Routledge.

Davidson, Basil. 1992. *The Black Man's Burden.* London: James Currey.

Dhonte, Pierre. 1997. *Conditionality As an Instrument of Borrower Credibility.* Washington, DC: IMF.

Elbadawi, I., D. Ghura and G. Uwujaren. 1992. *Why Structural Adjustment Has Not Succeed in Africa.* Washington DC: World Bank.

Engberg-Pedersen, P., P. Gibbon, P. Raikes and L. Udholt. 1996. *Limits of Adjustment in Africa.* London: James Currey.

Felix, D. 1977. "The Technological Factor in Socio-Economic Dualism Toward an Economy of Scale Paradigm for Development Theory", in M. Nash (ed.), *Essays on Economic Development and Cultural Change in Honour of Bert Hoselitz.* Chicago: University of Chicago.

Fukui, H. 1992. "The Japanese State and Economic Development: A Profile of a Nationalist-Paternalist Capitalist State", in R.P. Appelbaum and J. Henderson and (eds), *States and Development in the Asian Pacific Rim.* Newbury Park: Sage Publications.

Gendzier, I. 1985. *Managing Political Change: Social Scientists and the Third World.* Boulder, CO: Westview Press.

Gulhati, R. 1990. "Who Makes Economic Policy in Africa and How", *World Development, 8.*

Hawes, G. and H. Liu. 1993. "Explaining the Dynamics of the Southeast Asian Political Economy: State, Society, and the Search for Economic Growth", *World Politics,* 45:629–60.

Helleiner, G. 1994. "From Adjustment to Development in Sub-Saharan Africa: Consensus and Continuing Conflict", in G. Cornia and G. Helleiner (eds), *From Adjustment to Development in Africa: Conflict, Controversy, Convergence, Consensus?* London: Macmillan.

Hirschman, A. 1981. "The Changing Tolerance for Income Inequality in the Course of Economic Development", in Hirschman, A. (ed.), *Essays in Trespassing: Economics to Politics and Beyond.* Cambridge and New York: Cambridge University Press.

Hirschman, A. 1982. *Shifting Involvements.* Oxford: Blackwell Publisher.

Hobsbawm, E. 1996. "The Future of the State", *Development and Change,* 27:267–278.

Huntington, S. 1968. *Political Order in Changing Societies.* New Haven, Connecticut: Yale University Press.

Hutchful, E. 1995a. "Adjustment in Africa and Fifty Years of the Bretton Woods Institutions: Change or Consolidation", *Canadian Journal of Development Studies, XVI.*

Hutchful, E. 1995b. "The International Dimensions of the Democratisation Process", in E. Chole and J. Ibrahim (eds), *Democratisation Processes in Africa: Problems and Prospects.* Dakar: CODESRIA.

ILO. 1972. *Employment, Incomes and Equality: A Strategy for Increasing Productive Employment in Kenya.* ILO: Geneva.

IMF. 1997. *World Economic Outlook.* Washington, DC: IMF.

Johnson, H. 1967. "A Theoretical Model of Economic Nationalism in New and Developing Countries", in H.G. Johnston (ed.), *Economic Nationalism in Old and New States.* Chicago: University of Chicago Press.

Johnson, H. 1971. "A Word to the Third World: A Western Economist's Frank Advice", *Encounter.*

Jomo, K.S. 1996. *Lessons from Growth and Structural Change in the Second-Tier South East Asian Newly Industrialising Countries.* Geneva: UNCTAD.

Kahan, A. 1967. "Economic Nationalism in Britain in the Nineteenth Century", in H.G. Johnston (ed.), *Economic Nationalism in Old and New States.* Chicago: University of Chicago Press.

Killick, T. 1996. "Principals, Agents and the Limitations of BWI Conditionality", *World Economy,* 19.

Koo, H. and E.M. Kim. 1992. "The Developmental State and Capital Accumulation in South Korea", in R.P. Appelbaum and J. Henderson and (eds), *States and Development in the Asian Pacific Rim.* Newbury Park: Sage Publications.

Krugman, P. 1992. "Toward a Counter-Counterrevolution in Development Theory", in *World Bank Economic Review Supplement (Proceedings of the Annual Bank Conference on Development Economics, 15–39).*

Lipton, M. and M. Ravallion. 1995. "Poverty and Policy", in J.R. Behrman and T.N. Srinivasan (eds), *Handbook of Development Economics.* Amsterdam: Elsevier Science, B.V.

Mamdani, M. 1996. *Citizen and Subject: Contemporary Africa and the Legacy of Late Colonialism.* Princeton, NJ: Princeton University Press.

Mkandawire, T. 1994a. "Adjustment, Political Conditionality and Democratisation in Africa", in G. Cornia and G. Helleiner (eds), *From Adjustment to Development in Africa: Conflict, Controversy, Convergence, Consensus?* London: Macmillan.

Mkandawire, T. 1994b. "The Political Economy of Privatisation in Africa", in A. Cornia and G. Helleiner (eds), *From Adjustment to Development in Africa: Conflict, Controversy, Consensus?* London: Macmillan.

Mkandawire, T. and C.C. Soludo. 1999. *Our Continent, Our Future. African Perspectives on Structural Adjustment.* Trenton, NJ: African World Press.

Mkandawire, T. and A. Olukoshi. 1995. *Between Liberalisation and Repression: The Politics of Adjustment in Africa.* Dakar: CODESRIA.

Mosley, P. 1996. "The Failure of Aid and Adjustment Policies in Sub-Saharan Africa: Counter-examples and Policy Proposals", *Journal of African Economies,* 5:406–43.

Mosley, P., T. Subasat and J. Weeks. 1995. "Assessing Adjustment in Africa", *World Development,* 23:1459–1473.

Mosley, P. and J. Weeks. 1993. "Has Recovery Begun? Africa's Adjustment in the 1980s Revisited", *World Development,* 21:1583–1606.

Nkrumah, K. 1965. *Africa Must Unite*. New York: International Publishers.

N'zatioula Grovogui, S. 1996. *Sovereigns, Quasi-Sovereigns and African*. Minneapolis: University of Minnesota Press.

Olukoshi, A. 1996. "The Elusive Prince of Denmark: Structural Adjustment and the Crisis of Governance in Africa". CODESRIA Conference on African Perspectives on Structural Adjustment. Abidjan. Published by the Nordic Africa Institute in 1998 as Research report No. 108.

Oyejide, A., I. Elbadawi and P. Collier. 1997. "Introduction and Overview", in A. Oyejide, I. Elbadawi and P. Collier (eds), *Regional Integration and Trade Liberalisation in Sub-Saharan Africa*. London: Macmillan.

Paoha, M. K. 1996. "Globalisation and Poverty in South Asia Studies", *Millennium: Journal of International Studies*, 25.

Penrose, E. 1974 (2nd imprint). "The State and Multinational Enterprises in Less Developed Countries", in J.H. Dunning (ed.), *Economic Analysis and the Multinational Enterprise*. London: Allen & Unwin.

Platteau, J.-P. 1996. "The Evolutionary Theory of Land Rights as Applied to Sub-Saharan Africa: A Critical Assessment", *Development and Change*, Vol. 27, No. 1, January 1996.

Sandbrook, R. 1993. *The Politics of Africa's Economic Recovery*. Cambridge: Cambridge University Press.

Saul, J. 1973. "African Socialism in One Country: Tanzania", in G. Arrighi and J. Saul (eds), *Essays on the Political Economy of Africa*. New York: Monthly Review Press.

Seers, D. 1983. *The Political Economy of Nationalism*. Oxford: Oxford University Press.

Stiglitz, J. 1989. "Markets, Market Failures, and Development", *American Economic Review*, 79:197–203.

Summers, L. 1994. "Foreword", in S. Haggard and S. Webb (eds), *Voting for Reform*. New York: Oxford University Press.

Taylor, L. 1983. *Structuralist Macroeconomics*. New York: Basic Books.

UNDP. 1992. *Human Development Report 1992*. New York: United Nations.

UNDP. 1997. *Human Development Report 1997*. New York: United Nations.

Wade, R. 1991. *Governing Markets*. London: Macmillan.

World Bank. 1981. *Accelerated Development for Africa: An Agenda for Africa*. Washington, DC: World Bank.

World Bank. 1989. *Sub-Saharan Africa: From Crisis to Sustainable Growth*. Washington, DC: World Bank.

World Bank. 1994. *Adjustment in Africa: Reforms, Results and the Road Ahead*. Washington, DC: World Bank.

Young, C. 1988. "African Colonial State and Its Political Legacy", in D. Rothchild and N. Chazan (eds), *The Precarious Balance: State and Society in Africa*. Boulder, CO: Westview Press.

Poverty, Inequality and Security in South Africa

Stephan Klasen and Fani Zulu

Introduction

The end of apartheid in South Africa has considerably increased prospects for security for people in South as well as southern Africa. For South Africans, it has brought an end to armed struggle, forced removals and banishment, states of emergency, state and state-sanctioned violence and covert and overt security force activities. With the exception of some continuing problems in isolated areas, it has also sharply reduced the level of political violence between rival political groups. For the people of southern Africa, the end of apartheid has meant an end to overt and covert attempts to undermine the stability of regimes in the region. South Africa's membership in SADC and the OAU, and its recent efforts to mediate in conflicts across Africa has highlighted its new role as a stabilising and mediating force. Although some of its interventions in conflicts in the region—including its diplomatic efforts to resolve the conflict in the Democratic Republic of Congo and its controversial military intervention in Lesotho in 1998—have been poorly planned and executed, the South African government is committed to furthering security in the region.

At the same time, much remains to be done if South Africans (and southern Africans) are to enjoy security in the broader sense of the word, including economic and social security as well as protection from random events that threaten the physical and social well-being of the population. In particular, widespread poverty, high levels of vulnerability, high levels of inequality and associated political and social unrest, very high crime rates, and high rates of accidents threaten the safety and security of South Africans. While these issues affect all population groups to some extent, the poorest suffer the most.

This paper highlights these security issues facing the new South Africa and discusses policy options for promoting greater security for South Africans. Section 1 analyses poverty and inequality in South Africa and highlights its racial, regional, and gender dimensions. Section 2 examines some of the barriers and constraints poor people face when attempting to improve their economic well-being and links poverty to issues of security. These constraints include both lack of assets and services and high vulnerability to a variety of shocks. Section 3 looks at the role inequality plays in generating insecurity in South Africa, while Section 4 examines some of the responses made by people dealing with the these insecurities. The final section draws policy lessons from the foregoing discussion, highlighting the need to address, in a sustainable way, the security problems suffered by the population. Among the policy issues examined are the need for improved access to assets, services, and employment security for the poor; measures to enhance the physical safety of the population through reductions in accidents and crime; and ways to reduce inequality in order to promote economic and social stability. The section also briefly assesses the record of the new government in addressing these policy issues.

Poverty and inequality in South Africa

As shown in Table 1, South Africa fares very poorly in many social indicators when compared to countries with similar levels of per-capita income, and only little better in some of those indicators than much poorer countries in Sub-Saharan Africa. South Africa has a much higher poverty rate (measured at the purchasing power adjusted $1 per capita per day) than most comparable countries, and fares worse in most social indicators such as illiteracy, mortality, fertility, and access to safe water. Much of this poor performance is related to apartheid policies which focused resources and

Table 1. *Comparative social indicators: Selected countries*

	Thai-land	Po-land	Vene-zuela	Brazil	South Africa[c]	Ma-laysia	Chile	Kenya	Nigeria
GNP per capita US$ (1994)	2,410	2,410	2,760	2,970	3,040	3,480	3,520	250	280
Gini coefficient[*]	0.43	0.27	0.44	0.63	0.61	0.51	0.58	0.57	0.45
International poverty rate[*]	0.1	6.8	11.8	28.7	23.7	5.6	15.0	50.2	28.9
Life expectancy (years) (1994)	69	72	71	67	64	71	72	59	52
Infant mortality rate (1994)	36	15	32	56	50	12	12	59	81
Adult illiteracy rate (%) (1995)	6	_[b]	9	17	18	17	5	22	43
Total fertility rate (1994)	2.0	1.8	3.2	2.8	3.9	3.4	2.5	4.9	5.6
Access to safe water (%) 1993[a]	77	100	89	96	76	78	86	49	40

[a] Some data are for 1990.

[b] No comparable data are available.

[c] The South African data are an average of all races. There are large differences between the races in these social indicators.

[*] All Gini coefficients are based on income, except for those for sub-Saharan Africa which are based on expenditure (a Gini of 0 signifies absolute equality, and 1 absolute concentration). Gini coefficients and poverty rates are for different years in the late 1980s or early 1990s.

Source: Reconstruction and Development Programme (1995), World Bank (1994, 1996, 1997).

benefits on the White minority and which resulted in South Africa having one of the highest levels of inequality in the world with a Gini coefficient of 0.61.[1] Figure 1 illustrates the magnitude of this inequality by showing the distribution of consumption by household expenditure deciles, showing that the richest 10 per cent spend about 42 per cent of [national] expenditure, despite comprising only 6 per cent of the population.

Figure 1. *Inequality in South Africa*

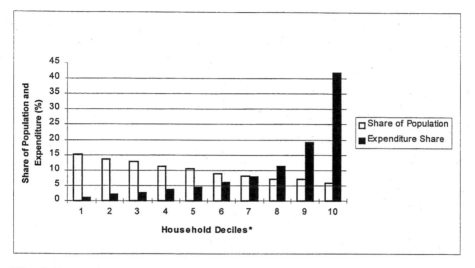

* Households are ranked by adult equivalent expenditure, in groups of 10% (deciles).
Source: Reconstruction and Development Programme (1995).

Table 2 shows the racial and geographical composition of each expenditure quintile (i.e. the poorest 20 per cent of households as measured by adult equivalent expenditures, the next richest quintile, etc.), based on the 1993 Southern Africa Labour and Demographic Research Unit (SALDRU) household survey.[2] Among the poorest quintile, 80 per cent are Africans in rural areas and another 17 per cent are Africans from urban and metropolitan areas. Among quintile 2, the proportions are similar, showing both the preponderance of Africans among the poor as well as the concentration of poverty in rural areas. In contrast, 71 per cent of the richest quintile are urban and metropolitan Whites. If one referred to the poorest 40 per cent of households as the poor (which would consist of about 53 per cent of the

---

[1] A Gini coefficient of zero signifies perfect equality; a Gini coefficient of one signifies all income accruing to the richest person.

[2] Expenditure levels were measured based on a household survey sampling 9,000 households in late 1993; to take account of different household compositions and differences in needs between children and adults, household expenditure is expressed in terms of expenditures per adult equivalent. Since poorer households are larger than richer households, nearly 29% of the total population lives in the poorest 20% of households. For details, see Klasen (1997a) or RDP (1995).

population, see RDP, 1995; Klasen, 1997a), we would thus find 75 per cent of the poor to be rural Africans, another 20 per cent to be urban and metropolitan Africans, about 4 per cent to be urban and metropolitan Coloureds, and well under 1 per cent to be Indians or Whites. By 1995, the situation appears to have changed only very slightly with Africans making up about 96 per cent of the poor and the share of Indians and Whites having increased to 1 per cent (May et al., 1998).[3]

Table 2. *Share of each quintile by race and location (1993)*

	Quintile 1 (Poorest)	Quintile 2	Poorest 40% (Poor)	Quintile 3	Quintile 4	Quintile 5 (Richest)	Total
Rural							
African	80.0%	66.6%	73.9%	45.5%	22.8%	4.5%	51.8%
Coloured	0.7%	0.6%	0.6%	0.8%	0.3%	0.0%	0.5%
Indian	0.0%	0.0%	0.0%	0.0%	0.0%	0.1%	0.0%
White	0.0%	0.0%	0.0%	0.2%	1.2%	6.4%	1.0%
Urban							
African	12.3%	12.8%	12.5%	17.3%	15.2%	2.3%	12.5%
Coloured	1.7%	4.3%	2.9%	4.4%	3.7%	0.6%	3.0%
Indian	0.0%	0.2%	0.1%	1.0%	5.8%	2.8%	1.5%
White	0.0%	0.2%	0.1%	0.2%	4.4%	20.6%	3.4%
Metropolitan							
African	4.8%	12.4%	8.3%	21.8%	23.8%	4.8%	12.8%
Coloured	0.5%	2.6%	1.5%	6.9%	12.7%	3.9%	4.5%
Indian	0.0%	0.0%	0.0%	1.4%	2.9%	3.3%	1.1%
White	0.0%	0.1%	0.1%	0.5%	6.9%	50.7%	7.7%
Total	100.0%	100.0%	100.0%	100.0%	100.0%	100.0%	100.0%

Source: Southern Africa Labour and Demographic Research Unit (SALDRU) (1993).

Figures 2, 3, and 4 (below) show poverty rates (defined as the percentage of people in the poorest two quintiles), the poverty gap (the average distance of a poor family's income from the poverty line), and the share of the poverty gap accounted for by race, gender, and education of the household head (e.g. the share of a total hypothetical transfer needed to lift the poor to the poverty line that would go to Africans). Figure 2 shows that Africans suffer from both higher poverty rates as well as deeper poverty (larger gaps to the poverty line), and thus make up 96 per cent of the national poverty gap, despite being only 77 per cent of the population. Similarly, female-headed households (both *de jure* and *de facto*) have much higher poverty rates, while the depth of poverty is similar among all types of households (Figure 3).[4]

---

[3] At the other end of the income spectrum, there have been some changes with Africans now making up some 25% of the population in the richest quintile. As a result, inequality among Africans, which was already considerable in 1993, has risen further. At the same time, inter-race inequality is still a more important factor in accounting for total inequality than intra-race inequality (Klasen, 1997a).

[4] *De jure* female-headed households refer to households which are officially headed by women. *De facto* female-headed households are headed by a male who is absent for most of the year.

Figure 2. *Poverty rates and poverty gap by race*

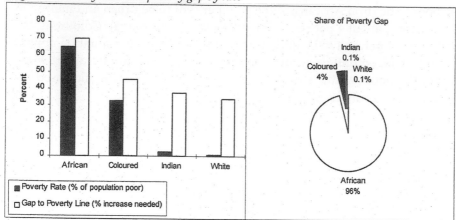

Source: Reconstruction and Development Programme (1995), own analysis.

Figure 3. *Poverty rates and poverty gap by household structure*

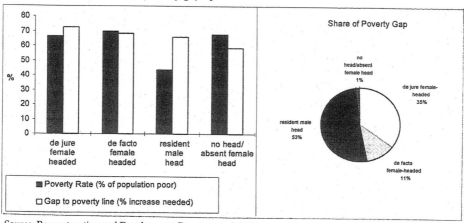

Source: Reconstruction and Development Programme (1995), own analysis.

Figure 4. *Poverty rates and poverty gap by education of household head*

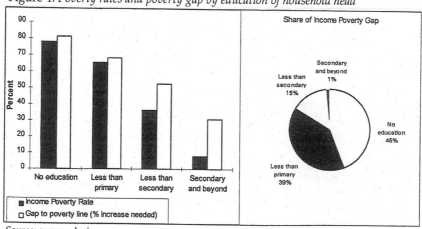

Source: own analysis.

Table 3. *Unemployment, participation, and sectoral employment by race, gender, and location (%)**

	All South Africans	Households ranked by consumption quintiles				
		Quintile 1 (Poorest)	Quintile 2	Quintile 3	Quintile 4	Quintile 5 (Richest)
Race						
African	38.3	54.3	44.2	32.0	19.7	13.1
Coloured	20.8	34.3	32.5	21.2	14.5	6.8
Indian	11.3	**	**	23.3	12.6	3.7
White	4.3	**	**	25.8	9.4	2.8
Gender						
Female	35.1	56.7	46.2	37.2	23.3	5.8
Male	25.5	50.2	40.5	24.4	13.2	3.3
Location						
Rural	39.7	53.7	44.3	30.6	13.2	5.9
Urban	25.6	49.9	38.5	30.3	16.1	4.2
Metropolitan	21.3	58.3	45.0	30.3	19.5	4.2
Total	29.9	53.4	43.3	30.4	17.1	4.4
Participation rate	61.1	49.5	55.4	62.5	69.5	76.5
Share working	42.7	22.9	31.3	43.3	57.6	73.0
Share citing illness/disability as cause for non-participation***	15.8	19.1	18.4	16.7	11.7	4.9
Share of people living in households with no one working	29.5	49.0	36.5	21.5	10.5	6.3
Share of workers in casual employment	11.4	19.2	15.5	12.2	6.5	8.7
Share of workers in agriculture and domestic service	21.9	58.0	37.3	23.5	11.0	3.2

* The unemployment rate is calculated by dividing the number of people aged 16–64 who are not working but would like to work (and are either actively seeking work or have given up looking) by the number of people in the labour force (defined as those currently employed plus those not working who would like to work).

** Too few observations in these cells to calculate reliable rates.

*** This is calculated as the number of people who cite illness or disability as the cause for non-participation in the labour force, as a percentage of people who are out of the (broadly defined) labour force and who are not in formal education.

Source: Reconstruction and Development Programme (1995), own analysis.

Less well-educated household heads also have much higher poverty rates and suffer from deeper poverty (Figure 4), underscoring the close linkages between poverty, education, and insecurity.

Poverty and insecurity

While low income is obviously a direct threat to the economic security of a household since it prevents the household from acquiring many important commodities and services that ensure a secure existence, the poor are burdened with additional constraints and burdens that threaten their security. In addition, many more people that may not have been poor at the time of the survey, are vulnerable to shocks and fluctuations in their incomes and resource bases that severely threaten their economic security. Let us deal with each of these issues in turn.

Both income poverty and income vulnerability are closely bound up with unemployment. As Table 3 shows, the poorest quintile have an unemployment rate of about 53 per cent. In addition, only about half of the working age population in the poorest quintile is in the labour force, so that less than a quarter of the people in the poorest quintile are actually working. As shown in Table 3, illness and disability are important reasons for non-participation among the poorest. Women have much higher unemployment rates than men, Africans have much higher unemployment rates than Whites and rural dwellers have much higher unemployment than urban and metropolitan residents. While many of the unemployed live in households where at least someone is employed, 49 per cent of people in the poorest quintile live in households where no one is employed.

In addition, the types of jobs held by the poorest are less secure and more vulnerable to economic and seasonal shocks. Twenty per cent of people in the poorest quintile have casual (as opposed to regular) employment characterised by short job tenure, poor job security, seasonal fluctuations, and low pay. Moreover, nearly 60 per cent of the poorest are working in agriculture and domestic service, which are very insecure, offer little protection and few benefits, and are subject to seasonal, weather, and economic fluctuations (Table 3).

Since 1993, the employment picture has become bleaker. Average unemployment rates rose to 37 per cent in 1997, and the poor suffer from employment rates of 60 per cent and more. This is also related to the long-term decline in employment in agriculture and domestic service, two important sectors of employment to the poor.

In addition, the non-employment sources of income of poor households illustrate the vulnerability of incomes. All sources show heavy dependence and vulnerability in relation to: other family members (remittances), the weather (agricultural income), local economic conditions (self-employment income), and state welfare provisions (social pensions and disability grants). Some sources are more reliable throughout the year than others. With the notable exception of the social pensions which are among the most reliable sources of income in terms of amounts and timeliness,[5] many of the other sources, in particular remittances, self-employment income, and income from agricultural activities, are notoriously unstable and depend in various ways on the goodwill of family members who are sending remittances, on the weather, and local economic conditions (Figure 5). For the poor, these same income sources are often particularly unreliable (which may be both a cause and a consequence of poverty). For example, only 25 per cent of households in the poorest quintile who are receiving remittances are receiv-

---

[5] They are, however, subject to annual budget cycles and policy-making which generates another dimension of vulnerability.

ing them at least monthly (in contrast to over 50 per cent in the richest quintile), making this income source particularly unstable and unreliable.

Figure 5. *Sources of income (%) for poor and ultra-poor households*

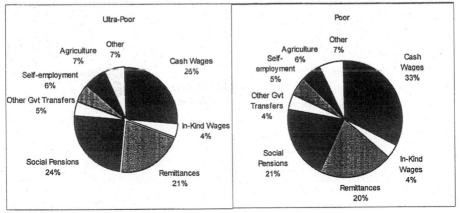

Source: own analysis.

Table 4. Educational attainment and enrolments by quintile

	Quintile 1 (Poorest)	Quintile 2	Poorest 40% (Poor)	Quintile 3	Quintile 4	Quintile 5 (Richest)	Total
Attainment (% of individuals 16+ who have achieved each level)							
No education	23.9	17.5	21.3	12.9	7.3	5.6	14.7
Primary-Incomplete	30.5	24.8	28.1	20.1	13.5	3.3	20.0
Primary-Complete	11.3	11.0	11.2	10.0	7.4	1.5	8.8
Secondary-Incomplete	30.1	38.4	34.6	44.6	48.6	27.3	37.5
Secondary-Complete	3.7	7.3	6.0	10.4	16.7	32.5	12.6
Tertiary-Incomplete	0.5	0.9	0.8	7.3	5.5	19.5	4.7
Tertiary degree				0.2	0.6	10.3	1.8
*Net enrolment rates:**							
Primary	85	87	86	88	89	90	87
Secondary	46	57	51	67	78	83	60
Tertiary	4	5	4	8	20	38	11

* Due to some children entering school later than normal and some children accelerating their education (i.e. moving to secondary education although they still are primary school age), net enrolment rates of 100% are unlikely to be achieved. For the calculation of primary school enrolment, the school age was assumed to be 6–12 years, for secondary 13–17, for tertiary 18–23.

Source: Reconstruction and Development Programme (1995).

Thus, both low levels and high variability of income are major sources of insecurity which affect the poor most severely, but can also throw higher income groups into poverty relatively quickly. Much of the lack of access to secure income sources is related to poor people's very low asset bases. These assets are physical as well as human assets, and relate to market as well as household production. As shown in Table 4, the poor have much worse human capital, as measured by educational attainment; together with Figure

4, it shows that poor education is both a cause as well as a consequence of poverty. While current enrolment rates point to improved access to education of the poor at the primary level, there remains considerable differential by income groups in educational attainment at the secondary and tertiary level. In addition, school quality and funds available per student also differ considerably by quintile, which will contribute to the inter-generational transmission of the cycle of poverty and poor education (Case and Deaton, 1996; Castro-Leal, 1995).

Apart from the problem of poor human resources, the poor suffer from low and insecure access to important physical and economic assets that could assist with market and domestic production. One of the most striking inequalities is access to agricultural land. In rural South Africa, the average White farm household owns about 530 ha, compared to only 2.2 ha for the average African farming household. In addition, there are massive inequalities in access to irrigation. About half the farmland owned by White farmers has access to irrigation, compared to only 2 per cent by Africans. These 30,000 White commercial farmers make up 50 per cent of total water use in South Africa (Government of South Africa, 1997; DWAF, 1997). To date, the agricultural users do not pay for the water, in many cases users do not even pay for the maintenance of the irrigation systems (about R20 b. worth of which were built and maintained by the state). Given the massive fluctuations in rainfall in most of the country, this inequality in access to subsidised irrigation has vast consequences average agricultural incomes as well as their variability (Government of South Africa, 1997: 21; World Bank, 1994).

Table 5. *Debt burden and source of credit*

	All South Africa	Households ranked by consumption quintiles				
		Quintile 1 (Poorest)	Quintile 2	Quintile 3	Quintile 4	Quintile 5 (Richest)
Amount owed (share of monthly expenditure)	161.0	33.4	40.7	56.6	104.4	226.0
Debt service (share of monthly expenditure)	8.7	9.8	7.8	8.0	10.3	8.7
Source of credit:						
Banks	8.4	0	0.4	1.8	6.1	27.0
Hire purchase	30.4	17.5	29.4	39.5	33.9	27.6
Shopkeepers	33.7	48.2	37.4	31.6	32.3	25.7
Relatives/friends	12.9	21.2	16.0	12.0	12.3	7.0
Other[*]	14.6	13.1	16.8	15.1	13.4	12.7

[*] Includes government schemes, NGOs, moneylenders, *stokvels*, burial societies, employers, and miscellaneous sources (none of which exceed 5% individually).
Source: Klasen, 1997a.

An important additional source of insecurity is the lack of access to reliable credit and financial services. The poor have to rely on informal sources of credit, and the ratio of repayment to debt stock indicate that these sources of funds carry much shorter maturity, higher repayments, and/or higher interest rates. Similarly, their reduced access to financial services more generally (including savings services) imposes additional costs, reduces their ability to stabilise incomes over time and necessitates more complex strategies of consumption smoothing (see Table 5).

Table 6. Inequalities in access to housing, services, and energy

	Percentage of households with:								
	Shack/ Trad.dw.	Crowd- ing	Electri- city	Piped water	Unclean water	Water inadequ.	Modern sanit.	No sanit.	Wood for cook.
African									
Rural									
1993	34.7	1.70	23.4	21.6	25.5	29.8	14.9	23.9	54.0
1994	47.1	1.72	16.4	28.5	27.9	26.5	20.4	20.4	52.5
1995	44.9	1.51	26.1	34.5	26.4	25.4	29.8	19.1	53.4
Urban/Metro									
1993	33.4	1.69	52.9	82.3	0.2	17.6	71.3	2.6	2.7
1994	19.7	1.56	67.4	85.8	0.4	8.3	75.1	1.8	3.0
1995	16.7	1.27	82.1	91.6	0.6	6.2	81.3	0.9	3.3
Total African									
1993	34.3	1.70	34.3	43.3	16.2	28.3	35.8	16.0	35.0
1994	35.6	1.65	37.8	52.6	16.4	18.9	43.4	12.6	31.7
1995	32.3	1.40	50.9	60.0	15.1	16.8	52.9	10.9	31.0
Coloured									
1993	4.3	1.43	83.6	79.4	0.4	6.7	88.0	2.8	4.0
1994	4.4	1.52	85.0	93.5	1.8	0.5	88.2	2.4	11.6
1995	5.3	1.32	84.7	92.2	1.9	1.5	81.5	3.2	14.3
Indian									
1993	1.2	0.97	100.0	99.2	0.0	0.0	99.6	0.0	0.0
1994	2.1	1.08	98.9	98.4	0.4	0.7	99.2	0.1	0.4
1995	1.2	0.85	98.9	98.0	0.0	0.5	99.3	0.0	0.4
White									
1993	0.4	0.52	99.8	99.7	0.0	0.0	99.8	0.0	0.3
1994	0.2	0.58	99.6	98.5	0.2	0.1	99.9	0.0	0.3
1995	0.3	0.49	99.7	97.2	0.4	0.4	99.7	0.0	0.4

Note: Column 1 refers to share of households living in shacks or traditional dwellings,[6] column 2 to the ratio of occupants to rooms in a house, column 3 to use of electricity as main source for lighting, column 4 to piped water in dwelling or on stand, column 5 to water from flowing rivers/streams, dams/stagnant water, or wells and springs, column 6 to the share responding water is mostly or never adequate (for 1993, sometimes or never), column 7 to flush toilets or improved latrines, column 9 to wood as the main source for cooking.
Source: SALDRU (1993), Central Statistical Services (1994, 1995)

In addition, poor households' lack of many basic assets both increases the burden of household production and threatens health and physical security. Table 6 shows that large portions of the population do not have access to reliable water supplies, decent housing, or safe forms of energy. This threatens security in several ways as it promotes poor health, leads to high rates of accidents and takes up valuable time (particularly women's time) in gathering

---

[6] In some cases, the housing classification was altered based on information on the wall materials (e.g. flats with corrugated iron or cardboard walls were reclassified as shacks, etc.).

water and wood. Rural African households without access to water and electricity spend an average of 4 hours a day fetching water and wood, leading to considerable *time poverty* among many rural dwellers (RDP, 1995; May, 1996); in addition, supplies are often unreliable and, in some places, very costly. While access to electricity and sanitation appears to have improved considerably between 1993 and 1995 (and have continued to improve since 1995), there is still a large proportion of the poor without access to safe water or electricity.

Poor forms of energy also promote considerable environmental and associated health problems, as shown in Table 7. Many African households live in households and in neighbourhoods that are prone to high levels of indoor and local air pollution, particularly in winter. Unsafe energy sources are not only a health threat, they are a major cause of accidents, particularly among children. They are related to frequent fires, which, according to a recently completed participatory poverty study, is one of the most important causes of massive poverty crises in poor households (especially in urban informal settlements, see May et al., 1997).

Table 7. *Share of households reporting difficulties breathing in winter because of smoke and pollution* (Urban areas only)

	African	Coloured	Indian	White
1994				
Difficult or very difficult	39.6	12.2	10.7	8.5
Some difficulty	15.1	9.9	9.0	6.8
1995[7]				
Difficult or very difficult	26.7	11.1	7.5	8.4
Some difficulty	19.6	12.8	10.6	7.2

Source: Central Statistical Services (1994, 1995).

Finally, high levels of accidents and criminal violence introduce a further level of insecurity, which threaten both the physical and the economic security of their victims. Tables 8 and 9 examine safety and security from several angles. Table 8 is based on perceptions of safety within the neighbourhood and in the home as well as reported changes in perceived safety compared to the previous year. The data on perceptions of safety in the home and the neighbourhood suggest a general worsening of safety, with particularly dramatic deterioration among Indians and Whites. It must be pointed out, however, that most households feel safe at home and in their neighbourhoods, and that Whites still feel safer at home and in their neighbourhoods than any other racial group. Africans reported in 1995 that they felt slightly

---

[7] The improvements observed for Africans are partly due to reclassification of some rural households in 1994 to urban households in 1995. When all (rural and urban) households are considered, however, the share reporting difficulty or great difficulty fell from 24.9% to 22.7%, while those reporting some difficulty rose from 12.6% to 17.5%.

less safe both in the home as well as in the neighbourhood; but when asked about changes in safety, more Africans reported that safety has improved rather than deteriorated.[8] In contrast, Whites' and Indians' perceptions of safety deteriorated, particularly in 1995.

Table 8. *Perceptions of safety and perceptions of changes in safety, 1994–1995*

| | Neighbourhood | | Home | | Safer-worse than a year ago[**] | |
	Unsafe[*] 1994	Unsafe 1995	Unsafe 1994	Unsafe 1995	1994	1995
Rural						
African	15.3%	16.1%	15.8%	15.8%	1.8%	8.3%
Coloured	2.3%	4.0%	1.7%	3.1%	5.4%	3.5%
White	9.8%	17.2%	5.6%	13.7%	-2.9%	-7.4%
Urban						
African	19.8%	21.9%	18.5%	19.2%	3.1%	14.8%
Coloured	21.2%	22.4%	14.2%	16.4%	-3.7%	-3.9%
Indian	13.2%	28.1%	10.2%	19.4%	-8.7%	-19.7%
White	10.2%	16.5%	6.4%	9.8%	-3.8%	-13.4%
Total						
African	17.2%	18.7%	16.9%	17.3%	2.4%	11.2%
Coloured	17.5%	18.5%	11.7%	13.6%	-1.9%	-2.4%
Indian	13.2%	28.1%	10.2%	19.4%	-8.7%	-19.7%
White	10.1%	16.6%	6.4%	10.2%	-3.8%	-12.7%
Total	15.7%	18.5%	14.2%	15.6%	0.5%	4.2%

[*] Refers to the percentage of households feeling rather unsafe or very unsafe.

[**] This refers to the share of households reporting that they feel safer than a year ago minus those that report that they feel less safe.

Source: Central Statistical Services (1994, 1995).

Table 9 allows for a comparison of levels of crime in the period 1990–1995. While levels of politically motivated public violence have reduced sharply (a major success of the peaceful transition), overall crime rates show an upward trend. The number of murders appears to have stabilised at an extremely high level[9] and the number of rapes and serious assaults has increased dramatically. Similarly, property crimes (robberies, vehicle thefts, housebreaking) have also increased considerably.[10] This rise in crime levels goes as far back as the 1980s, when there was intense public concern about the political conflict and public violence, coupled with a racially biased approach to crime prevention. Consequently, crime did not enjoy the high profile on the political agenda that it has now.

---

[8] While these results appear inconsistent, they may be partly reconciled by the fact that fewer people reported to be feeling 'very unsafe' rather than just rather 'unsafe'.

[9] South Africa continues to have one of the highest murder rates in the world at about 35/100,000 (South Africa Foundation, 1996).

[10] A proportion of robbery and vehicle theft and hijacking may in fact be fraud against insurance companies, so that these reported figures should be treated with some caution.

Surveys suggest that Africans and Coloureds, particularly in urban areas, suffer from particularly high rates of rape and murder, while urban Indians and Whites suffer from high levels of property crimes (robberies, vehicle thefts, etc). Crime levels in rural areas are considerably lower, although far from negligible (SALDRU, 1993; CSS, 1995).

Table 9. *Numbers of reported crimes (1990–1995)*

Crime	1990	1991	1992	1993	1994	1995
Public violence	4,756	2,402	2,250	5,696	961	750
Rape	20,321	22,749	24,316	27,039	32,003	36,888
Serious assault	123,639	129,241	135,991	144,750	156,838	171,656
Murder	18,569	17,812	19,384	19,584	18,285	18,983
Housebreaking	158,838	185,660	181,026	185,299	196,146	214,854
Robbery	61,025	68,907	78,447	87,083	95,198	102,809
Vehicle theft	68,254	71,069	71,315	77,890	94,239	97,947
Truck hijacking	-	500	586	616	836	1,692
Fraud	49,396	55,178	57,958	55,787	54,626	52,684

Source: The NEDCOR Project on Crime, Violence and Investment, June 1996.

Apart from crime, accidents and disasters are a major source of insecurity in South Africa. South Africa has one of the highest traffic accident fatality rates in the world (Table 10). With 10,256 traffic-related deaths in 1995, South Africa has a rate of 10.4 road fatalities per 100 million kilometres travelled, about five times the rate prevailing in Europe (Council for Scientific and Industrial Research, 1996). Particularly noteworthy is that more than 40 per cent of fatalities in traffic accidents are pedestrians (ibid.).[11]

Table 10. *Traffic accidents and their consequences*

Injuries and deaths in traffic accidents, 1991–95	Fatal	Serious	Minor	Total
1991	11069	34765	90612	136446
1993	9470	33555	85130	128155
1995	10256	39510	96350	146055
Fatalities by status	Driver	Passenger	Pedestrian	Total
1991	2832	3340	4897	11069
1993	2543	2812	4115	9470
1995	2792	3299	4165	10256

Source: CSIR (1996).

For other accidents, particularly domestic accidents, there are fewer reliable statistics, but the levels of accidents relating to burns and fires are very high in many townships and rural areas. Apart from unsafe energy, low quality

---

[11] This astounding statistic is, in part, related to the combination of very good roads, very fast vehicles, and very little effective separation of pedestrians and traffic on most roads, particularly in rural areas, and the influence of alcohol (among both drivers and pedestrians).

housing and poorly designed traffic systems, alcohol abuse plays a prominent role in many domestic and road accidents, as well as in many incidences of violence. Finally, a range of disasters, including floods and fires, hurt the urban poor living in informal settlements and present a major source of economic insecurity to them (May, 1997).

The effects of accidents, disasters, and crime are different for different groups. The critical difference is that most wealthier people are insured against losses of property and health risks, while most of the poor are not. Therefore, accidents and crises tend to throw poor people immediately into desperate financial straits and can lead to a downward spiral into destitution (May, 1997).

One way to get a summary assessment of the impact of these types of insecurity on health and physical safety is to examine the causes of death of South Africans. Table 11 shows that unnatural causes of death are responsible for 11–26 per cent of the potential years of life lost,[12] depending on the estimate. This is one of the highest rates in the developing world. In addition, diseases related to unsafe water, poor sanitation, poor housing and insufficient access to health care (mainly infectious and respiratory diseases) account for another 27 per cent of potential years of life lost. These figures show clearly that there are considerable human costs to insecurity.

Table 11. *Potential years of life lost by cause (1990)*[*]

	Reported[**]	Estimated[**]
Perinatal	19.8	22.1
Infectious	17.4	14.4
Respiratory	9.3	13.1
of which TB		4.3
Circulatory	8.1	6.1
Total Injuries	25.6	10.9
of which transport	5.6	1.6
of which homicide/suicide	6.5	2.3
Cancer	5.8	1.6
Nutritional Deficiency		3.4
Other/Ill-defined[***]	14.0	30.1

[*] Potential years of life lost (PYLL) count the number of years people die before age 65 to give a sense of the importance of specific causes of death. The total PYLL in 1990 was estimated to be 4.4 million (Bradshaw et al., 1994).

[**] Reported is based on actually reported causes of death while estimated adjusts reported figures for known incidences of under-reporting, especially among the African community where only about 55% of all deaths were reported in 1990. Thus the reported figures are biased towards Whites and urban groups.

[***] Many death certificates do not state a cause, as the deaths were not witnessed by a medical professional; the high rate of ill-defined causes of death is a symptom of poor access to health care.

Sources: Bradshaw et al. (1994); Bourne (1994).

---

[12] Potential years of life lost refer to deaths that occur before age 65. For example, the death of a one year old would represent 64 potential years of life lost; that of a 50 year old only 15 years lost.

Disability is another major problem associated with the combination of poverty, poor health access, and the effects of accidents and violence. Table 12 shows self-reported rates of disability by race and age. Africans and Coloured adults have much higher rates of physical and mental disability which, as was shown in Table 3, significantly influences their ability to participate in the labour force. As the rates shown in the table are self-reported, they should be treated with some caution, since both awareness and perceptions of disability may influence reporting.[13]

Table 12. *Disability rates by race and age (1995)*

	Sight	Hearing/Speech	Physical	Mental
Under 18 years				
African	1.24	0.47	0.34	0.11
Coloured	1.04	0.42	0.42	0.24
Indian	0.72	0.48	0.16	0.48
White	1.24	0.22	0.15	0.15
18-64 years				
African	3.40	0.86	2.38	0.67
Coloured	2.50	0.88	3.91	0.66
Indian	3.04	0.61	1.64	0.38
White	1.90	0.85	1.30	0.38
64+ years				
African	12.66	3.85	7.34	0.38
Coloured	12.75	4.37	7.16	0.62
Indian	8.69	3.01	8.41	0.00
White	5.09	5.37	3.46	0.83
Total	2.8	0.87	1.69	0.44

Source: Central Statistical Services (1995).

Inequality and insecurity

Some causes of insecurity are, in important ways, related to inequality. As already indicated in Table 1, South Africa's poor social indicators, compared to other middle-income countries, are directly related to inequality. Lower inequality would be likely to reduce differentials in access to basic services, as well as health and education imbalances, all of which were identified as major sources of insecurity among the poor. Conversely, public policy to lower the differentials in access to health, education, and services would help reduce income inequality.

Secondly, the levels of crime, violence, and accidents are partly related to the levels of inequality. While causes of crime and violence are complex and do not lend themselves to easy characterisation, the combination of poverty and unemployment (particularly youth unemployment) for one

[13] For example, it may well be the case that the low rate of mental disability among African children is related to the fact that slight mental disabilities have not been detected to the extent that they have been among other groups. Also, perceptions of illness are importantly influenced by access to health services and awareness of health conditions (Sen, 1992).

group of the population and very high levels of wealth, income, status, and power for other groups is likely to contribute to high levels of crime and violence.[14] Furthermore, the increase in crime and violence, particularly since 1991, is an unfortunate side effect of an otherwise positive political, social and economic transition. It may be unfortunate, but understandable, that the whole of South Africa dedicated all its energy and effort to the negotiation of a new political order in the period 1990–1994, rather than to the control of crime and violence of a non-political nature. However, the consequences of this choice are seriously threatening the credibility and maybe the survival of the new democratic order.

The occurrence of accidents is, in many cases, directly related to the lack of access to safe forms of energy and poor housing, which in turn leads to an inordinate number of domestic accidents involving burns and fires, particularly among children. Similarly, South Africa's high levels of traffic accidents are, in part, related to the inequality in wealth and lifestyles. The extensive and high-quality road network (with the exception of the homelands) serves the dual purposes of a fast means of traffic for many powerful vehicles as well as a main avenue of pedestrian travel, particularly in peri-urban and rural areas. There is also some evidence that poverty, unemployment, and inequality are related to some social pathologies including high rates of alcohol abuse, which are related to many instances of accidents and violence (May, 1997).

Finally, inequality has a direct impact on political and social stability and security. While the transition to the new government has been remarkably smooth in many ways, the transition from apartheid to the government of national unity and the first years of the new government have been characterised by considerable struggles over economic policy, particularly labour market policy. Examples include a general strike over labour market clauses in the new constitution, considerable struggles over labour relations bills and basic conditions of employment, and the publication of diametrically opposed growth strategies by business and organised labour. Part of the reason for these struggles is related to differences in ideology and visions of economic policy, and is thus part of a healthy debate in a democratic society. But the intensity of the debates appears related to struggles over redistribution and inequality and linked to the aspirations of the newly enfranchised majority which are, in important ways, patterned along the lives led by the wealthy White community (Moller, 1997).[15] The intensity of these

---

[14] Clearly, low employment prospects and poverty, combined with high potential returns for criminal activity increase the incentives for criminal activities (Becker, 1965). Other factors that need to be considered are the very poor effectiveness of the police and the criminal justice system in dealing with crime, which is related to low trust of the police in communities, police corruption, low motivation and pay for the police, out-dated techniques and poor training, and a slow and ineffective criminal justice system.

[15] The nature of these struggles cannot also simply be understood as poor *versus* rich. Organised labour does not, on the whole, represent the poorest part of the community, as its members

struggles and the means with which they have been fought have served to weaken the stability of economic policy-making and public confidence in the government and the country.

In addition, there have been instances of the poor taking matters into their own hands. Examples include land invasions for housing near urban areas and continued reluctance to pay for services and rents in many urban and metropolitan areas. The outcome has been considerable volatility of foreign investment, sharp fluctuations of the exchange rate, insecurity about government policy, and slow investment and job creation.

Responses to insecurity

As shown above, many South Africans, particularly the poor, are suffering from considerable levels of economic and social insecurity. In order to minimise the risks associated with this insecurity, the affected people have adopted a variety of strategies to minimise its impact.

Table 13. *Source of income by quintile (1993)*

	Quintile 1 (Poorest)	Quintile 2	Quintile 3	Quintile 4	Quintile 5 (Richest)	Total
Remittances						
-cash	39.5%	43.7%	33.0%	17.0%	7.1%	28.1%
-in kind	10.4%	16.5%	15.2%	6.9%	2.5%	10.3%
Old age pension	42.0%	31.8%	23.0%	12.2%	5.1%	22.8%
Disability grant	4.8%	5.3%	4.4%	2.5%	0.9%	3.6%
Unemployment ins.	1.2%	1.2%	1.1%	1.0%	1.0%	1.1%
Maintenance grant	0.2%	1.0%	1.3%	0.6%	0.2%	0.6%
Self-employment	10.0%	11.9%	14.9%	13.6%	14.2%	12.9%
Agriculture	33.6%	28.0%	15.6%	6.9%	4.3%	17.7%
Wage	36.3%	48.8%	63.7%	78.9%	79.8%	61.5%
Private/ Civil service pension	0.9%	1.9%	2.4%	4.0%	14.5%	4.7%
Capital earnings	0.2%	0.3%	0.3%	1.2%	13.8%	3.1%
Total	179.2%	190.4%	174.9%	144.8%	143.3%	166.5%

The percentages above refer to the share of households reporting the listed sources of income as one of their sources (multiple listings possible).
Source: SALDRU (1993).

As already suggested by Figure 5, the poor appear to rely on multiple sources of income. Part of the reason for this is that none of the sources individually would be able to sustain a livelihood. In addition, however, reliance on multiple income sources minimises the risks inherent in many of them. As shown in Table 13, many poor people rely on a combination of agriculture, informal sector activities (mostly small trading activities, *shebeens* (township bars), sewing and selling clothes, and small repair and craft

---

are drawn predominantly from quintiles 3 and 4. At the same time, these struggles are related to the large differences in wealth and life-style between them and the White minority and the leaders of the business community.

operations), wage income, as well as government transfers. The table under-states the multitude of income sources, as many households rely on the earnings of more than one wage earner and the informal and agricultural activities of more than one member of the household. While these strategies of diversifying income sources increase the chances of the poor to survive in the face of low and uncertain incomes, they also entrap people in a state of poverty as they make it more difficult to increase their productivity, spe-cialise, invest, and escape the shifting menu of low-productivity activities (May, 1996; May et al., 1998).

In addition, it appears that livelihood strategies include changes in household structure and formation that increases the economic security of the poor. For example, there is considerable evidence that households form around people with secure incomes. In rural areas, those with the most se-cure income sources are often old-age pensioners, who therefore have be-come the focus of household formation in poor rural areas. While this type of strategy solves short-term problems of economic necessity, it generates another type of poverty trap as it often takes people away from where em-ployment and informal sector opportunities are (and to rural areas where opportunities are few), and it generates other forms of insecurity, in particu-lar the death of the person receiving the pension (Case and Deaton, 1998; Klasen and Woolard, 1998).

Responses to other types of insecurity also contribute to considerable economic inefficiencies and lead to distortions. For example, private protec-tion against crime is a growth industry in South Africa. The NEDCOR pro-ject on crime calculated that the total costs of crime, including private pro-tection spending, direct losses, and the costs of policing and the criminal jus-tice system, amounted to at least R31.3 b. (about $ 7 b. or $180 per capita) in 1996/97, equivalent to 5.6 per cent of GDP.

Much spending intended to reduce susceptibility to crime is indirect as it consists of choices of neighbourhoods, types of housing, type of enter-tainment sought, methods and location of shopping, means of transportation used, etc. While there are few precise data and serious conceptual and measurement issues, it is clear that in high-crime areas such as Gauteng, people's choices in all the above-mentioned dimensions are influenced by crime. As a result, people prefer to live in clusters of houses with centralised security and surrounded by high walls or fences, prefer to travel by car, shop and seek entertainment in enclosed malls, and are willing to travel long distances to work if these behaviours increase perceived security. All impose considerable costs and distort spending patterns.

Finally, those who can afford it continue to seek and maintain the ability to emigrate as another way to reduce their perceived sense of insecurity re-lated to crime and the economic future of South Africa. This is not only costly (materially and psychologically) to those considering emigration, but also imposes costs on the rest of society that rely on the active participation of its skilled and professional labour force.[16]

Clearly, insecurity is very costly for those who suffer from it. It imposes considerable direct costs, reduces the returns on their income-earning strategies and, in the case of the poor, may help entrap them in their poverty. At the same time, it imposes considerable social costs as it reduces the productivity of assets (both physical and human), leads to distorted and inefficient developments, and wastes resources. Thus increasing economic and social security is not only beneficial to those suffering from insecurity, but also promotes economic growth and social welfare.

Conclusion: Policies to increase economic and social security

As it is the poor who suffer most from insecurity, measures to promote their economic security should receive highest priority. Many of the problems of the poor are related to their very poor asset base (land, credit, savings, human resources, and time) which forces them to engage in the menu of low-productivity livelihood strategies described. This link between insecurity and lack of assets highlights the importance of increasing the asset base of the poor. As most poor people live in rural areas, increasing their access to land, agricultural support and credit may therefore be among the most important elements of a strategy to reduce insecurity for the poor. In addition, efforts to reduce the inherent risks in agricultural production (e.g. irrigation, drought and pest-resistant crops) could be particularly valuable.[17]

A critical complement to such a strategy is the reduction of *time poverty* of many rural households that would enable them to effectively develop and use a greater asset base. In this context, assistance that reduces the time spent on daily survival activities (esp. collection of water and firewood, transport, etc.) would be most critical. Thus the extension of reliable rural water supplies, assistance with energy (electricity and/or biomass fuels) and support for rural transport may be most important.

To help the poor deal with inevitable fluctuations in their fortunes, greater access to means of saving, investing, and borrowing will be critical to increasing their security. Expanding the formal financial network and supporting the development of informal (but reliable) savings and credit institutions in rural areas will be critical.

---

[16] There is little reliable data on emigration. There are frequent suggestions, however, that there is a considerable willingness among young, skilled Whites to emigrate (often in relation to studying abroad or initiated by short-term employment abroad). There are more indications, however, that a larger share of Whites attempts to keep the option of emigrating open through transfers of funds abroad, maintenance of contacts, regular visits, etc.

[17] Such a strategy should not necessarily generate a class of full-time farmers; instead, it may be more feasible and useful to enable the poor to generate a greater share of their incomes from agriculture in a more secure manner. In that sense, increasing and giving greater security to the land-holdings of all the rural poor may be more useful than transferring the ownership of commercial farming operations.

In addition, the development of human resources through the provision of high-quality education will be an important element in increasing the assets of the poor, both in rural areas as well as improving their economic prospects elsewhere.

The existing social safety net, especially the social pensions, has brought a greater sense of economic security for many poor households. To the extent possible, it is important to extend the scope of this safety net to help other marginal groups in society more effectively. An enhanced social security system should emphasise integration into the economy (rather than ex clusive focus on cash assistance). Policies supportive of integration into the economy might include help with job searches, training, public works employment and assistance with setting up businesses, in addition to cash assistance to vulnerable groups.

Finally, for the rural poor as well as the urban poor, greater employment opportunities, and greater employment security will be critical. The only reliable and sustainable employment strategy is through pro-poor economic and employment growth that will reduce the current slump in the labour market and will generate more economic opportunities for the poor. While the impact of pro-poor growth may take a while before it sustainably increases the security and remuneration of employees, intermediary strategies that could be considered are pro-poor labour-intensive public works programmes (such as the 'working for water' programme); support for more labour-intensive agricultural production; heavy investment in education and training; assistance in informal sector activities through credit, advice, assistance; and favourable treatment by tax and regulatory authorities.

Efforts to deal with insecurity associated with crime and violence will necessitate not only great efforts to increase the effectiveness of the police and the criminal justice system (as well as their openness and accountability) and a reduction in widespread gun ownership, but generation of economic and social alternatives to crime and criminal behaviour of unemployed youth. To the extent that growth and employment creation will take place, they may contribute to the solution of the problem; to the extent that there is a vicious cycle that first needs to be broken, more will be needed to provide economic and social alternatives for youth to prevent descent into crime.

Greater recognition of the devastating effects of accidents and violence on the security of individuals, especially the poor, is needed. Measures to combat this impact include better housing and greater access to safe forms of energy, greater attempts to ensure road safety,[18] reduction of alcohol abuse and its impact on accidents and violence,[19] and mechanisms that en-

---

[18] Measures include greater separation of pedestrians and car traffic; separation between types of traffic, speed limits, and greater enforcement of alcohol limits (Barss et al., 1992).

[19] Taxation has been found to be one of the most effective ways to reduce consumption of alcohol, particularly among young people who are typically most frequently involved in alcohol-related accidents and violence (Barss et al., 1992).

able victims of accidents and violence to deal more effectively with their economic consequences.

Finally, policies to reduce existing inequality could enhance security considerably for several reasons. First, inequality itself is the source of considerable economic and social instability and insecurity. Second, inequality may prevent the government from combining policies to ensure efficient allocation of scarce economic, environmental, and fiscal resources with policies promoting equity and redress of past inequities. As argued elsewhere (Klasen, 1997b), greater reliance on market-based mechanisms to deal with emerging scarcities of vital resources such as water, energy, and land (while being the most efficient solution to address these issues), could perpetuate existing inequalities in endowments and be perceived as iniquitous. Third, measures to address inequality (either through the tax and expenditure systems or through reallocation of assets and resources) could help mobilise the resources that are in turn needed to provide the assets vitally needed by the poor.[20]

It is fortunate that the new government has recognised most of the issues mentioned above and has been determined to address these problems of insecurity. At the same time, not all dimensions of security have been enhanced. Policies implemented by the new government that have successfully enhanced the security of all, and the poor in particular, have been the rapid extension of water supply and electricity in rural and township areas, the expansion of access to free primary health care, and the maintenance of the social pensions which constitute an important safety net for the poor. On the other hand, the provision of housing has seriously lagged, as has the restructuring of the education and health systems to improve quality and coverage of their services. Crime rates remain extremely high and accidents and disasters still take a large toll, although there have been considerable efforts recently to improve road safety. Finally, economic performance has been poor in the past years and has contributed to rapidly rising unemployment rates and increased insecurity for many South Africans.

The transition from apartheid and the installation of the new government in South Africa have already enhanced the security of South Africans and Southern Africans in a variety of dimensions. But great challenges must be resolved if South Africans are to enjoy security in the broad conception of the term.

---

[20] Many of the programmes developed by government to address poverty and inequality rely on fiscal transfers (e.g. land reform, housing program, rural water supply program, public works programs) that enable the poor to acquire assets and improve their access to services and employment. Given the tight overall fiscal situation and the need to distribute the resources to a large part of the population who are poor or vulnerable, existing resources will not be sufficient to effectively implement many of the programs at the scale required.

References

Barss, P. et al. 1992. *Injuries in Developing Countries: Epidemiology and Policy.* New York: Oxford University Press.

Becker, G. 1965. *The Economics of Crime and Punishment.* Chicago: University of Chicago Press.

Bourne, D. 1994. *Analysis of Mortality Data for 1990.* Mimeograph. Cape Town: University of Cape Town.

Bradshaw, D. et al. 1994. *Estimated Causes of Death Profiles for the Nine New Provinces.* Cape Town: Medical Research Council.

Case, A. and A. Deaton. 1996. *School Quality and Educational Outcomes in South Africa. Mimeograph.* Princeton: Princeton University.

Case, A. and A. Deaton. 1998. "Large Cash Transfers to the Elderly in South Africa", *Economic Journal* 108:1330–61.

Castro-Leal, F. 1995. *Public Education Spending and the Poor.* Mimeograph. Washington DC: The World Bank.

Central Statistical Services (CSS). 1994. *October Household Survey 1994.* Pretoria: CSS.

Central Statistical Services (CSS). 1995. *October Household Survey 1995.* Pretoria: CSS.

Council for Scientifical and Industrial Research (CSIR). 1996. *Road Fatalities in South Africa.* Pretoria: CSIR-Transport Branch.

Department of Water Affairs and Forestry (DWAF). 1997. *Overview of Water Resources Availability and Utilisation in South Africa.* Pretoria: DWAF.

Government of South Africa. 1997. *White Paper on a National Water Policy for South Africa.* Pretoria: Government Printers.

Klasen, S. 1997a. Poverty, "Inequality, and Deprivation in South Africa: An Analysis of the 1993 SALDRU Survey", *Social Indicator Research,* 41:51–94.

Klasen, S. 1997b. "Social, Economic, and Environmental Limits to 'Late Developers' in South Africa?" Paper prepared for Conference on "Population, Consumption, and Development". King's College, Cambridge October 24–25, 1997.

Klasen, S. and I. Woolard. 1998. *Unemployment, Household Formation, Poverty and Nutrition in South Africa.* Mimeographed, University of Munich.

May, J. 1996. *The Experience and Persistence of Poverty in Rural Areas.* Durban: Data Research Africa.

May, J. 1997. *The South African Participatory Poverty Assessment.* Durban: Data Research Africa.

May, J. et al. 1998. *Poverty and Inequality in South Africa.* Durban: Data Research Africa.

Moller, V. 1997. "Aspirations, Consumption, and Conflict in the New South Africa". Paper prepared for "Conference on Population, Consumption, and Developmentt". King's College, Cambridge October 24–25, 1997.

NEDCOR. 1996. *The NEDCOR Project on Crime, Violence, and Investment.* Johannesburg: NEDCOR.

Sen, A. 1992. *Inequality Reexamined.* New York: Oxford University Press.

South Africa Foundation. 1996. *Growth for All.* Johannesburg: South Africa Foundation.

Southern African Labour and Demographic Research Unit (SALDRU). 1993. *The South African Living Standards and Development Survey.* Cape Town: SALDRU.

Reconstruction and Development Programme (RDP). 1995. *Key Indicators of Poverty in South Africa.* Pretoria: RDP.

World Bank. 1994. *South African Agriculture: Structure, Performance, and Options for the Future.* Informal Discussion Paper on Aspects of the Economy of South Africa No. 6. Washington DC: The World Bank.

World Bank. 1996, 1997. *World Development Report 1996, 1997.* Washington DC: The World Bank.

Health and Security in sub-Saharan Africa

William Pick

Introduction

The African continent faces enormous health challenges. Not only does sub-Saharan Africa have a large proportion of poor people, it is challenged by a lack of security that includes but goes beyond military security. Good health is a function of a secure physical and psychological environment as much as it is a function of good nutrition and quality health care. Sub-Saharan Africa has poorer health statistics than the rest of the world's poor nations, as manifested by a higher infant mortality rate and poorer life expectancy. The poor health status of Africans is a function of a number of complex but interrelated factors. These include a lack of political commitment to dealing with poor health, civil conflict, drought, declining commodity prices and the effects of structural adjustment programs.

The lack of food security, often the consequence of drought or civil conflict, has had devastating effects on health. The economic consequences of diseases such as AIDS, malaria, onchocerciasis and tuberculosis, among others, continue to have major implications for Africans' productivity, undermining the economic security of many countries and communities. Establishing economic, environmental, political and military security in Africa should be seen as central to any attempt at improving the health status of Africans. This paper argues that Africa has major health problems, that they stem from the lack of a number of securities, that military conflict is an important but transient cause of poor health, and that the lack of security (broadly defined) is, in turn, a function of the poor health status of the people of sub-Saharan Africa.

It further argues that only collective, multi-sectoral efforts can impact on poor health status, and indeed on poverty. The paper concludes with the argument that the security of wealthy nations is dependent on security and stability in sub-Saharan Africa.

Security and health

Given the historical changes in the concept of security described by Emma Rothschild (1995), it is easy to understand the link between health and security. Two examples of this direct link are the need for food security and appeals for household water security in Africa. The consonance of calls for securing these life-sustaining items with the Declaration of Alma Ata on Primary Health Care and the generally held view that food, water, sanitation and refuse removal are the major contributors to good health, bear testimony to the synergy between health and security (UNICEF/WHO, 1978). At the same time, a narrower military definition of security is not independent of health. For example, school health services in the United Kingdom were instituted because public authorities realised that war recruits were in such poor health that they would not make good soldiers.[1] Thus a separation between health and security is, at best, a matter of convenience.

Tracking the major features of health in sub-Saharan Africa

Sub-Saharan Africa (SSA) has an infant mortality rate which is 55 percent higher and life expectancy which is 11 years lower than those in the rest of the world's low-income developing countries (IBRD/WB, 1994). Its maternal mortality is almost double that found in other low-income countries. The AIDS epidemic has assumed enormous proportions and millions suffer from malaria and tuberculosis every year. All this notwithstanding, the health experience in sub-Saharan Africa has been mixed. The past 25 years have seen a reduction in the infant mortality rate by almost a third, an increase in the average life expectancy by 10 years, and an increase in the proportion of the African population with access to safe water from 14–40 percent. It is, however, important not to view Africa as a homogeneous continent. There are substantial variations in mortality between countries in Africa. For example, the death rate among children under the age of five ranges from more than 200 deaths per 1,000 live births in Mali, Angola and Mozambique to fewer than 100 in Botswana and Zimbabwe. Maternal deaths, similarly, range from 83 per 100,000 live births in Zimbabwe to 2,000 and more in Mali. Variations occur within countries as well, largely on the basis of socio-economic status but also depending on urban or rural location and ethnicity. Childhood mortality in urban areas can be 20–45 percent lower than in rural areas in countries like Zimbabwe, Togo, Sudan and Uganda. The well-known association between maternal education and child survival is illustrated by the fact that children born to women with no education are two to four times more likely to die than children born to married women with secondary education. Africa also has some of the highest teenage pregnancy rates in the world with up to 40 percent of births in Côte d'Ivoire, Nigeria and Mauritania to adolescent mothers.

Ethnic differences in mortality are a function of both different attitudes and perceptions of health and disease as well as unequal access to social and economic opportunities.

---

[1] Interestingly, the recruits were being enlisted for the British Army fighting a war against the Boers in South Africa.

Causes of death in sub-Saharan Africa

The major causes of death in SSA are preventable infectious and parasitic diseases. Perinatal, infectious and parasitic diseases account for 75 percent of all infant deaths. Infectious and parasitic diseases account for 71 percent of deaths between the ages of one and four and 62 percent of deaths in those aged five to fourteen. Prior to the AIDS epidemic, these diseases accounted for more than half the adult deaths in SSA (IBRD/WB, 1994). With the advent of AIDS, this picture has deteriorated with an estimated one in 40 adults in SSA now infected with HIV. In many African countries, AIDS has become the leading cause of death for adults.

In addition to its pre-existing burden of disease, Africa has also experienced newly emerging and re-emerging diseases. Malaria continues to be Africa's leading cause of morbidity, followed by respiratory infections and diarrhoeal diseases. The number of cases of malaria has been increasing alarmingly in recent years and the annual percentage increase has been estimated at 7 percent in Zambia, 10 percent in Togo and 21 percent in Rwanda. Tuberculosis has also been on the increase in Africa and this has been compounded by the AIDS epidemic. It is estimated that 9 million Africans are infected by the virus and approximately 2 million have full-blown AIDS. In recent years, Africa has seen the re-emergence of cholera as a major problem.

Unequal access to health care poses another challenge to the continent. The rural and periurban poor are particularly disadvantaged. In Côte d'Ivoire, it is estimated that only 11 percent of the rural population have to travel less than an hour to get to the nearest health facility. The figure for Somalia is 15 percent, for Rwanda 25 percent, and 30 percent for Liberia, Niger and Nigeria (IBRD/WB, 1994). In some countries, coverage of rural populations is good. In Botswana the proportion of rural poor within an hour of a health facility is 85 percent and in Tanzania it is 73 percent. This is largely the result of concerted efforts by these governments to provide access to health care for the rural poor. Urban bias in the provision of health facilities is reflected in Nigeria where three-quarters of public and private health facilities are located in urban areas, where only 30 percent of the population reside. Similarly, Nairobi has one doctor for 500 people while some rural areas in Kenya have one doctor for 16,000 people (IBRD/WB, 1994).

The poor in periurban areas are equally under-served. Not only is access to sophisticated private health care facilities limited, but the sprawling informal settlements on the fringe of the city are often 'ruralised', i.e. they lack safe water and sanitation. In Africa, the growth of cities will pose the major risk to health and security in the 21st century.

Coupled with the deteriorating health situation in Africa is the high population growth rate, estimated to be 3 percent per annum. Should this rate not decline, the continent's estimated population of 502 million could increase to 1.2 billion by the year 2025. The effect of population pressure on the environment and on resources is enormous and a reduction in demographic pressure is a prerequisite for security of any kind. Much of the military instability in Africa can be ascribed to competition for scarce resources, including natural resources.

How is this gloomy picture of health in Africa related to security? As indicated above security—human security—is concerned with human life and dignity and not weapons and military activity. Human security, therefore, has many dimensions; the Human Development Report of 1994 argues that health security is one of its many components (UNDP 1994: Chapter Two, 'New Dimensions of Human Security'). I would argue that health security encompasses all the components of human security. Some of the diverse aspects of health and security in Africa are discussed in the following section and include military security, political security, economic security, food security, environmental security, personal security and community security.

Health and military security

The lack of military security is reflected by the failure of countries in SSA to contain military spending at a time when global military spending was declining.[2] This lack of military security on the African continent has both direct and indirect health effects. Apart from the obvious effects of armed conflict on health, the drain on Africa's financial resources is devastating.

In SSA the proportion of regional GDP spent on arms increased from 0.7 percent in 1960 to 3 percent in 1991 (UNDP 1994: Chapter Two) in spite of the fact that almost half of the African population continues to live in poverty. Globally, it would cost about 12 percent of military spending to provide primary health care for all, eliminate severe malnutrition, reduce moderate malnutrition by half and provide safe drinking water for all (UNDP 1994: Chapter Two). In addition, only 4 percent of military spending would reduce adult illiteracy by half, provide universal primary education and educate women to the same level as men. A reduction in military expenditure would have even greater benefits for Africa. The well-known improvements in child survival and health that accompany female education would translate into enormous health benefits for the region. It is even more difficult to justify such high military spending given that the chances of dying from malnutrition and preventable diseases are 33 times greater than dying from the effects of war.

The lack of military security leads to other indirect adverse effects on health. Military conflict has led to an enormous refugee problem in the region (Table 1) with appalling consequences for the health of those who es-

---

[2] Between 1987 and 1994 a 3.6 percent annual reduction of military expenditure worldwide produced a cumulative peace dividend of US$395 billion (UNDP, 1994: 58 fig. 3.5).

cape death. The outbreaks of infectious disease epidemics (such as cholera) in refugee camps have been well documented. In addition, military conflict has also been associated with the spread of HIV/AIDS; the disease has accompanied troop movements in countries such as Mozambique (Baldro, 1990).

Table 1. *Refugees in selected African countries, 1992*

Country	Refugees
Mozambique	1,730,000
Somalia	870,000
Ethiopia	840,000
Liberia	670,000
Angola	400,000
Sudan	270,000

Source: UNDP 1994.

A further mechanism by which the lack of military security affects health in SSA is the migration of health professionals (usually trained at great cost by governments) away from African conflicts to richer countries in the North. Those who migrate tend to be the most highly-trained. For example, about 60 percent of the doctors trained in Ghana in the early 1980s have left the country (UNDP 1994: Chapter Two). It has been estimated that the average loss incurred when a doctor emigrates from Nigeria is US$ 30,000. If we examine the provision of health care personnel on the continent, we find that SSA is worse off than not only developed countries, but also other developing countries (Table 2).

Table 2. *Supply of human resources in health services, 1985–90*

	Sub-Saharan African countries	All developing countries	Industrial countries	World
Population/doctor	10,800	1,400	300	800
Population/nurse	12,100	1,700	170	530
Nurses/doctor	5.0	1.0	2.0	1.5

Source: WHO 1988, 1992, cited in *Better Health in Africa*, IBRD/WB, 1994.

Africa has an estimated 66,000 doctors and 500,000 nurses, and an unknown number of therapists, technicians, dentists, and other categories of health care personnel (IBRD/WB, 1994). However, the supply within the continent is varied and unequal. For example, the doctor-population ratio in Burkina Faso and Mozambique was estimated at 1:50,000 in 1985–90; that for Nigeria and Zimbabwe was estimated at 1:6,000. In South Africa, it was 1:1,600. South Africa is exceptional—it has an estimated 26,000 doctors while the rest of the continent has 40,000 (IBRD/WB, 1994). Similarly, the nurse-population ratio varies considerably across the continent. In Burkina Faso and

Mozambique, it was 1:4,000 in 1989–90; 1:1,000 in Nigeria and Zimbabwe; and 1:266 in South Africa. Within countries, the distribution of personnel is equally inequitable with a concentration in urban areas, among the high income categories and in the private sector. All these ratios show an improvement on the figures for 1970, except in the case of Mozambique, where the situation has become worse. Though the doctor-population ratio improved in the 1960s and 1970s, Africa was the only region in the world where the number of doctors per 10,000 people declined from 1980 to 1986. This is largely due to the emigration of health personnel, which increases at times of military upheaval.

Commendable attempts have been made to stem the haemorrhage of health personnel from Africa. Community service after qualification is but one of many attempts to recoup public investment in the training of health professionals. In South Africa, an interesting experiment is underway. Foreign doctors are not licensed to practice in the country unless recruited through government-to-government contracts. Doctors are recruited from Northern countries with an oversupply of doctors, such as Germany. Through this policy, doctors in undersupplied African countries are not lured to South Africa and the flow of health personnel is reversed to a certain extent.

Political insecurity

In many parts of the world, expenditure on military security is a function of political insecurity and the military is not infrequently used to suppress political opposition. Sub-Saharan Africa is no exception, and this lack of political security has both direct and indirect health consequences. A useful measure of political security is the ratio between military spending and social spending (spending on health and education). This is illustrated for selected countries in SSA in Table 3. It is clear, therefore, that apart from the direct effects of a state of political insecurity, the direct impact of high military spending on health and welfare budgets is considerable.

Table 3. *Ratio of military to social spending, 1990–91*
(Military spending as a percentage of combined spending on health and education)

Angola	208
Somalia	200
Ethiopia	190

Source: Human Development Report 1994.

For comparison, it should be noted that Syria had a ratio of 373 percent, Oman 293 percent and Iraq 271 percent for the same year.

Environmental security and its relevance to disease control strategies

A healthy physical environment is a prerequisite for human existence. The strain on the environment posed by rapid industrialisation and population pressure is enormous. Africa, in comparison with other continents such as Europe, is relatively under-populated, despite its high population growth rate. This could be due partly to 500 years of active de-population of the fittest and most fertile through slavery, as well as to the inhospitable climate and high incidence of disease in many parts of the subcontinent. However, Africa has not been spared the ravages of environmental exploitation, driven by an insatiable search for wealth, first through a process of colonisation and more recently through a more subtle process of economic exploitation of the continent's resources. The execution of opponents of such environmental exploitation in Nigeria bears testimony to the ongoing struggle to secure the African environment.

One of the major environmental disasters in SSA is deforestation accompanied by increased desertification. In the past 50 years 65 million hectares of productive land has become desert. Much of this deforestation is a result of the growing prevalence of crops such as tobacco, which require curing methods based on wood burning. It has been estimated that one tree is burned for every 300 cigarettes produced in developing countries (Muller, 1978). The fuel requirements of tobacco curing have led to vast areas in countries such as Malawi being deforested (ibid.).

But the growth of tobacco farming has other environmental effects that have a direct bearing on health. The soil in which tobacco grows often becomes of such poor quality that chemical fertilisers are needed. These fertilisers leach out of the soil and affect health. Tobacco has furthermore displaced food crops because it earns foreign exchange, which poor African governments find attractive and which structural adjustment policies encourage.

Growing water scarcity has posed a major hazard to health. As indicated earlier, lack of safe water is a leading contributor to death and disease in Africa. Diarrhoeal disease deaths can be reduced by 50 percent or more if safe water is provided (Esrey et al., 1991). In Mozambique, the outbreaks of plague in the 1970s and in 1994 were associated with drought accompanied by the centripetal movement of wild rodents towards domestic rodents and the hunting of rodents by humans in search of sustenance.

There is a further relationship between environmental security and political (and military) security which could have adverse effects on the health of Africans. Africa has more than 50 international drainage basins but there are not many international agreements on the protection and use of water sources within them. Water scarcity could become a prime cause of military insecurity, with all its attendant health problems.

Environmental security also implies the adequate and safe disposal of human waste. Deaths from diarrhoeal diseases can be reduced by between

22 percent and 36 percent if excreta disposal systems are improved (Daniels et al., 1990). Worm loads, especially in children, are a function of inadequate excreta disposal systems. Children not only suffer from anaemia due to worm infestation, but their school performance also suffers. Poor school performance eventually leads to poor economic performance, and lack of income limits access to health care.

Population pressure

The growing population of Africa has led to the occupation of land that would normally be uninhabited because of lack of water and the occurrence of disease. More and more people have settled in these marginal areas, with adverse health consequences. Similarly, increasing (and in some cases rapid) urbanisation leads to informal settlements in the most environmentally hazardous parts of cities. These settlements are often close to industrial waste sites and exposed to potentially hazardous substances. These informal settlements are often located below the flood line and are thus prone to inundation and infectious diseases.

Food security

While the world's production of food is sufficient to feed everyone, a lack of access to food—largely because of lack of income—has led to the food crisis facing many countries. In the late 1980s, 40 out of 68 low-income countries with a food deficit failed to provide for the basic nutritional requirements of their populations. Of these, 29 were in Africa. The World Bank has estimated that 340 million people in developing countries could not afford a diet that would prevent serious health risk and 730 million could not meet the dietary requirements of an active life, and 50 percent of these were in Africa. Economies in Africa grew by an estimated 1.5 percent per annum between 1990 and 1994, at only half the population growth rate. At the same time, agricultural production dropped to a negative growth of –2.4 percent in 1991–1992 and Africa's food self-sufficiency ratio dropped from 102 in 1960–70 to 75 in 1978–82 (Dinar, 1995). The challenge facing the continent is enormous. Within the next three decades, Africa's food requirements will triple while the per capita arable land is expected to halve.

Despite this gloomy picture, however, it should be noted that cereal production has increased in the highlands of SSA while growth in maize production has been significant in southern Africa over the past three decades. On the other hand, the meat sufficiency ratio dropped to 91.4 percent in 1994, which led to imports of animal foodstuffs at prices beyond the reach of vulnerable groups (Dinar, 1995).

The lack of food security manifests itself in malnutrition and an increased prevalence of, and mortality from, infectious disease as the human immune system fails to cope with the load of pathogenic organisms. It has been estimated that the number of undernourished people in Africa has grown from 100 million in 1960 to almost 200 million. Poor nutrition has direct and adverse effects on the educational performance of children. Well-nourished children are school-ready earlier than poorly-nourished children. A study in Nepal has shown that only 5 percent of nutritionally stunted children will attend school, compared to 27 percent of children that are nutritionally sound (World Bank, 1993). Well-nourished children also perform better at school. And girls, who are more likely to suffer from iron and iodine deficiencies that cause them to drop out of school, are particularly vulnerable. This effect on education has implications not only for the economy but also for the health of the offspring of the poorly nourished. The adverse health effects of food insecurity are therefore inter-generational, not only through the direct relationship between maternal nutrition and low birth weight but through perpetuation of the cycle of poor nutrition, poor education, low productivity, low income and poor health.

Conversely, the presence of diseases has adverse effects on food production. AIDS has had a devastating effect on food security through its direct effects on economic (and thus food) production, because it is a disease that affects people in their most productive years. In addition, individual treatment costs, on average, are estimated to be about 150 percent of annual per capita income. In poor countries, the impact of AIDS on national economies has major implications for food security. It is estimated that the epidemic has slowed the growth in per capita income by 0.6 percent per year in 10 of the worst-affected countries in SSA. However, the lack of food security in Africa stems mainly from land degradation, desertification, political and military instability, and the low priority generally given to food production by governments (UNDP Special Initiative booklet). This situation has been compounded in some countries by the effects of structural adjustment, which has often been accompanied by the removal of food subsidies. This benefited the farmers but meant malnutrition in poor families in mainly periurban areas.

Climatological security

The relationship between health and climatological security is related in many ways to environmental security. Africa is a continent burdened by climates that encourage the proliferation of vectors that bring disease to many of its inhabitants. The prevalence of malaria, onchocerciasis, schistosomiasis, filariasis, and many other diseases is a function of the African climate. The relationship between climate and health has been described since the time of Hippocrates. Today there is a general consensus that man has altered the global climate, and that these climatological changes have consequences for health. Direct effects include heat waves that lead to mortality from cardiovascular disease while indirect effects include the influence on vector- and water-borne diseases. Climate changes, which include alterations in temperature and rainfall, have led to the emergence of new diseases and the re-emergence of diseases that had been brought under control through immunisation and other public health measures. Vector-borne diseases such as malaria, plague and trypanosomiasis and water-borne diseases such as cholera are re-emerging and spreading as a consequence of climate change. The health effects of El Nino-induced drought in southern Africa included famine with resultant nutritional diseases, the death of 370,000 head of cattle, a 70 percent reduction in crop production and outbreaks of plague in Mozambique in 1994 (Aragon et al., 1997). The subsequent cold phase (La Nina) produced floods in southern Africa that led to a resurgence of malaria.

The contribution of man to global climate change has far-reaching implications not only for health but also human survival. The emission of greenhouse gases needs to be reduced if climatological security is to be provided not only to Africans, but to all populations in the world. Man's modern addiction to fossil fuels is in need of a cure in order to secure the climatological stability so necessary for healthful human existence.

Economic security

'Poverty is the world's deadliest disease' (WHO, 1995). Given the poor economic scenario referred to above, donor agencies (notably the World Bank and the International Monetary Fund) began to take a serious interest in the economic security of African countries. The stabilisation of African national economies, in the early eighties was intended as a short-term intervention. Structural adjustment was intended to correct longer-term economic policies that could lead to a reversal of poor economic performance. The reduction in state spending that accompanied stabilisation and adjustment inevitably led to less spending on health and welfare, with disastrous consequences for health, especially of the most vulnerable groups in society (WHO/WFP, 1989). Ethiopia experienced a rise in child mortality from 32:1,000 in 1980 to 38:1,000 in 1985; Mali from 34:1,000 in 1980 to 43:1,000 in 1985; and Tanzania 19:1,000 in 1980 to 22:1,000 in 1985.

In eight out of ten countries in which UNICEF studied the effects of recession and structural adjustment on health, the nutritional status of children had deteriorated; the same research showed a reversal after 20 years of decline in child mortality in three out of eight countries (Monekosso, 1993). The adverse health effects of structural adjustment have been acknowledged by the World Bank and structural adjustment loans are now conditional upon there being no reduction in health expenditure (Elmendorf, 1996). Table 4 indicates the changes in World Bank policy in recent years. However, a decline in health expenditure is but one of the consequences of structural adjustment as certain services, notably mobile maternal and child health services, had been curtailed in many countries. In addition, the gains made in the control of malaria and schistosomiasis, for example, were lost

due to the decreased health budgets that accompanied adjustment programmes.

Table 4. *Health variables in African structural adjustment loans, FY87–FY95*

Number of SALs	57
Number (%) of SALs with health-related fiscal measures	39 (68%)
Number of SALs (%) with health sector policy actions	23 (40%)
Health-related conditions as share of total SAL conditions	11%

Source: Elmendorf, 1996.

Another consequence of economic insecurity is the loss of health personnel
from rural to urban areas, and more importantly, to other, usually richer
countries, with disastrous consequences for the already under-supplied
continent. Adjustment programmes that encourage governments to produce
commodities and crops for export have led to a concentration on the production of tobacco in some African countries. This pressure to acquire foreign exchange obscures the fact that the economic benefits of tobacco production are outweighed by the long-term health care costs.

Personal security

For many people personal security is jeopardised by crime, especially violent crime. Crime in Africa is increasing. Women are particularly vulnerable.
It has been estimated that a third of the wives in developing countries are
battered. In addition, crimes such as car thefts are on the increase. In Kenya,
3,300 car thefts were reported in 1993, a 200 percent increase over the 1991
figure. In South Africa, the highway death toll in 1993 was 10,000—three
times the number of deaths from political violence. Violence against children
takes many forms from child labour to child prostitution. These are both
social and public health problems and many stem from poverty and gender
inequality. People cannot be regarded as healthy if their personal security
cannot be assured.

Community security

Membership of a group such as a family, community, clan, or an organisation provides a certain degree of security. However, membership in disadvantaged groups can also lead to oppression through bonded labour and
slavery, affecting women in particular. Another price paid for such community identity is the genital mutilation that follows from the practice of female
circumcision practised in some communities. However, the growing opposition to this practice may eventually lead to its abolition. The ethnic conflicts
that occur all over the world are a function of a lack of community security.
The declaration of 1993 as the Year of Indigenous Peoples by the United
Nations, which signified its concern with the lack of community security

and the 'ethnic cleansing' perpetrated on the continent and beyond, is further evidence of the direct relationship between health and security. The oppression of ethnic minorities (in some cases, notably South Africa, ethnic majorities are oppressed) has direct consequences for their health through homicide, lack of access to resources and lack of adequate health care.

Conclusion

Lack of security leads to poor health and that poor health leads to inadequate security. How then can the situation be improved? Given the complexity of health and security in Africa, simultaneous intervention on a number of fronts is the only way to address the challenges facing the continent. It is clear that all the different types of security are interrelated. To maintain military security, all the other forms of security will need attention. Because of the vastness and heterogeneity of the African continent, there is a need for action at both local and regional levels. Individual African countries are too weak in terms of population and economic power to address the major challenges to human security on the continent. The maturity of nations is measured by their ability to cooperate. The spirit of the Abuja Treaty is a useful guide for the policymaking and planning which needs to take place at regional and sub-regional levels. An important pre-requisite for security in Africa is support for fledgling organisations such as the Economic Community of West African States (ECOWAS), the Economic Community of Central African States (ECCAS), and the Southern African Development Community (SADC), among others. Cooperation agreements are more easily established on health matters than on many other issues. These agreements could form the basis for ensuring the other securities discussed in this paper. The tendency of the international community to view Africa as a single entity is erroneous. A strongly-supported regional approach that simultaneously promotes local capacity development holds the key to ensuring health and security in Africa.

Some of the central pillars around which improved health and security in Africa ought to be built include:

– The adoption of sound economic policies which do not affect health adversely. In this regard, regional economic cooperation holds most promise.
– The management of population growth within a framework of multisectoral development with particular emphasis on the rights and roles of women.
– Stronger government focus on food production, including greater support to research into agriculture and food production. The extended use of early-warning systems for famine and climatological disasters.

- National and regional measures to manage natural resources and to prevent environmental degradation.
- The rapid implementation of primary health care as defined at Alma Ata in 1978.
- The establishment of a culture of human rights in all nations on the continent.

These general principles should be underscored by greater advocacy by public health professionals, non-government organisations and donor agencies. The persuasive arguments so eloquently spelled out in the 1993 *World Development Report* should leave no one in doubt as to the wisdom of such a focus. It is clearly impossible to meet all the health needs of Africa and resources will have to be carefully allocated to cost-effective interventions. Priority health-specific interventions include the provision of affordable primary health care packages (that should include immunisation, reproductive and women's health services, the treatment of endemic diseases and the provision of adequate supplies of essential drugs). Other priorities include the increased coverage of the population by primary health care services and the increased gender sensitisation of the health services. Apart from investments in water and sanitation, the most important investment that can be made for better health is in the education of women. Such prioritised investment in health will provide greater security for all Africans.

But health and security in Africa need to be seen in a global context; they are not the responsibility of Africans alone. The world community has an important role to play in creating the climate in which Africa can be rehabilitated. The struggle to recover from the ravages of five centuries of slavery and colonialism in Africa is a struggle for all civilised people. But Africa should not be seen merely as a place in need of humanitarian aid. On the contrary, the African continent offers a potentially lucrative market for goods and services from many parts of the world. The developed world cannot be secure unless Africa is secure. The sleeping giant that is Africa has undreamed-of riches that will remain inaccessible as long as hunger, disease and poverty prevail. A secure, healthy Africa means a secure, healthy world.

References

Aragon, M., A. Barreto, P. Epstein. 1997. "Drought and Health Implications in Mozambique", *Medicine and Global Survival* (in press).

Baldro, M. and J. Cabral. 1990. "Low Intensity Wars and Social Determination of the HIV Transmission: The Search for a New Paradigm to Guide Research and Control of the HIV-AIDS Pandemic", in Stein, Z. and A. Zwi (eds), *Action on Aids in Southern Africa*. Paper presented at the Maputo Conference on "Health in Transition in Southern Africa", Mozambique, April 1990. New York, NY State Psychiatric Institute and Columbia University in NY City: Committee for Health in Southern Africa (CHISA) and HIV Center for Clinical and Behavioral Studies.

Daniels D.L., S.N. Cousens, L.N. Makoae, R.G. Feachem. 1990. "A Case-Control Study of the Impact of Improved Sanitation on Diarrhoea Morbidity in Lesotho", *Bulletin of the World Health Organisation*, 68(4):455–63.

Dinar, A. 1995. *Food Security and Food Self-Sufficiency in Africa*. University of Pennsylvania.

Elmendorf, A.E. 1996. *Health Reform and the World Bank in Africa*. Takemi Seminar, Harvard School of Public Health, 1996.

Esrey S.A, J.B. Potash, L. Roberts, C. Schiff. 1991. "Effects of Improved Water Supply and Sanitation (excreta disposal) on Ascaris, Diarrhoea, Dracunculiasis, Hookworm, Schistosomiasis and Trachoma", *Bulletin of the World Health Organisation*, 69(5):602–21.

IBRD/WB. 1994. *Better Health in Africa: Experience and Lessons Learned*. Washington, DC: The International Bank for Reconstruction and Development/The World Bank

Monekosso, G.L. 1993. "Economic Crises and Structural Adjustment Programmes in Africa— Their Impact on Health and Social Services and How People are Managing to Survive". Keynote Address at a World Health Organisation/Confederation of African Medical Associations and Societies Round Table Conference, Maseru, Lesotho, 1993.

Muller, M. 1978. *Tobacco and the Third World: Tomorrow's Epidemic?* London: War on Want.

Rothschild, E. 1995. "What Is Security?", *Daedalus*, 1995; 124(3):53–79.

UNICEF/WHO. 1978. *Primary Health Care*.

UNDP (United Nations Development Programme). 1994. *Human Development Report 1994*. New York: Oxford University Press.

UNDP (United Nations Development Programme). *The United Nations System-Wide Special Initiative on Africa Booklet*.

World Bank. 1993. *World Development Report. Investing in Health*. New York: Oxford University Press.

WHO. 1995. *Bridging the Gaps. World Health Report*. Geneva: World Health Organisation.

WHO/WFP. 1989. *Paper on Structural Adjustment, Health, Nutrition and Food Aid in the African Region*. Prepared for the International Conference on the Human Dimension of Africa's Economic Recovery. Zimbabwe: WHO Regional Office for Africa.

Meeting the Goals of the 1990 World Summit on Children: Health and Nutritional Status of Children in sub-Saharan Africa

Omar B. Ahmad

Introduction

Over the last quarter of a century, sub-Saharan Africa has experienced a substantial reduction in overall rates of child mortality. However, they remain far higher than the figures for other developing regions of the world. Many lives continue to be lost unnecessarily. In 1985–1990, for instance, the annual death toll for children under five years was estimated at about 4.1 million (Heligman et al., 1993:9–41). Among the survivors, a majority will grow up without the most basic requirements for a healthy life—a safe environment for growth and development, education, adequate food, clean water, decent sanitation facilities and a minimum set of essential health care services. Those who are fit enough to survive these hardships are often condemned to a life of ignorance, malnutrition, disease and poverty. Those who survive to adulthood are often permanently handicapped by a reduction in their capacity to learn and to earn.

In recognition of this potential hopelessness, many health intervention programmes in sub-Saharan Africa are shifting their focus from simply concern for child survival to a broader concern for the overall quality of child life. To this end, in 1978 the World Health Assembly set, as its major objective, the goal of reducing mortality further and ensuring a longer and healthier life for all children by the year 2000. Similarly, the USAID Child Survival Initiative (1985) aimed to reduce the infant mortality levels of participating countries from an average of 97 infant deaths per 1,000 live births to less than 75 deaths per 1,000 live births. These ambitious goals were to be realised through improvements in immunisation coverage, greater use of oral rehydration therapy, improvement in the health and nutritional status of mothers and children and reduction in the number of high-risk births. The goals of the 159 participating countries at the 1990 World Summit for Children were no less ambitious—reduction in infant and under-five child mortality to 50 and 70 deaths per 1,000 live births respectively, or by one-third, whichever is less (UNICEF, 1991); improvement in birth-weights and reduction in the prevalence of malnutrition. The specific strategies for achieving these broad sets of objectives were left to the individual countries.

At the time of these declarations, the year 2000 seemed far off. Today, it is less than a year away. Overall, sub-Saharan Africa continues to carry a fairly high burden of morbidity and mortality. At the country level, however, there are different degrees of success. The aim of the present paper is to take stock of the progress made so far using available health indicators. The paper will assess how much more work is to be done if these countries are to achieve the stated objectives of:

i)   achieving a rate of 50 infant deaths and 70 under-five deaths per 1,000 live births by the year 2000;

ii) reducing the prevalence of common diseases and improving their management;

iii) improving the nutritional status of children; and

iv) improving immunisation coverage.

To this end, comparative health and nutrition data from the Demographic and Health Surveys (DHS) for 17 sub-Saharan African Countries are used in this study. These surveys were conducted between 1990 and 1996:

Burkina Faso	(BF, 1993)	Benin	(BN, 1996)
Cameroon	(CM, 1991)	Côte d'Ivoire	(CI, 1994)
Ghana	(GH, 1993)	Guinea	(GU, 1992)
Kenya	(KE, 1993)	Madagascar	(MD, 1992)
Malawi	(MW, 1992)	Namibia	(NM, 1992)
Niger	(NI, 1992)	Nigeria	(NG, 1990)
Rwanda	(RW, 1992)	Zambia	(ZM, 1992)
Zimbabwe	(ZW, 1994)	Senegal	(SN, 1992/3)
Tanzania	(TZ, 1991/2)		

These surveys are designed to provide information on levels and trends in fertility rates, infant and child mortality rates, family planning practices and maternal and child health including the nutritional status of children. The data are also intended to form the basis for comparative evaluation of family planning, health and nutrition programmes at the international level.

The 17 countries comprise a population of 275 million out of an estimated population of 570 million for the whole sub-Saharan region (Table 1). The level of urbanisation ranges from less than 5 per cent in Malawi and Rwanda to over 40 per cent in Benin and Zambia (Table 1). The average life expectancy varies from as low as 44 for males in Guinea, Malawi and Niger to as high as 61 for females in Zimbabwe and Kenya (Table 1). Between the

Omar B. Ahmad

Table 1. *Current population, level of urbanization, life expectancy, fertility trends and modern contraceptive prevalence for selected countries in sub-Saharan Africa*

Country	Population size in million	Urban %	Life expectancy Male	Female	Total fertility rate (DHS) 1980–89	1990–96	Contraceptive prevalence (%)
Benin	5	40	49	52	7.1	6.3	3.4
Burkina Faso	10	6	47	50	7.2	6.9	4
Cameroun	12	20	54	58	6.3	5.8	4
Côte d'Ivoire	13	27	53	59	6.8	5.7	6
Ghana	16	29	54	58	6.4	5.5	10
Guinea	6	27	44	44	6.1	5.7	1.5
Kenya	26	10	57	61	6.7	5.4	27
Madagascar	12	14	50	53	6.4	6.1	5
Malawi	9	2	44	45	8.0	6.7	7
Namibia	2	19	58	60	-	5.4	26
Niger	8	9	44	48	7.0	7.4	2
Nigeria	102	20	50	50	6.3	6.0	4
Rwanda	7	3	45	48	8.5	6.2	13
Senegal	8	33	48	50	6.3	6.0	5
Tanzania	26	7	49	52	6.5	6.3	7
Zambia	8	42	46	49	7.4	6.5	9
Zimbabwe	10	17	58	61	5.5	4.3	42
Overall	275	18	50	53	6.8	6.0	11

Source: National Research Council (1990), Table 2-1, Pg. 15.

Table 2. *Trends in child mortality rates per 1000 live births, by country* Pre-1960 through 1985 and the most recent DHS estimates for 1990–96. Based on the probability of dying by age 5.

Country	Pre-1960	1960	1965	1970	1975	1980	1985	(DHS) 1990–96
Ghana	370	220	210	185	170	155	160	119
Nigeria	-	-	-	-	-	195	190	193
Zimbabwe	-	160	155	145	140	135	95	76
Kenya	260	210	185	165	145	125	100	96
Malawi	-	360	345	335	320	285	-	234
Tanzania	260	240	235	225	215	-	-	154
Zambia	-	220	190	180	165	150	-	191
Namibia	-	-	-	-	-	-	-	84
Guinea	380	-	-	-	-	-	-	252
Burkina Faso	420	315	295	275	255	220	215	187
Cameroun	290	-	235	220	185	-	-	125
Côte d'Ivoire	-	-	265	245	210	165	140	150
Benin	360	-	-	255	240	200	-	184
Senegal	375	300	295	285	265	220	190	132
Niger	300	-	-	-	-	-	-	318
Rwanda	-	240	220	225	210	-	-	151
Madagascar	-	-	-	-	-	-	-	162

Source: Hill (1992).

period 1980–1989 and 1990–1996, the mean total fertility rate (TFR) for all 17 countries dropped by about 12 per cent, from 6.8 to 6.0. The average level of contraceptive prevalence is about 11 per cent for all countries, with a range between 2 per cent (Niger) and 42 per cent (Zimbabwe) (Table 1). In a historical context, these indices represent significant achievements. In a global context, they are less impressive. The overall picture is thus one of a relatively large population with high rates of natural increase, urbanisation and poverty. The implications of these indices for population growth and development are quite serious.

Mortality

Over the last thirty-odd years, child mortality has dropped significantly in each country. Table 2 shows the trends in country-specific child mortality rates from before 1960 to 1996. There are, however, wide differences in the degree of progress achieved by each country. For the period 1990–1996, the levels range between 76 deaths per 1,000 live births in Zimbabwe to about 318 deaths per 1,000 in Niger. Figure 1 shows the trend in the probability of dying by the age of five for five selected countries—Ghana, Zimbabwe, Kenya, Burkina Faso and Senegal. All five have experienced significant changes in under-five mortality, but Senegal appears to have achieved the most sustained progress. In contrast, the decline in Kenya appears to have levelled off. Figure 2 shows the levels of infant mortality for the 17 countries. Only Namibia and Zimbabwe have rates below 60 per 1,000 live births. Four other countries, Kenya, Cameroon, Ghana and Senegal, have rates between 60 and 70 per 1,000 live births. The rest have infant mortality rates above 80 per 1,000 live births. Figure 3 shows the percentage declines in infant and child mortality rates needed to meet the goals envisaged by the year 2000 objective. The majority of countries need a decline of between 40 and 70 per cent in infant mortality rates and between 40 and 80 per cent in under-five mortality rates in order to meet the targets. For most of the countries, therefore, the task of attaining the declared targets is almost impossible. In fact, of the 17 countries, only Zimbabwe is likely to achieve the stipulated mortality targets.

To make matters worse, these summary national statistics tend to hide significant socio-economic differences. Table 3 shows the country-specific infant and under-five mortality rates by residence and education level. In general, infant mortality rates are higher in rural than in urban areas. In some cases, the difference is as much as 60 per cent (Senegal, Guinea and Niger). Similar urban-rural differences are also observed in under-five mortality rates. Educational differences are even wider. In some cases, such as Ghana, the infant mortality rate is about three times higher among women with no education than among those with secondary or higher education. In the case of under-five mortality, the educational difference is four times as much.

Figure 1.

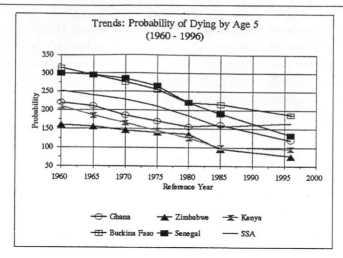

Figure 2.

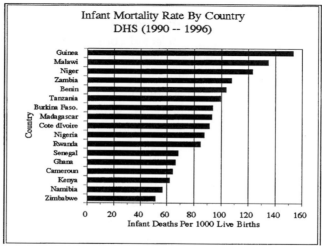

Figure 3.

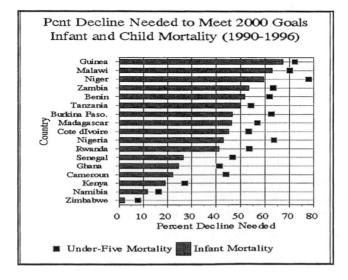

Table 3. *Infant and under-five mortality rates for the ten-year period preceding the survey date, by residence and education*

Country	Residence				Maternal education			
	Infant mortality ($_1q_0$)		Under-five mortality ($_5q_0$)		Infant mortality ($_1q_0$)		Under-five mortality ($_5q_0$)	
	Urban	Rural	Urban	Rural	Secondary/ Higher	No education	Secondary Higher	No education
Zimbabwe	44.3	53.6	63.0	80.3	38.6	61.6	56.6	93.1
Kenya	45.5	64.9	75.4	95.6	34.8	66.3	53.7	99.8
Namibia	63.1	60.7	86.3	94.2	57.0	57.9	75.8	96.9
Ghana	54.9	82.2	89.9	149.2	28.2	87.1	40.7	165.7
Senegal	54.5	86.7	101.8	184.2	32.1	81.1	52.4	170.7
Côte d'Ivoire	74.7	99.7	120.2	165.2	61.0	98.8	92.6	160.9
Cameroun	71.7	86.1	120.3	158.9	50.6	113.1	80.3	198.4
Nigeria	75.4	95.8	129.8	207.7	48.6	95.9	77.3	210.1
Madagascar	74.7	106.8	142.1	183.2	48.4	137.6	66.1	222.5
Burkina Faso	76.4	113.0	148.4	214.4	52.8	111.3	86.8	211.7
Benin	84.4	112.3	150.0	199.5	49.9	108.4	76.7	193.7
Zambia	78.0	115.8	150.8	201.2	79.4	114.9	134.8	204.4
Rwanda	87.5	90.3	154.6	162.8	62.8	97.3	91.2	176.9
Tanzania	108.3	97.2	159.2	152.2	71.8	103.3	100.8	162.3
Guinea	107.8	167.1	175.5	275.8	89.4	158.4	137.0	258.0
Malawi	118.1	138.0	205.4	243.9	61.2	142.8	127.3	254.9
Niger	89.0	142.6	210.3	346.8	101.9	137.0	207.9	334.0
All countries	77.0	100.8	134.3	183.2	57.0	104.3	91.6	189.1

Source: DHS 1990–1996.

Fertility

As mortality declines, the general expectation is that parents become more confident that their children will survive. As a result, the desire for children falls and the demand for contraceptives increases. Indeed, most major areas of the developing world experienced sharp declines in fertility in 1965–70 and 1980–1985, largely in response to substantial reductions in mortality levels. In some countries, especially in Asia, the Near East, North Africa and Latin America, the magnitude of the decline represented as much as 47 per cent of the difference between their TFR at the beginning of this period (about 6.0) and the replacement level fertility (2.10) (Freedman and Blanc, 1991). In contrast to these regions, sub-Saharan Africa experienced very little fertility change over the same period. Birth rates have remained close to 50 per 1,000. Table 1 shows the estimated total fertility rate for each country for two specific points in time during the intervals 1980–1989 and 1990–1996. It also shows the contraceptive prevalence rate for the period 1990–1996. Figure 4 shows a plot of the TFR against the contraceptive prevalence rate (CPR) for the 17 countries, and the predicted regression line. Only Zimbabwe has a TFR below 4.5. Most of the countries have TFRs close to 6.0 and CPRs well under 15 per cent. Three countries have CPRs above 25 per cent (Kenya, Namibia and Zimbabwe). In general, it appears that the higher the CPR, the lower the fertility rate. Some countries have TFRs that are well above what their current CPR would suggest; others have TFRs that are below their predicted values (e.g. Senegal, Niger and Zambia).

Figure 4.

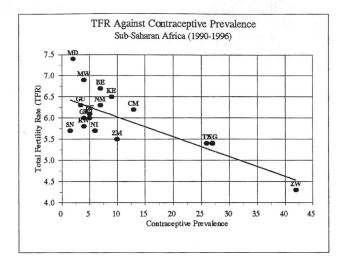

The current levels of contraceptive use are so low that the possibility of a significant short-term fertility decline operating through the adoption of birth control technology is rather limited. Given this context, it seems fairly reasonable to conclude that the rate of population growth is unlikely to slow down any time soon. The implications for socio-economic development are enormous. The UN's medium-term projection indicates that the population of the region will increase to about 1.4 billion by 2025. Furthermore, while the proportion of children that are dying is decreasing, the phenomenal increase in the size of the base population implies that the actual number of child lives that are lost at various ages will be tremendous. In a 1989 publication, the World Bank concluded that:

> Significant improvement in living standards cannot be achieved over the long term unless population growth is slowed. Going by current trends, Africa will increasingly be unable to feed its children or find jobs for its school-leavers. (1989:40)

If the sub-region is to achieve any meaningful socio-economic development, therefore, a lot more needs to be done to control fertility, achieve further reduction in mortality and improve living standards and the quality of life. The evidence from this and other studies suggests that where contraceptive prevalence is high, fertility decline is remarkable, and vice versa. Also, women who use contraceptives show more marked declines in fertility than non-users. It appears, therefore, that Africa's development is closely linked to efforts to achieve a sustained fertility reduction.

Reproductive health

Worldwide, it is estimated that close to 500,000 maternal deaths occur annually. The majority of these deaths occur in the less developed countries, especially those in Africa. Many of these deaths are due to causes that are largely preventable. Often, lack of access to appropriate obstetric emergency care aggravates complications that may arise during pregnancy, childbirth or puerperium. In addition to these, there are other non-obstetric factors that may aggravate or be aggravated by pregnancy. Among these factors are nutritional status (including anaemia and PEM), nervous system disorders, cardio-respiratory problems, sexually transmitted diseases and other infections. Strategies to reduce maternal mortality and improve other maternity outcomes must include the provision of quality antenatal care, delivery and postpartum care, nutrition, etc.

Antenatal care

Timely and good antenatal care (ANC) can substantially improve obstetric outcomes and reduce maternal mortality by:

- Providing preventive care information to women and their families.
- Establishing rapport between women and their providers early in the pregnancy.
- Offering an opportunity for the early detection and treatment of illnesses related to pregnancy, e.g., anaemia.
- Providing an opportunity for administering a variety of preventive interventions including tetanus toxoid immunisation, nutrition education and family planning counselling.
- Helping in the identification and monitoring of high-risk pregnancies.

The standard recommendation is that all pregnant women should have at least three antenatal care visits, with at least one visit during each trimester of pregnancy. In addition to frequency of visits, the quality of the care provided is essential in ensuring successful delivery. Among the indicators of quality of ANC are i) access to a trained antenatal care provider, ii) immunisation with tetanus toxoid (TT) (at least one TT injection given during pregnancy if the woman is not already fully immunised), and iii) delivery by a trained attendant (a doctor, a nurse, a nurse midwife or a paramedic). Traditional birth attendants, even if reported as 'trained', are not included in this definition.

Figure 5 shows a plot of the proportion of births with no prior antenatal care for 15 of the 17 countries in the current series. In the majority of countries, the proportion of births with no prior antenatal care is around 20 per cent or less. In Malawi, Zambia, Zimbabwe, Rwanda, Kenya and Tanzania, the corresponding figure is less than 10 per cent. At the other extreme are countries such as Niger where close to 70 per cent of births have had no prior antenatal care. These aggregate figures conceal severe socio-economic differences by residence and education (Table 4). In all countries, urban residents tend to have greater access to antenatal care than do rural residents. There are, however, wide variations in the levels of inequality among countries.

Figure 5.

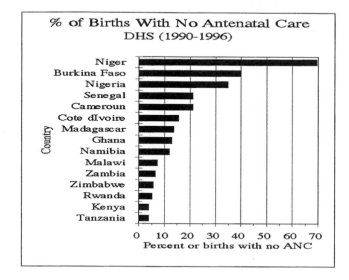

Table 4. *Differentials in antenatal care (ANC) coverage*
Percentage of recent live births for which women received antenatal care from a medically trained person, by residence, level education and maternal age.

Country	Percent of births with prior ANC	Type of place of residence		Highest educational level			Maternal age at birth (years)		
		Urban	Rural	None	Primary	Secondary Higher	<20	20–34	35+
Benin	-	-	-	-	-	-	-	-	-
Burkina	58.5	94.9	52.5	55.1	82.5	94.8	57.4	59.3	56.5
Cameroun	78.6	91.7	70.3	56.5	93.7	98.1	78.3	79.5	74.3
Côte d'Ivoire	83.2	96.3	76.5	78.3	91.1	97.8	82.7	84.0	80.0
Ghana	85.6	96.3	81.4	75.0	91.9	99.2	87.4	86.3	80.5
Guinea	-	-	-	-	-	-	-	-	-
Kenya	94.8	97.3	94.4	87.8	95.8	98.2	93.4	95.3	93.8
Madagascar	77.9	86.7	76.6	59.7	80.0	90.4	75.3	78.3	79.8
Malawi	90.1	-	-	85.8	94.5	97.0	92.0	91.1	84.9
Namibia	87.1	89.8	85.8	69.3	89.6	93.0	85.6	88.4	83.6
Niger	29.9	85.7	19.8	26.5	60.0	91.7	30.2	30.2	28.2
Nigeria	58.8	84.4	52.0	45.8	75.3	92.5	50.7	61.7	53.9
Rwanda	94.4	97.1	94.3	92.0	96.3	98.9	93.6	94.9	92.9
Senegal	73.6	94.1	63.2	68.8	93.7	98.0	70.6	75.0	70.6
Tanzania	91.8	97.8	90.2	86.3	94.5	99.1	91.7	92.4	89.1
Zambia	92.2	98.1	87.1	80.5	93.5	98.4	91.9	92.9	89.4
Zimbabwe	93.1	95.4	92.3	91.8	90.9	96.4	95.5	93.2	89.0
All countries	79.3	93.3	74.0	70.6	88.2	96.2	78.4	80.2	76.4

Source: DHS 1990–1996.

Table 5. *Frequency and timing of antenatal care (ANC) visits*
Percent distribution of recent births by number of antenatal care visits, and by the stage of
pregnancy at the time of the first ANC visit.

	Time of first ANC visit			Proportion with 3 or more visits and first visit before 7th month of pregnancy					
					Residence		Education		
	No prior ANC visits	Before the 7th month	Median month at first visit	As percent of all births	Urban	Rural	None	Secondary/ Higher
Benin	-	-	-	-	-	-	-	-
Burkina Faso	40.0	48.6	4.8	37.2	72.6	31.3	33.6	77.0
Cameroun	21.0	73.6	4.3	63.2	76.1	54.8	38.0	88.8
Côte d'Ivoire	15.5	67.7	5.4	45.9	59.9	38.7	37.8	74.6
Ghana	12.7	78.2	4.5	69.5	86.0	63.1	55.4	94.3
Guinea	-	-	-	-	-	-	-	-
Kenya	3.8	78.9	5.6	74.3	78.0	73.8	68.0	80.0
Madagascar	13.6	72.3	5.4	60.4	69.8	59.0	46.1	75.0
Malawi	7.2	74.0	5.9	70.5	66.4	74.2	83.6	70.2
Namibia	11.8	76.8	4.8	62.5	67.0	60.3	45.2	72.7
Niger	69.5	26.5	4.6	18.9	63.1	10.9	16.0	76.6
Nigeria	34.7	52.6	5.3	49.3	73.4	42.9	37.1	82.3
Rwanda	5.1	51.1	6.9	34.9	58.6	33.7	32.6	58.5
Senegal	21.1	68.8	3.9	51.9	74.1	40.6	45.8	86.7
Tanzania	3.7	83.2	5.6	78.9	80.2	78.6	74.0	84.1
Zambia	6.4	80.8	5.6	74.1	78.7	70.1	59.7	84.1
Zimbabwe	5.6	81.0	5.1	78.1	75.4	79.0	74.1	81.6
All countries	18.1	67.6	5.2	58.0	72.0	54.1	49.8	79.1

Source: DHS 1990—996.

Table 6. *Differentials in tetanus toxoid coverage*
Percentage of recent live births for which women received at least one tetanus toxoid injection
during pregnancy, by residence, level of education and maternal age.

Country	Percent of births where mother received any TT	Type of place of residence		Highest educational level			Maternal age at birth (years)		
		Urban	Rural	None	Primary	Secondary Higher	<20	20–34	35+
Benin	-	-	-	-	-	-	-	-	-
Burkina Faso	64.9	92.2	60.3	62.3	82.3	91.7	57.9	66.5	65.3
Cameroun	70.7	83.1	62.8	51.4	84.2	87.2	72.5	70.8	66.8
Côte d'Ivoire	75.3	88.2	68.7	69.2	84.7	94.7	77.8	75.0	72.2
Ghana	78.4	91.2	73.4	68.4	83.9	95.1	75.9	80.7	69.8
Guinea	-	-	-	-	-	-	-	-	-
Kenya	91.3	95.2	90.7	86.3	91.4	95.3	90.0	92.0	89.1
Madagascar	60.1	72.2	58.3	49.4	60.0	71.1	57.7	60.9	59.6
Malawi	87.0	-	-	82.6	91.5	93.8	89.9	88.4	79.4
Namibia	64.1	59.5	66.4	49.6	68.9	64.5	61.1	64.4	66.0
Niger	23.8	76.8	14.2	20.9	45.9	84.5	22.8	24.6	20.8
Nigeria	54.6	78.3	48.2	42.9	70.1	82.8	46.4	57.4	49.9
Rwanda	90.8	91.0	90.8	89.1	92.1	95.1	91.5	91.6	87.9
Senegal	71.4	88.6	62.7	67.3	88.7	91.3	66.8	73.0	69.6
Tanzania	90.5	93.4	89.8	86.2	92.8	95.2	92.6	90.7	87.1
Zambia	81.9	87.8	76.7	68.0	83.3	89.2	81.2	82.7	78.5
Zimbabwe	83.3	85.8	82.5	79.7	81.8	86.7	88.7	83.7	74.1
All countries	72.5	84.5	67.5	64.9	80.1	87.9	71.5	73.5	69.1

Source: DHS 1990–1996.

Figure 6.

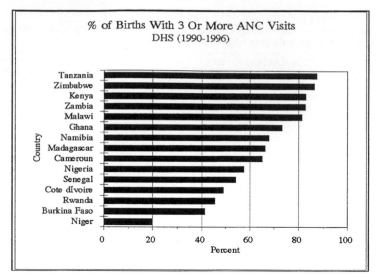

Table 5 shows the frequency and timing of antenatal care visits. It appears that a majority of women start antenatal care before the third trimester. The corresponding proportion varies from about 27 per cent in Niger to 83 per cent in Zimbabwe, with most countries falling between 68 and 83 per cent. The median month of first ANC visit ranges from four months in Senegal to seven months in Rwanda. The proportion of births with at least three antenatal care visits is less than 80 per cent in all countries except Tanzania, Zimbabwe, Kenya, Zambia and Malawi (Figure 6). In Niger this figure is just about 20 per cent. The median number of visits ranges from less than one in Niger to about six in Zimbabwe. Again, there are significant socio-economic differences within countries, especially by education (Table 5).

Tetanus toxoid immunisation

The practice of vaccinating pregnant women to protect newborns from neonatal tetanus has spread widely over the last 10–20 years. The World Health Organisation (WHO) recommends five doses of tetanus toxoid injection for all women. The first two doses are to be administered during the first pregnancy. The third, fourth and fifth doses are to be administered at yearly intervals or during the three succeeding pregnancies, whichever is earlier. If completed, this regime is believed to provide lifelong protection (WHO, 1987). The DHS data on tetanus toxoid immunisations is limited to births occurring in the three to five years preceding the survey date. It is, therefore, not possible to make any reliable conjecture about protection levels. In about 73 per cent of births, mothers did get tetanus toxoid vaccination (Table 6). Again, there are wide differences among countries and, within countries, among different socio-economic groups (Table 6).

Delivery care

Most pregnancies result in the delivery of a healthy baby. But many women who may not fit the traditional definition of a high-risk group may nevertheless develop unanticipated complications such as excessive bleeding, eclamptic convulsions and obstructed labour during delivery. Prompt recognition and referral can be lifesaving. Attention from a medically trained person during labour and delivery can facilitate such referral and is a key objective of the safe motherhood initiative.

In the current data, only 48 per cent of births in sub-Saharan Africa were delivered by a trained person (Table 7). Figures vary from under 15 per cent in Niger to about 69 per cent in Zimbabwe. As expected, urban births are more likely to be delivered by a trained attendant than rural births (Table 7). Births to women with secondary or higher education are on the average about three times as likely to be attended to by a trained person, as are births to women with no education (Table 7).

The place of delivery can have a profound impact on obstetric outcomes (Koblinsky et al., 1995). Delivery complications such as obstructed labour and haemorrhage can be more effectively managed when they occur in hospital. Less than 50 per cent of all deliveries in sub-Saharan Africa occur in a health care facility. Figures vary from about 16 per cent in Niger to over 67 per cent in Namibia (Figure 7). In conformity with the typical distribution of resources, urban births are about twice as likely to occur in a health facility as rural births. The relationship between level of education and the chance of hospital delivery is positive and monotonous.

Nutritional status

Low birth weight (LBW)

Studies have demonstrated a strong association between low birth weight (<2.5 kg) and infant morbidity and mortality (McCormick, 1985; Fauveau et al., 1990). In the present series, the prevalence of low birth weight is about 11 per cent on average. This represents about one low birth weight baby for every 10 births in sub-Saharan Africa. There are considerable variations by country from about six per cent in Cameroon to about 17 per cent in Madagascar (Figure 8). The rate is lowest among births to urban women and women with secondary or higher education. There is also a clear age effect. The rate is usually highest among births to teenage mothers and lowest among births to mothers over 35 years, except in the case of Nigeria where, paradoxically, the highest prevalence of LBW occurs among older women and the lowest among teenage mothers (Tables available). It is important to keep in mind that these data refer only to children who have been weighed and may indeed be an underestimate.

Table 7. *Differentials in access to delivery by trained person*
Percentage of recent live births delivered by a trained person, by residence, level of education and maternal age.

Country	Percent of births attended to by doctor, nurse, or midwife	Type of place of residence		Highest educational level			Maternal age at birth (years)		
		Urban	Rural	None	Primary	Secondary Higher	<20	20–34	35+
Benin	-	-	-	-	-	-	-	-	-
Benin	-	-	-	-	-	-	-	-	-
Burkina Faso	41.4	91.6	33.0	37.0	70.1	92.0	42.9	41.8	37.9
Cameroun	63.5	83.3	50.9	35.7	81.1	90.5	62.0	64.6	60.8
Côte d'Ivoire	45.4	76.3	29.6	36.9	55.4	81.4	48.7	45.1	41.7
Ghana	43.7	80.8	29.4	23.9	54.1	84.4	47.6	45.0	34.9
Guinea	-	-	-	-	-	-	-	-	-
Kenya	45.1	79.7	40.1	22.4	42.3	73.1	50.9	46.5	30.3
Madagascar	56.7	82.9	52.8	38.4	55.4	78.7	52.2	58.0	56.7
Malawi	54.9	-	-	44.7	64.0	91.1	57.1	56.9	46.1
Namibia	68.2	86.2	59.4	42.7	63.8	89.5	75.7	70.1	55.0
Niger	14.9	69.9	4.9	12.1	34.8	82.4	14.0	14.8	16.5
Nigeria	33.0	60.8	25.6	17.4	50.4	78.4	25.4	35.0	32.1
Rwanda	25.9	67.1	23.7	18.5	28.7	65.5	42.4	26.5	17.7
Senegal	47.2	84.1	28.5	39.5	76.9	92.7	44.8	48.1	45.9
Tanzania	53.1	85.7	44.7	37.9	60.3	83.7	56.5	53.2	48.4
Zambia	50.4	79.0	25.6	21.6	48.0	82.8	50.2	52.0	42.5
Zimbabwe	69.4	91.1	61.7	42.0	62.7	87.5	71.4	71.0	57.8
All countries	47.5	79.9	36.4	31.4	56.5	83.6	49.5	48.6	41.6

Source: DHS 1990–1996.

Table 8. *Initial breast-feeding*
Percentage of children born in the three years preceding the survey who were 'ever breast-fed' (i.e. given breast milk, regardless of frequency or duration), by sex, residence and maternal education.

Country	Percentage 'ever breast-fed'					
	Sex		Residence		Education	
	Male	Female	Urban	Rural	No Education	Sec/Higher
Guinea	93.5	92.7	93.2	93.1	93.5	91.9
Namibia	94.1	95.7	91.8	96.4	96.5	93.6
Ghana	96.7	97.6	97.7	96.9	96.8	98.4
Benin	95.8	97.7	96.5	96.9	97.2	96.8
Nigeria	96.3	97.1	96.3	96.9	96.9	97.5
Malawi	97.0	96.7	95.8	97.0	97.6	96.1
Kenya	96.9	97.2	97.2	97.0	96.7	98.2
Rwanda	97.2	97.3	96.2	97.3	96.1	-
Madagascar	96.7	97.8	95.9	97.4	96.4	97.2
Senegal	97.0	98.1	97.8	97.5	97.7	97.3
Niger	97.8	97.4	98.2	97.5	97.5	-
Zambia	97.3	97.7	97.4	97.6	97.8	97.9
Tanzania	97.5	97.7	95.6	97.7	97.6	97.6
Burkina Faso	97.9	97.7	97.7	97.8	97.9	95.3
Cameroun	97.0	97.4	96.1	97.8	96.9	96.8
Côte d'Ivoire	97.3	98.1	96.4	98.4	98.2	94.0
Zimbabwe	98.9	98.9	98.7	98.7	98.9	98.6
All countries	96.8	97.2	96.4	97.2	97.1	96.5

Source: DHS 1990–1996.

Figure 7.

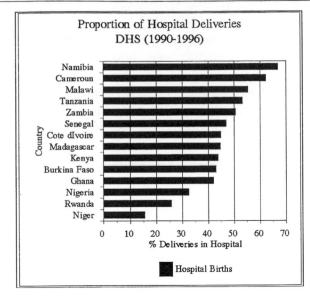

Figure 8.

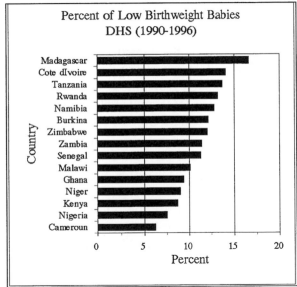

Breast-feeding and food supplementation

The superiority of breast milk as infant food is well established. In addition to being the most natural food for the infant, it provides some protection against infection. With the increasing use of bottle-feeding, some observers have expressed the fear that over time, fewer and fewer educated women will initiate breast-feeding. Response to the questions on 'ever breast-fed' children are used as proxy in determining the proportion of women who initiate any breast-feeding at all. In the present analysis, the values range between 92 and 99 per cent in rural areas and between 92 and 99 per cent in urban areas (Table 8). These figures seem to indicate that initiation of breast-feeding is still the norm in sub-Saharan Africa, even among the educated (Table 8).

Below the age of two months, very few children are introduced to solid/mushy foods except in Guinea, Cameroon and Malawi, where more than 15 per cent of babies are already on food supplements. By the age of six months, a substantial proportion of breast feeding children is already on solid/mushy foods (Figure 9). The figures vary from 29 per cent in Guinea to more than 90 per cent in Kenya. Guinea is peculiar in that even at 24 months, only about 57 per cent of breast feeding children are on food supplements.

Anthropometry

There is strong evidence that most of the growth retardation observed in developing countries begins in the first two to three years of life. Data from the nutrition Collaborative Research Support Programme (CRSP) indicate that most of the deceleration in growth occurs before the age of two (Calloway et al., 1992). Long-term prospective studies in rural Guatemala also indicate that growth retardation is largely confined to the first few years of life. This period corresponds to the transitional period of a shift from total dependence on maternal milk to complete reliance on the local diet. Available evidence indicates that such growth loss is often not regained during later childhood and adolescence (Martorell et al., 1990; Martorell et al., 1994; Haupsie et al., 1980; Billewicz and McGregor, 1982). The reasons for this are not clear.

There are various measures of physical well-being in children, but the most effective are anthropometric measures. One-time anthropometric assessment of height and weight can be expressed in a variety of indices of nutritional status. A child is classified as undernourished if (s)he measures two standard deviations below the mean for the reference population. *Stunting* reflects past or chronic undernutrition and is defined as deficient height for a given age measure. *Wasting* reflects acute undernutrition and is defined as deficient weight for a given height measure. *Underweight,* which captures low weight in relation to age, may be due to either chronic or acute undernutrition, and is thus a composite measure of nutritional status.

The prevalence of *acute undernutrition* (wasting) among children under six months varies from less than 1 per cent in Cameroon and Madagascar to more than 9 per cent in Guinea (Table 9). The rate increases with age to peak at between 12 and 23 months and drops thereafter (Figure 10). This seems to be the general age-pattern in all the countries. In general, the prevalence of acute undernutrition appears to be higher in West than in East Africa, at all ages. It is higher among males than females, rural than urban residents, and women with no education than those with secondary education.

The prevalence of *chronic undernutrition* (stunting) is generally higher than that of acute undernutrition at all ages (compare Tables 9 and 10). It in

Figure 9.

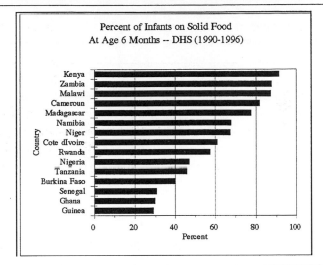

Figure 10.

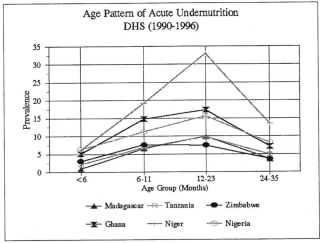

Figure 11.

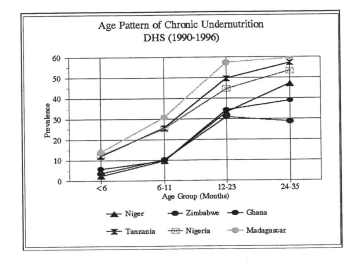

Table 9. *Nutritional status*
Percentage of children 1–35 months of age who are classified as acutely undernourished by age
of child at survey.

Country	Age-specific prevalence of acute undernutrition			
	<6 months	6–11 months	12–23 months	24–35 months
Cameroun	0.5	3.4	7.3	1.9
Madagascar	0.9	6.5	9.9	3.6
Tanzania	2.1	6.8	9.8	4.9
Zambia	2.1	5.7	9.9	4.9
Malawi	2.4	7.0	11.2	3.9
Zimbabwe	3.0	7.6	7.4	3.6
Senegal	3.4	2.3	15.8	7.5
Côte d'Ivoire	3.5	9.5	13.2	5.2
Kenya	4.3	4.8	10.0	5.4
Namibia	4.7	7.2	12.6	8.4
Ghana	5.1	14.8	17.3	7.1
Niger	6.1	19.2	33.0	13.5
Benin	6.2	19.5	19.1	10.5
Nigeria	6.3	11.2	15.6	8.2
Rwanda	6.3	6.7	7.4	3.0
Burkina Faso	9.3	20.2	26.4	10.7
Guinea	-	-	-	-
Average	4.1	9.5	14.1	6.4

Source: DHS 1990–1996.

Table 10. *Nutritional status*
Percentage of children 1–35 months of age who are classified as chronically undernourished by
age.

Country	Age-specific prevalence of acute undernutrition			
	<6 months	6–11 months	12–23 months	24–35 months
Cameroun	0.5	3.4	7.3	1.9
Cameroun	1.7	8.9	28.5	31.3
Niger	2.3	9.7	33.3	47.1
Senegal	3.2	10.9	23.4	28.8
Zimbabwe	3.5	10.2	31.0	28.7
Burkina Faso	3.6	10.6	31.7	38.2
Ghana	5.7	9.7	34.3	38.9
Côte d'Ivoire	6.0	13.4	30.9	34.9
Kenya	7.5	18.1	40.3	37.7
Benin	8.5	13.4	30.6	38.4
Zambia	9.1	22.1	47.8	49.3
Malawi	10.4	26.9	52.0	59.5
Rwanda	11.1	32.8	54.4	49.4
Tanzania	12.0	25.6	49.5	57.2
Nigeria	12.4	25.3	44.6	53.3
Namibia	13.2	23.9	37.4	32.9
Madagascar	13.9	30.8	57.3	59.5
Guinea	-	-	-	-
All countries	7.8	18.3	39.2	42.8

Source: DHS 1990–1996.

creases sharply with age until about 12–23 months (Figure 11). After this period marked variations appear between countries. In some the prevalence continues to rise with age, in others it levels off, and in still others the prevalence begins to drop. It is higher among male children, rural children and children of women with no education. Children whose mothers have no education are one to three times more likely to be chronically undernourished than children whose mothers have secondary education.

Childhood Immunisation

Increasing the proportion of children fully immunised against the most common childhood diseases is one of the most effective strategies for improving child survival. It is no wonder, therefore, that during the 1980s mass immunisation programmes became a major focus of many child survival initiatives throughout the world. Among the recommended vaccinations for children during the first year of life are BCG, at least three doses of DPT (diphtheria, pertussis and tetanus) and oral polio vaccines,

The current data suggest that vaccination coverage varies substantially across countries and between different socio-economic groups within the same country (Figures 12 and 13). As expected, urban children are more likely to have been vaccinated than are rural children. However, the urban-rural differences are wider in some countries than in others (Figure 12). For instance, in Niger, more than 90 per cent of urban children have had some vaccination compared to only 30 per cent of rural children. There are also substantial differences by level of education (Figure 13). In all the countries (except Cameroon and Nigeria), more than 95 per cent of children whose mothers have secondary or higher education have been vaccinated. In contrast, in a majority of the 17 countries, between 10 and 20 per cent of children whose mothers have had no education did not get vaccinated at all. The corresponding figures range from less than 4 per cent in Rwanda to more than 51 per cent in Nigeria (Figure 13). In general, coverage appears to be much higher in eastern and southern African countries than in the western African countries.

Childhood morbidity

It is estimated that more than 14 million deaths occur among children under five years of age. Among the leading causes of mortality in the first five years of life are malaria, diarrhoea, acute respiratory infections, and the vaccine-preventable diseases such as tuberculosis, measles, diphtheria, pertussis, tetanus, and poliomyelitis. Malnutrition appears to play a critical role in childhood morbidity and mortality (Black, 1991). The DHS survey collects data on episodes of childhood fever, cough with rapid respiration and diarrhoea for the periods i) 24 hours and ii) two weeks before the survey.

Table 11. *History of fever, diarrhea and cough with rapid breathing episodes in the last two weeks*
Percentage of children under 3 years with these symptoms 2 weeks before the survey by age of the child.

Country	Prevalence of fever by age				Prevalence of diarrhea by age				Prevalence of cough and rapid breathing by age			
	<6 months (A)	6–11 months (B)	12–23 months (C)	24–35 months (D)	<6 months (A)	6–11 months (B)	12–23 months (C)	24–35 months (D)	<6 months (A)	6–11 months (B)	12–23 months (C)	24–35 months (D)
Ghana	17.5	33.1	30.0	28.5	14.9	24.9	23.9	17.0	9.3	15.5	11.1	6.8
Nigeria	25.4	37.4	41.4	34.9	11.7	26.3	29.3	20.7	7.0	8.9	9.5	5.9
Zambia	32.8	54.4	54.2	46.8	14.5	33.4	36.4	24.0	11.9	18.3	15.6	11.4
Kenya	37.3	55.1	50.1	42.5	15.0	23.8	24.4	13.0	18.5	22.6	24.0	19.0
Malawi	42.8	49.0	52.1	42.1	17.4	41.7	36.2	21.2	18.4	22.7	17.7	14.0
Tanzania	27.4	43.8	40.8	30.3	11.5	26.1	21.1	10.5	6.2	16.2	11.6	6.1
Namibia	34.2	45.3	42.1	32.9	13.4	34.1	32.5	21.0	20.2	23.7	202.0	18.8
Guinea	38.2	43.2	45.0	37.5	16.2	19.2	21.6	21.4	18.5	15.4	18.2	14.5
Burkina Faso	34.7	48.2	45.3	36.3	17.0	28.3	33.4	23.7	13.6	17.5	12.4	10.7
Cameroun	19.8	30.4	27.7	23.5	7.3	28.4	28.2	20.5	10.4	10.8	11.8	8.6
Senegal	42.9	56.2	49.1	37.5	22.9	32.8	33.1	20.5	19.6	20.8	18.4	12.6
Niger	43.4	58.4	56.0	46.3	27.1	45.6	40.3	29.1	14.5	8.1	13.9	23.8
Rwanda	42.3	60.8	57.5	37.5	21.1	39.4	37.3	20.1	37.4	45.1	39.2	31.3
Madagascar	19.1	35.7	33.4	30.4	11.6	22.5	19.7	12.2	20.2	23.5	17.7	16.1
Benin	-	-	-	-	13.8	32.6	32.3	23.3	13.7	19.9	17.2	12.7
Zimbabwe	-	-	-	-	13.8	33.2	31.4	15.6	23.4	33.7	26.2	20.8
Côte d'Ivoire	-	-	-	-	11.1	23.8	25.3	19.9	12.6	17.7	14.6	11.0
All countries	32.7	46.5	44.6	36.2	15.3	30.4	29.8	19.6	16.2	20.0	17.6	14.4

Source: DHS 1990–1996.

Figure 12.

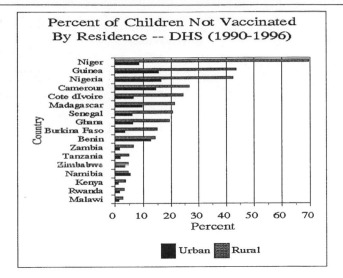

Figure 13.

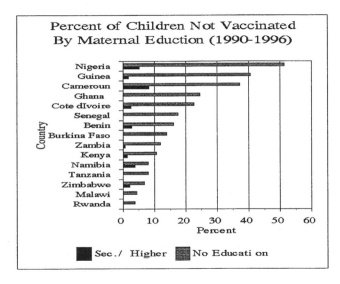

Table 11 shows the prevalence of fever, diarrhoea and cough two weeks before the survey date by age of child.

On average about 33 per cent of sub-Saharan African children would have had an episode of fever by the age of six months. This figure rises to about 47 per cent by the age of one year and drops to about 36 per cent by the age of three years. Figure 14 shows a plot of the age-pattern of fever for a selected number of countries. In each case, the prevalence of fever rises with the age of the child to peak at around six months. Generally, the age-pattern of the prevalence of diarrhoea and cough with rapid breathing is similar to that for fever (Table 11, Figures 15 and 16). The age-specific pattern of prevalence of these conditions may be related to at least two factors: (i) increased exposure of the child to the general household environment, and (ii) the initiation of food supplementation at about six months.

Figure 14.

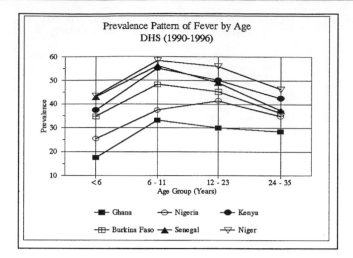

Figure 15.

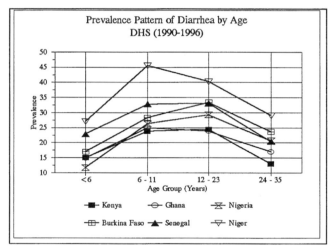

Figure 16.

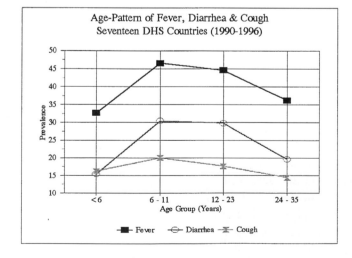

The year 2000 objectives: Can they be met?

Almost all countries in sub-Saharan Africa have committed themselves to these goals and to the goals of health for all by the year 2000. There is a genuine desire on the part of governments to meet the stipulated targets. Since the declarations highlighted in the introduction of this chapter were made 20 years ago, a lot has changed. There has been a significant improvement in overall sub-regional figures on access to antenatal care, delivery care and immunisation services. More children are given oral rehydration therapy during diarrhoea episodes. Today, fewer children are dying from diarrhoea, measles, diphtheria and other disease than in 1978. Smallpox has been eradicated. Overall infant, child and under-five mortality rates have dropped significantly.

These impressive sub-regional summary figures tend to hide serious differences among countries and among groups within the same country. As the present analysis has demonstrated, there are wide variations in access to a variety of services. For instance, the proportion of births with no prior antenatal care varies from less than 4 per cent in Kenya and Tanzania to about 70 per cent in Niger. Similarly, the proportion of births that occur in hospitals and maternity homes ranges from less than 15 per cent in Niger to more than 65 per cent in Namibia. Similar variations are seen in access to contraceptive technology, delivery care by trained personnel, frequency of visits to antenatal facilities, immunisation against vaccine-preventable diseases, etc. These country-specific differences in access to services tend to correlate well with differences in morbidity and mortality levels. The probability of dying by the age of one year is 51 per 1,000 live births in Zimbabwe compared to 153 per 1,000 in Guinea—a three-fold difference. Under-five mortality is around 76 per 1,000 in Zimbabwe compared to 252 per 1,000 in Guinea, representing more than a three-fold difference.

Differences within countries are sometimes even wider than inter-country differences. Within the broad groups, some people have greater disadvantages than others. The rural areas are heavily disadvantaged. Better-educated individuals have greater access to all resources than the less educated. In Niger, for instance, 86 per cent of urban residents have access to antenatal care, compared to only 20 per cent of rural residents. There are also wide international differences in socio-economic disparities. In contrast to Niger, Zimbabwe has a more equitable access to antenatal care: 95 per cent for urban as compared to 92 per cent of rural. Similar differentials are also observed in access to services such as family planning, delivery, etc. Socio-economic differentials in mortality are equally marked. In Ghana, for instance, births to women with no education show three times higher infant mortality rates and about four times higher under-five mortality rates than births to women with secondary or higher education.

These severe socio-economic differences are largely due to the fact that in almost all sub-Saharan African countries, progress has not been equitably distributed. Furthermore, the declines in fertility that are expected to accompany substantial declines in mortality have not occurred. As a result, the sub-region is characterised by high rates of natural increase. Most countries in the sub-region are increasing at an average annual rate of about 3 per cent. The sheer size of this population increase, coupled with the severe lack of resources implies persistent shortfalls in infrastructural development—schools, roads, hospitals, etc. Lack of economic opportunities in the rural areas has led to massive rural-urban migration with devastating consequences for the limited services that are available. Rising unemployment, a high dependency ratio and a high rate of growth of poverty are bound to have serious implications for development. It is estimated that some 200 million people in this region are income-poor (The World Bank, 1999).

In comparison with other regions of the world, sub-Saharan Africa has a very high prevalence of low birth weight babies and acute and chronic undernutrition. A substantial proportion of children suffer from fever, cough with rapid breathing and/or diarrhoea. The level of mortality is still very, very high. Children are plagued with illnesses just when their bodies and minds are in their formative stages. Women suffer more than men from poverty, disease, lack of credit and discrimination. Over a quarter of a million of women die annually from pregnancy-related conditions.

If the sub-region is to achieve any meaningful socio-economic development, fertility control must be paramount on the agenda. Any attempt to lower mortality further requires considerable efforts at narrowing the group differentials. This demands substantial improvements in people's living conditions, guaranteed employment and access to a basic package of quality health care. Among the strategies that can reduce fertility and improve quality of life are:

–   Greater commitment of sub-regional governments to improving the living conditions of their people.
–   Greater commitment to genuine and effective population control measures, rather than mere sloganeering.
–   Lowering physical and cultural barriers to contraceptive use.
–   Improving the accessibility and availability of family planning services, especially in the rural areas where the bulk of the population resides.
–   Improving the quality of family planning services.
–   Intensification of programmes that benefit women in terms of knowledge and use of contraceptives.
–   Improving training of family planning nurses and the provision of greater incentives to supply services to remote rural communities.
–   Targeting of specific at-risk groups for concentrated service delivery.
–   Improving access to maternal and child health services including prenatal care, delivery care, postpartum care and well-baby care.

Unfortunately, however, this region is also one of the most unstable in the world. Persistent conflicts and insecurity, poor economic performance and the scourge of AIDS are all conspiring to make further significant improvements in the human condition unlikely, at least in the foreseeable future. Even today, about 30 per cent of the sub-Saharan population will not survive to the age of 40, compared to about 9 per cent for East Asia.

In conclusion, one could state, without running the risk of controversy, that for most of sub-Saharan Africa, the goals set at the World Summit on Children cannot be realised any time soon. The level of commitment needed, in terms of resources and political will, is simply tremendous. Solutions are likely to emerge not at the governmental level, but largely as a result of the individual's desire to make progress.

References

Bankole, A. and C.F. Westoff. 1995. "Childbearing Attitudes and Intentions", *DHS Comparative Studies*, No. 17, DHS, Macro International Inc.

Bhatia, J.C. 1993. "Levels and Causes of Maternal Mortality in Southern India", *Studies in Family Planning*, 245 (5):310–318.

Billewicz, W.Z. and I.A. McGregor. 1982. "A Birth-to-Maturity Longitudinal Study of Heights and Weights in Two West African (Gambian) Villages, 1951–1975", *Annals of Human Biology*, 9 (4):309–320.

Black, R.E. 1991. "Would the Control of Childhood Infectious Diseases Reduce Malnutrition?", *Acta Paediatr Scand Suppl.*, 374:133–40.

Boerma, T. (1986). "Monitoring and Evaluation of Health Interventions; Age- and Cause-Specific Mortality and Morbidity in Childhood". Paper presented at the International Epidemiologist Association conference, Nairobi, Kenya.

Calloway, D.H., S. Murphy, J. Balderstone, O. Receveur, D. Lein, and M. Hudes, 1992. *Village Nutrition in Egypt, Kenya, and Mexico: Looking across the CRSP Projects*. University of California, Berkeley. Mimeographed.

Cohen, B. 1993. "Fertility Levels, Differentials and Trends", in K. Foote, K. Hill and L. Martin (eds), *Demographic Change in Sub-Saharan Africa*. Panel on the Population Dynamics of Sub-Saharan Africa, Committee on Population. Washington, DC: National Academy Press.

Fauveau, V., B. Wojtyniak, G. Mostafa, A.M. Sarder, and J. Chakraborty. 1990. "Perinatal Mortality in Matlab, Bangladesh: A Community-Based Study", *International Journal of Epidemiology*, 19(3):606–612.

Fauveau, V., M.A. Koenig, J. Chakraborty, and A.I. Chowdhury. 1988. "Causes of Maternal Mortality in Rural Bangladesh, 1976–1985", *World Health Organization Bulletin*, 66(5):643–651.

Freedman, R. and A.K. Blanc. 1991. "Fertility Transition: An Update". Paper presented at the DHS World Conference, Washington, DC, August 5–7, 1991.

Goldstein, H., and J.M. Tanner. 1980. "Ecological Considerations in the Creation and Use of Child Growth Standards", *Lancet*, 1:582–588.

Graitcer, P.L., and E.M. Gentry. 1981. "Measuring Children: One Reference for All", *Lancet*, 2:297–299.

Hauspie, R.C., S.R. Das, M.A. Preece, and J.M. Tanner. 1980. "A Longitudinal Study of the Growth in Height of Boys and Girls of West Bengal (India) Aged Six Months to 20 Years", *Annals of Human Biology*, 7 (5):429–441.

Heligman, L., N. Chen, and O. Babakol. 1993. "Shifts in the Structure of Population and Deaths in less Developed Regions", in Gribble, J.N. and S.H. Preston (eds), *The Epidemiological Transition: Policy Planning and Implications for Developing Countries*. Washington, DC: National Academy Press.

Hauspie, R.C., S.R. Das, M.A. Preece, and J.M. Tanner. 1980. "A Longitudinal Study of the Growth in Height of Boys and Girls of West Bengal (India) Aged Six Months to 20 Years", *Annals of Human Biology,* 7 (5):429–441.

Heligman, L., N. Chen, and O. Babakol. 1993. "Shifts in the Structure of Population and Deaths in less Developed Regions", in Gribble, J.N. and S.H. Preston (eds), *The Epidemiological Transition: Policy Planning and Implications for Developing Countries.* Washington, DC: National Academy Press.

Hill, A.L.L. 1992. "Trends in Childhood Mortality in Sub-Saharan Africa", in G. Pison, E. van de Walle, and M. Sala-Diakanda (eds), *Mortality and Society in Sub-Saharan Africa.* Oxford: Clarendon Press.

Kane, T.T., A.A. El-Kady, S. Saleh, M. Hage, J. Stanback, and L. Potter. 1992. "Maternal Mortality in Gaza, Egypt: Magnitude, Causes, and Prevention", *Studies in Family Planning,* 23(1):45–57.

Koblinsky, M., K., McLaurin, P. Russell-Brown, and P. Gorbach (eds). 1995. *Indicators for Reproductive Health Program Evaluation Report of the Subcommittee on Safe Pregnancy.* The Evaluation Project, Carolina Population Center.

Kwast, B.E., R.W. Rochat, and W. Kidane-Mariam. 1986. "Maternal Mortality in Addis Ababa, Ethiopia", *Studies in Family Planning,* 17(6):288–301.

Martorell, R., J. Rivera, and H. Kaplowitz. 1990. "Consequences of Stunting in Early Childhood for Adult Body Size in Rural Guatemala", *Annals,* Nestlé, 48:85–92.

Martorell, R., L.K. Khan, and D.G. Schroeder. 1994. "Reversibility of Stunting: Epidemiological Findings in Children from Developing Countries", *European Journal of Clinical Nutrition,* 48 (Supplement 1):S45–S57.

Martorell, R. 1995. "Promoting Healthy Growth: Rationale and Benefits", in Pinstrup-Andersen, P., D. Pelletier and H. Alderman (eds), *Child Growth and Nutrition in Developing Countries: Priorities for Action.* Ithaca: Cornell University Press.

McCormick, M.C. 1985. "The Contribution of Low Birth Weight to Infant Mortality and Childhood Morbidity", *New England Journal of Medicine* 312:82–90. United Nations. 1989. *World Population Prospects.* New York: United Nations.

Rhode, J. 1988. "Beyond Survival: Promoting Healthy Growth", *Indian Journal of Pediatrics,* 55:S3–S8.

Satyanarayana, K, A.N. Naidu, and B.S.N. Rao. 1979. "Nutritional Deprivation in Childhood and the Body Size, Activity, and Physical Work Capacity of Young Boys", *American Journal of Clinical Nutrition,* 32 (9):1769–1775.

United Nations Children's Fund. 1991. *The State of the World's Children 1991.* Oxford: Oxford University Press.

Waterlow, J.C., R. Buzina, W. Keller, J.M. Lane, M.Z. Nichaman, and J.M. Tanner. 1977. "The Presentation and Use of Height and Weight Data for Comparing the Nutritional Status of Groups of Children under the Age of 10 Years.", *Bulletin of the World Health Organization,* 55 (4):489–498.

WHO. 1987. *WHO Expert Committee on Biological Standardization.* (Meeting held in Geneva 1–8 December 1986). WHO Monograph. Technical Report No. 60. Geneva: WHO.

The World Bank. 1999. *World Development Report, 1999.*

Conflict Prevention and Early-Warning Systems

J. 'Bayo Adekanye

Introduction

Much of this analysis proceeds from the findings of research studies conducted by the author between May 1994 and September 1997 while he was Programme Leader of the Ethnic and Nationalist Conflicts Programme at the International Peace Research Institute in Oslo (PRIO). The most relevant among the published results of this research are listed in the selected references at the end of the paper. The paper begins with an overview of the phenomenon of rising social and ethnic conflict general to contemporary Africa, and the remedial measures used so far by the international community for dealing with the problem.

The most prominent of these measures consists of attempts to build indigenous capacity in defence and security management—what has come to be euphemistically termed 'training for peacekeeping'. Such measures assume, erroneously, that the security issues thrown up by Africa's current circumstances are basically military in the conventional sense, rather than political-economic in their nature and determinations as well as consequences. But the critical question to pose is whether the measures are appropriately conceived and targeted. To be sure, many of the factors and forces responsible for the raging conflicts in Africa lie in the impoverishing socio-economic burden of debt and adjustment and the stresses of environmental and human insecurity. These factors combine with the pressures of democratisation, including the contradictions of domination, marginalisation and demands for empowerment. These are classified among what I call the major proximate causes, accelerators, or precipitating conditions of conflict, as opposed to the structural and predispositional variables in the background. Included in the latter set are pervasive poverty, underdevelopment, inequality of access and opportunity, differences between groups and/or classes, and the inchoate character of state structures. It is argued that policy and action aimed at conflict management, resolution or prevention will find it more productive (at least in the short to medium term) to concentrate remedial efforts at the former level. The paper proceeds to formulate a strategy for designing appropriate conflict prevention measures based on the causal scheme that we have just suggested, which differentiates between the two groups of factors—the structural and predispositional variables and the more proximate causes or precipitants—and targets appropriate and quick remedial measures accordingly. The paper ends with an analysis of the role of triggers in conflict anticipation and prevention.

Ubiquity of armed conflicts

Violent social and ethnic conflict has emerged as a dominant feature of political life in much of contemporary Africa. Among the first horrific cases to draw international attention and concern were the genocides in Liberia, Somalia, Sierra Leone, Rwanda and Burundi, all states that have come to be labelled as 'collapsed' or 'failed' states.

Their precursors include a number of others referred to as newly 'reconstructed' states. Including cases like Chad, Uganda, Ethiopia, Mozambique, South Africa and Mali, this category refers to those states that have managed to transit from war to peace, from conflict to what has come to be called the post-conflict phase, from authoritarian breakdowns to democratic beginnings. But this does not mean that the transitional governments that succeeded to power in such states are consolidated. The root causes of conflict are yet to be addressed. In addition, other problems thrown up by the transition process have been added on to the conflict resolution agenda: problems of demobilising and reinserting ex-combatants, the return and reintegration of refugees, the problems of surplus arms and banditry, balancing the short-term imperatives of inter-elite accommodation and power-sharing against the regime's need for political inclusion. Therefore, the standing danger of a return to war is much greater than most analysts would like to believe.[1] For a very long time, the predictions of most analysts pointed towards Mobutu's Zaire simply disintegrating along ethnoregional fault-lines. This eventuality appears, at least for now, to have been staved off. But current concerns include Moi's Kenya; Nigeria is clearly hovering on the brink for reasons that we spell out towards the conclusion of the paper.

In other parts of West Africa, the old north-south divide between Tuaregs/Arabs and black Africans has not only resurfaced but has become more acute. It has rekindled memories of the old slave trade, making the task of administering many of the states of the sub-region, particularly Mauritania, Mali and Niger, very difficult. Although we have earlier described one of these states as having moved on from the stage of armed conflict, there is always the potential of a new conflict capable of returning any of the affected nations to a state of war.

The people of the Casamance region continue with their armed secessionist struggle against the Senegalese state, while there are simmering con-

---

[1] This threat is the subject of a recently concluded research project on disarming ethnic guerrillas. The results of the research are being currently interpreted, and therefore not part of our present analysis.

flicts in the relations of the Anglophone minority elements of south-western Cameroon with the rest of what they regard as a Francophile-dominated state. Tanzania's union with the islands of Zanzibar and Pemba has come under severe strain and is threatening to break up.

The upsurge of Islamic fundamentalism can be observed across much of North Africa. In Algeria, where it has been most prominent, the radical Islamicist front feeds on the disillusionment of millions of Algerians not only with the rump of the old FLN/military regime that has ruled the country since independence in 1962, but in large part because of the present conditions of economic and social impoverishment. Similar factors underlie the difficulties in the Sudan, although there the problem derives mainly from the long and costly war that the Khartoum-based, Arabised regime to the north has been fighting with the peoples of the south for nearly 30 years.

In most parts of the Horn of Africa, as indeed across the Sahelian region, the pressures of ecological disaster, corrupt and centralised state rule, war and debt have forced many groups long known for their nomadic lifestyle to revive pre-colonial strategies for 'surviving at the margins', leaving the constituent state units of the region literally bursting at the seams. The ongoing inter-clan rivalries and struggles that followed the collapse of Siad Barre's rule in 1991 in the ex-Somali territorial space constitute a good example.

The character of conflicts

It should be clear from this brief overview that while conflict has been a general feature of much of the continent, its nature has tended to differ across countries and regions. Variations depend on the configuration of a given society, the balance of social class over ethno-regional forces and the location of the society concerned along the homogeneity-heterogeneity continuum. Such considerations determine, for example, whether particular conflicts stay contained within a given state's boundaries and functions (that is, they are waged within the framework of a unified political structure), or spill over into centrifugal channels. It is nevertheless remarkable that, in spite of the inchoate and heterogeneous composition of nearly all these states, most of the organised rebellions with which they have had to contend over the last 10 to 20 years have been fought within the framework of the post-colonial state. But it is also true that the region has recorded the highest rate of state 'collapse' or 'failure', amounting in effect to experiences that call into question the character of most of these states as presently constituted, and suggest that they might be replaced by other forms. The possibility of disintegration is not ruled out.

A prominent feature of Africa's current civil-military history is the ease with which the regular armies and regimes of an increasing number of authoritarian multi-ethnic states have been fought, defeated, overthrown and replaced by insurgent guerrilla forces organised from among their own citizens. Congo-Brazzaville and the Democratic Republic of Congo (formerly

Zaire) are the latest examples; earlier cases were Uganda, Ethiopia/Eritrea, Somalia and Rwanda. There are indications that we may not have seen the end of this phenomenon. Such successful 'wars of liberation', wresting power from native tyrannical regimes, used to be considered an impossibility in Africa.

However, in almost all the cases surveyed, conflicts have either been preceded by or benefited from at least four major factors: the mobilisation of disaffected segments or classes; an upsurge of civil society groups; interests and demands; and changes pointing to authoritarian breakdowns on the one hand and democratic beginnings on the other.

Above all, the struggles that have been principally about democracy have tended to combine two foci of resistance: one against the state, which is seen as increasingly coercive and negligent of its primary welfare responsibilities; and the other against the externally imposed structural adjustment programme (SAP), because of its pauperising impact. To be sure, the patently anti-SAP dimensions of current conflicts, meaning the proverbial food riots, workers' strikes and rising wave of peasant revolts induced by globalisation and adjustment, have tended to take place side by side with overtly ethnic wars, struggles for identity and religious fundamentalism.

Interests in conflict prevention

Naturally, the international community has come to be concerned about these conflicts and to manifest active interest in their reduction, management and prevention. Evidence of this concern abounds. There have been countless international gatherings, conferences and workshops on the issue. Then there are the many commissioned studies, published books, monographs and other works on conflict, its prevention and early-warning systems in Africa. The literature on the subject continues to grow. Another piece of evidence: the US Congress passed a whole bill on the problem, the African Conflict Resolution Act (1994), almost on the heels of the genocide in Rwanda. Also, the United Nations under Dr Boutros-Ghali launched the system-wide New Initiative on Africa. (More on this later.) Finally, the international community's interest in the domain shows also in the increasing level of material, manpower and logistical support being given to an Organisation of African Unity (OAU)-based conflict-resolution mechanism.

Laudable though all this interest is, the core of most international strategies emphasises the need to give support to and help with the strengthening of Africa's capacity for security management, including what has come to be referred to as 'training for peacekeeping'. This approach has seen the US, for example, pouring money and material into rebuilding the armed forces of friendly African states and retraining them for peacekeeping functions. For the French, the so-called new emphasis amounts to no more than the refurbishing of the long-accustomed neo-colonial scheme (including defence treaties, bases, and other privileges), but now re-packaged as 'pan-African peacekeeping forces'. Then there are the geopolitical interests preventing major powers like France, Britain and America from agreeing to common conflict prevention measures. The approach to given potential conflict situations, whether in Rwanda, Zaire or Nigeria, continues to be guided by considerations about who controls what in terms of spheres of influence. In short, the emphasis remains predicated on the methods of the Cold War, particularly in the use of military means as a conflict prevention resource.

But the critical question is: Are such measures appropriately conceived and sufficiently targeted? To be sure, the security issues thrown up by Africa's current conditions are not military in the conventional sense, but basically political-economic in their nature and determinations as well as consequences. They are about helping people to regain their job security, income security, food security, health security, shelter security, social security, individual security, and the security of life itself. In short, security in Africa is largely about guaranteeing citizens and marginalised social groups equal opportunity and access as well as self-actualisation. Besides, have not many of the military establishments here—through the parasitic proclivities they had been exhibiting, the excessive pressures exerted on their countries' much-diminished foreign exchange resources, and their contribution towards the stifling of grassroots participation in governance and development—emerged in fact as part of the problem? These are the issues at the heart of the quest for common security across the continent, and they go beyond the use of force, as we elaborate later. In short, *aiming at breaking out of the 'impoverishment equals rising conflicts' equation*. Better still, *bringing the human security provisions back in* is the key. Unless and until such considerations orient the strategy of conflict prevention, it will be impossible for any policy or action measure to prove sustainable. This assumes an understanding of the linkage between adequate conflict diagnosis and conflict prevention; this understanding is an important first step towards any sustainable strategy of action in the domain.

Understanding the linkage between conflict diagnosis and conflict prevention

A long-standing truism about the art of conflict resolution, going back to the very foundation of political science, affirms the linkage between adequate conflict diagnosis and conflict prevention. An understanding of this relationship is necessary if policymakers' efforts are to yield positive results. But diagnosis is of no use unless it is ultimately related to the search for solutions. As a founding father of the discipline, Aristotle once put it thus: 'To know the causes which destroy constitutions is also to know the causes which ensure their preservation.' In other words, analysis of what causes conflicts is an important first step for any policymaker who would avoid them. The presumption here is that such analysis would be good and sound and help in the choice (if not also in the initial design) of the most appropriate remedial measures for dealing with given conflicts. To summarise the essence of the now familiar analogy to the body politic borrowed from the medical field: 1) a doctor cannot treat an illness until and unless he/she has first made a diagnosis; 2) the diagnosis must be correct and sound if the therapy prescribed is to prove efficacious; and 3) the therapy prescribed must suit the diagnosis made. The procedures for understanding conflict prevention and the design of appropriate early-warning systems in Africa should follow a similar logic.

Let me illustrate the point with a few examples. Among the phenomena that have come to attract the growing concern and interest of the international community in recent times are the former child soldiers (and prospects of their rehabilitation in post-conflict society), child labour (whose conditions are sometimes akin to slavery), female graduate prostitutes (some of them forced to leave their homelands for the streets of Western capitals like Rome, Paris, London, and Amsterdam in search of hard currency), the trade in narcotics (into which increasing numbers of African farmers who have been forced to abandon traditional crops for export are now moving, partly due to low earnings and partly due to protectionist barriers in the North) and illegal trafficking in surplus small arms (together with their cross-border transfers and linkages). The strategies for dealing with these phenomena tend to lie in the adoption of new conventions, or the streamlining of existing ones, followed by reminders to the signatory nations of their obligations.

This is certainly the case with the problem of 'child soldiers' whose deployment in many of today's raging wars has shocked most members of the international community, including non-governmental organisations (NGOs) and relief agencies, and justifiably so. But how efficacious are such new conventions for dealing with the problem? With many of these countries' schools and colleges either completely closed, or the fees for attending them jacked up far beyond the means of most parents, have not tens of millions of Africa's children simply found themselves forced out of school by prevailing economic policies? If you then factor in the 'sapped'[2] conditions in which most households now find themselves, the break up of social institutions and mores, including families, and the fundamental insecurity facing all, increasing numbers of these children may find that the most socially meaningful and economically rewarding activity is to join a rebel fighting force. Entering into new conventions on the rights of children or strengthening existing ones may be laudable but as a strategy, it fails to address the proximate causes of the problem, namely relieving these societies of the acute economic stresses and deprivations that make employment as 'child soldiers' the only relevant future for most young boys and girls.

---

[2] 'Sapped' is a play on words derived from the Structural Adjustment Programmes (SAPs) undertaken by many African countries in the 1980s and 1990s.

A related problem also plaguing those African states currently engaged in post-conflict peace-building, as previously mentioned, concerns the large distribution of 'surplus arms' circulating outside of state defence forces. It is known that resort to the use of these illegally stocked 'surplus arms' accounts for much of the rising incidence of criminal violence, particularly banditry and armed robbery. An effective programme of disarmament has been suggested for coping with the problem. But it is difficult to see how this can be achieved. To begin with, the strategy assumes that resort to arms is the original source of the raging instabilities and conflicts rather than a reflection of other underlying factors, including the need for security. Besides, as many researchers working on the problems of disarmament and demobilisation in Africa's post-conflict states have found, arms have come to have an economic as well as a security value for those who possess them. For many of the former soldiers and also their counterparts among the citizenry, guns have long been part of their cultural existence, their very means of livelihood. This explains why disarmament has not proven to be as successful as demobilisation. And one is not likely to get those possessing arms to freely turn all of them in unless and until the fundamental economic, security and cultural needs necessitating the retention of weapons are addressed.

By logical extension, it would amount to a poor diagnosis and/or application of wrong therapy to suggest that the solution to the problem of rising conflicts in Africa today lies in merely pouring more money, arms and equipment into beefing up the 'peacekeeping' and 'security-tending' (a euphemism for war-making) capacity of African states or their sub-regional organisations (e.g. Economic Community Monitoring Group (ECOMOG) for West Africa, Southern African Development Community (SADC) for Southern Africa, and Intergovernmental Authority on Drought and Development (IGADD) for the Horn), as if the problem were of essentially military origin. For the international community to move towards its stated objective of helping with the reduction of conflict on the continent, it is important that not only a correct and sound diagnosis of these conflicts be made, but that the remedial measures prescribed be appropriate as well as suitable. A basic and rather commonsensical proposition, one would have thought, but which would seem to have until now been disregarded! Perhaps it is no longer possible or in the interests of all of us to continue to disregard it.

Factors and forces behind the recent explosion of conflicts

Many of the *precipitating* conditions of conflict in Africa today lie in the intertwining of socio-economic burdens of debt and structural adjustment, the stresses of environmental and human insecurity and the pressures of democratisation, including the contradiction of forces of marginalisation or domination and demands for empowerment. Their combined effect has produced the alarming rise in social and ethnic tension and conflict. The links are very well established and documented in the literature, including some of this author's recent writings in the field. Policy and action should target these areas—and urgently too—if the international community is to move towards its recently stated objective of helping with conflict prevention and resolution and the formulation of strategies for promoting sustainable peace and development in Africa.

Fortunately, there is now growing recognition in the international community of the fact that the very programmes of its own agencies in Africa, particularly the IMF and World Bank with their imposed political-economic package of structural adjustment programmes, have significantly encouraged the new social and ethnic tensions and conflicts. But that recognition came too late for many of the states, or rather not until a number of them had been thrown into violent conflicts. One of the calculated objectives of SAPs was to 'roll back the state'. But one of the effects of that programme in Africa has been reneging on the commitments made by states to the eradication of poverty, hunger, ignorance, disease and other obstacles to the realisation of full human potential. The latter in turn has left many millions in Africa fighting for basic survival, seeming to return the people to the Hobbesian, 'pre-developmental state' of things when life itself was 'solitary, poor, nasty, brutish, and short'. The implications of the cutbacks in spending on social programmes, particularly education, health, housing, the abolition of food and agricultural subsidies and the removal of employment generation almost completely from the list of governmental responsibilities were that all the developmental gains of the 1960s and 1970s were brought to nought.

That the programme has exacerbated Africa's poverty and conflicts has now come to be conceded by most, though sometimes grudgingly. It was presupposed, for example, by the UN's New Initiative on Africa, launched in April 1996. It sought to bring together all the United Nations specialised agencies with experience in Africa, namely Economic Commission for Africa (ECA), the UN Development Programme (UNDP), UNICEF, UNESCO, the World Health Organisation (WHO), the Food and Agriculture Organisation (FAO), the International Labour Organisation (ILO), along with the Bretton Woods institutions, to mount a concerted international attack on the crisis of debt and economic and social stagnation still plaguing much of Africa. The programme also affirmed the existence of linkages between impoverishing conditions and rising conflict that many researchers, scholars and commentators have been writing or talking about for some time now. 'In Africa, Unattended Poverty Leads to Conflict,' wrote the new ECA Executive-Secretary K.Y. Amoako and the UNDP Administrator James Gustave Speth in a joint article preparatory to the launching of that UN Initiative (*International Herald Tribune*, 21 March 1996, p.8).

Certainly, the UN document's emphasis on renewing public investments in health, education and other areas of skill acquisition implies a reaffirmation of the long-known research finding that human resource development is indispensable for achieving economic and social growth or, for that matter, recovery. Which is interesting, because these are areas where most of these countries' capital stocks have been depleted by SAPs. The interconnections of proposed public investment in the social sphere with support for an active strategy on Africa's external debt on the one hand and Africa's need to develop its own conflict-resolution capacity on the other also imply an acknowledgement of the linkages between the debt-cum-adjustment burden, rising poverty and increasing conflict. Special emphasis was also placed by the Initiative on the need to control land degradation and desertification, encourage irrigation and improve soil quality. These measures were clearly designed to improve food security for most of the population, and to provide relief from debilitating ecological disasters, both natural and man-made. African leaders' efforts to improve governance was also to be bolstered under the Initiative through supporting the civil services to better manage development, building independent judicial systems, strengthening the functioning of parliaments and electoral processes and making public administration more accountable. Even the World Bank (judging from the *World Development Report*, 1996) has now moved away from the earlier 'markets-solve-everything' view to concede that *a revitalised (not weak) state* is and has been essential everywhere for building adequate national infrastructure required for the development of markets. Right on target!

But this new emphasis would need to be not only backed up by concrete measures but, perhaps even more importantly, supplemented by action aimed at *tackling the debt question*, considering its link to the impoverishment/conflict nexus. The campaign to 'Give Africa a Fresh Start' through debt reduction or even forgiveness (to which many of the international development agencies and NGOs have subscribed) was born out of the realisation that the debt burden is clearly unsustainable; and that concerted, drastic action would have to be taken to relieve most of the economically poor, badly endowed and severely indebted countries. This would be the only way to permit them to move forward economically and socially. Some of the once war-ravaged economies such as those of Uganda and Ethiopia that have recovered and now appear to be growing will also need to be helped on this front if they are not to falter again.

Strategy for designing appropriate conflict prevention measures

Locating the outbreak of violent ethnic conflict in the proximate causes of rising debt burden, the stresses of demographic and human insecurity and the pressures of democratisation—what we have classified as the precipitants or accelerators of conflicts, rather than the background structural and predispositional conditions—has considerable implications for the strategy of designing conflict prevention measures. We must now proceed to spell these out. One of the important points stemming from the analysis, for example, is that it forces one to *rethink the whole business of differences between groups* (say, those between the Rwandan/Burundian Hutus and Tutsis, whether real or putative) *being considered causes of conflict*. The point is that, although important, what we have called the structural and predispositional variables at best only point to the existence of conflict potential, but cannot explain the actual occurrence of a given conflict. Structural background variables, or predispositions of conflict, need other factors or forces to activate them, in order for an actual conflict to break out. The corollary is that there is nothing in the existence of differences between groups in terms of language, culture, religion, class and social organisation per se that explains, or can and must explain, outbreaks of violent social and ethnic conflict. Precipitating factors, accelerators, and conflict triggers are required to set off such outbreaks. These other ingredients are to be sought outside of the set of variables often referred to in the literature as the *root causes of conflict*, or what we typify here as the structural background conditions or preconditions, and especially in the more dynamic factors and forces, those we call the proximate causes, precipitants or accelerators of conflict. By extension, policy and action aimed at conflict prevention, management and resolution will find it more useful and productive of quicker results to concentrate remedial efforts at the second level. Also, working to remove the root causes of conflict is a much slower, more difficult, and less easily attainable task (at least in the short to medium term) than attempting to prevent conflict acceleration and exacerbation.

There is an additional reason for wanting to begin by targeting policy and action at the second level: most of the *urgent danger-signals or triggering circumstances and events* are located in this area. Equally important is the crucial problem of sequencing and timing. Obviously, not all times are equally appropriate for initiating preventive action. This may well depend in part on how good one's sense of anticipation is. However, what seems relatively obvious (and emerges as a lesson learnt from all the conflict cases surveyed above) is that by the time one begins to look for triggering events, circumstances and the like, one already has in hand *potentially explosive conflict materials waiting only to be ignited*. The ultimate objective of strategy and therefore the test of its success or failure, of course, is *not to wait for the explosion to take place before initiating preventive action*. The last statement takes us straight to a discussion of the role of triggers in conflict occurrence, anticipation or prevention, the last issue in our subject of analysis.

Role of triggers in conflict anticipation

Very often, the events or circumstances triggering the outbreak of major conflicts tend to come from obscure and unforeseen sources. Thus the April 6, 1994 plane crash in which the presidents of the two fatuously linked states of Rwanda and Burundi (both Hutus) lost their lives, supplied the spark for the genocidal explosion that followed. It was not the first time, of course, that the death of an important conflict group leader, or the assassination of a ruler, or even a mere shooting incident served as a catalyst for violent conflict. From Burundi's history alone, we have evidence of at least one other instance: the first popularly elected president of the Burundian state and himself a Hutu, Melchior Ndadaye, was assassinated together with other important Hutu political figures in a coup organised by elements from the Tutsi-dominated army barely three months after being sworn into office (October 23, 1993), and almost instantaneously the country was thrown into one of those frenzies of genocidal and counter-genocidal slaughters which have become identified with the politics of the area.

The latter illustration also brings out another important element, the catalytic role that an ethnically skewed military coup d'état can play in unleashing bloody inter-ethnic (or inter-religious) war—especially where such a coup is directed at a sectional takeover of power, preventing the constitutional loss of power to others, or aborting an ethnic (or religious) opponent's electoral mandate to govern. Students of military-ethnic relations have long remarked on the conflict-triggering effect of such sectional use of force on a deeply divided society. Nor is the Burundian case cited above the only one. There are similar illustrations in the experiences of many other countries, including Nigeria (both current and past), Sierra Leone, Liberia, Uganda, Algeria (current), Cyprus, and Sri Lanka (formerly Ceylon). Of course, elections will present a potential danger-signal for conflict in any deeply divided society.

But the catalysts for conflict may also have come from government responses or policy measures in relation to issues of inter-ethnic import. The range here is obviously unlimited, and could include such activities or policies as tampering with election results, census counts, or formulas determining revenue allocation; the promulgation of one language out of a competing set as the official language for use in schools or as a requirement for recruitment into the state's public service; moves changing a secular multi-religious state into a theocracy, whether real or perceived; the announcement of austerity measures; the imposition of levies, laws, or regulations considered by others as burdensome, unjust, or discriminatory; the support or termination of social programmes affecting the ethnic division of labour; appointments to top organs of state power, particularly political, bureaucratic, judicial, and above all military; selective actions taken in support of the desecration of holy rites, pilgrimages, or shrines; police brutality; soldiers shooting at and killing individuals in a mob; raising the ante on repression, or initiating reforms aimed at accommodation; a major policy setback; and the sheer announcement effects of any of these. Examples illustrating these are too many to list here.

Defeat in war, perhaps followed by the disintegration of a ruling regime and even the breakdown of the state itself, may be seized upon by long-oppressed factions or groups as an opportunity to break away from the control of the dominant groups, thereby sparking off the 'war of all against all', as was the experience of Somalia in 1991 in the immediate aftermath of the collapse of the Siad Barre rule. Factors triggering the war in northern Mali included the expulsion in early 1990 of some 18,000 Tuaregs who had been previously living in Algeria. The returnees included many who had not only received military training but also had fighting experience in desert wars, having once enlisted in Gaddafi's Islamic legion in Chad and the Middle East.

The catalyst could be a series of chance incidents (or better still accidents) coming out of the blue, such as a natural disaster, unfavourable weather or a bad harvest. These events might be coupled with some psychic interpretations of any such incidents as regards their timing, duration, and consequence. There is also the role that instant rumours play in the activation of conflicts, something again that the Rwandan case of 1994 brought out. Finally, if only because of the interconnectedness of today's global community, external developments, including their possible contagion effects, as well as expectations of external support, and of course the timing of any of these, all have a way of dramatically impacting upon conflict processes within states.

These are a few of the possible catalysts of conflict that immediately come to mind. Nor do any of these triggers necessarily work in isolation. It is possible to imagine a series of triggers or catalysts working in the context of what one can consider as triggering circumstances. The important thing to bear in mind is that they all relate to a whole complex of intangible circumstances (call them the stochastic variables) behind the onset of social and ethnic conflicts that could easily have been termed 'chance' for want of a better word. It is a term perhaps meant to capture that grey area where *elements of spontaneity and organisation criss-cross in the concatenation of events that sparks violent social and ethnic conflicts*. But the term may be considerably misleading. Are we saying, for example, that the Rwandan genocide that followed the April 6, 1994 plane crash was entirely fortuitous? Was there not something in the systematic nature of the genocidal attacks directed against the Tutsi minority, although those massacres included some Hutu moderate elements too, that should point to elements of considerable organisation, leadership, and co-ordination being involved? Also, from a previous study of this particular case, there were enough indications from not just the structural background conditions, but even more importantly the proximate pressures of debt burden combined with rising demographic insecurity, and the arraying of the forces of democratisation against entrenched ethnic privilege, to suggest that the ethnic conflagration that followed could not have been accidental.

In other words, even though many events may be unpredictable and seem fortuitous and beyond human agency, incidents that provide sparks for the outbreak of violent ethnic conflict do not operate in a vacuum.

Rather, such triggering events or circumstances are linked to the scheme of things and very often derive their causal significance from being part of other and much broader factors and forces, particularly those variables which we earlier classified as the complex of accelerators or precipitants of conflict. The challenge facing conflict prevention and the designing of appropriate early-warning systems is in how to anticipate the 'finite' trigger before intervening, when from all accounts or indicators available from objective sources (e.g. human rights monitors, development aid workers, NGOs, international bodies and agencies, etc), a given case may already have been on the brink of conflict explosion, that is, long 'ripe for conflict prevention'. The Nigerian case comes to mind, and there could perhaps be no better illustrative material with which to conclude.

The current pro-democracy struggles raging in Nigeria are taking place against the background of great economic depression created by past and continuing mismanagement and corruption, the burden of huge external debts and acute conditions of general impoverishment. The first and most immediate cause of the crisis (the catalyst) was the annulment by the military regime of the results of the June 12, 1993 presidential election, which was to have ended the second period of military rule and ushered in the Third Republic. Adjudged one of the most peaceful, fair and free elections to be conducted in the country's history, it is widely believed to have been won by a southern business tycoon turned political leader, Chief M.K.O. Abiola. Apparently, some powerful northern interests close to the Sokoto caliphate were unhappy about the imminent change in the locus of power and sought to use a faction of the military high command to block Abiola's accession to the presidency. Since the annulment, the country has not known peace as successive regimes from Babangida's, through the military-contrived interim national government under Shonekan, and now to Abacha's own have been faced with *a rising wave of civilian resistance*. Thus, the struggles currently raging in Nigeria are as much a reaction against worsening economic conditions, particularly the general impoverishment on account of debt and adjustment, as they are against continued military authoritarian rule, domestic mismanagement and corruption. This explains why the June 12 event, one of the catalysts of the struggle, has come to provoke such an explosion in civil society and to throw up newly organised social groups and forces as well as to mobilise all in joint opposition to continued military rule.

Since late 1993, there had been evidence that the Nigerian pro-democracy forces might have been shifting their strategies from passive resistance and non-violent civil disobedience and becoming increasingly militant and even militarised. It is all too evident from the rise in incidents of sabotage of strategic installations, bombings, hijacking and the shooting down of government aeroplanes and assassination attempts on regime collaborators. Perhaps even more worrisome is the establishment by some exiled opposition elements of what is known as the 'National Liberation Council of Nigeria' as a sort of government-in-exile, including a military wing which is said to be committed to overthrowing the regime by armed struggle, if necessary. The opposition now owns and operates a powerful private short wave radio broadcasting facility for beaming insurrectionary news from abroad directly into Nigeria. These militant acts of the opposition in turn have had the effect of provoking even greater repression by the military, with the vicious cycle of violence producing further counter-violence, thereby edging the country closer to the brink of the precipice. Also, for the first time in the history of that country, an increasing number of its citizens turned political or environmental refugees are being processed for either asylum or landed immigrant status in the West, particularly Britain, Canada and the US. These include the cream of the country's highly skilled professionals and trained personnel, who are being lost through a brain drain. In the neighbouring Benin republic a number of camps for Ogoni refugees fleeing the repression of Nigeria's military authorities are reported to have been set up.

All these and many other things add up to serious and disturbing signs that, should another civil war result from either a misreading or the mismanagement of the country's accumulated crisis potential, it might spell disintegration for Nigeria. The onset of such a war of disintegration, along with the sheer scale of inter-ethnic violence, cost in human lives, physical destruction and massive refugee flows that this *worst-case scenario* portends, could throw up enormous security problems and a humanitarian catastrophe for the whole West African sub-region, dwarfing those of the former Yugoslavia. For such is Nigeria's strategic significance, including the size of population (some 100 millions, the largest on the continent), territorial size, ethno-political make-up, and the size of the national economy (the second largest in Africa) inextricably coupled with the other economies in the sub-region, that an outbreak of this kind is simply too horrific to contemplate. But precisely for this reason the international community cannot afford to wait for 'the finite trigger' from the blue (say, the death of the imprisoned leader of the pro-democracy opposition movement, for example), since the danger-signals from the Nigerian case are urgent enough for timely preventive action to be mounted.

Conclusion

This paper is about a strategy for designing appropriate conflict prevention measures in Africa based on a causal scheme that first differentiates between two groups of factors involved in conflict occurrence (namely the structural and predispositional variables, and the more proximate causes or precipitants) and then targeting appropriate and quick remedial measures accordingly. The objective of policy must be to reduce rising conditions of impoverishment arising from debt and adjustment burdens, environmental and human insecurity, and the contradictions of domination, marginalisation and demands for empowerment, if the level and intensity of conflicts are to decrease. The argument basically is about how and why not to wait for the 'finite trigger' before mounting the necessary preventive action. The concluding, major part of the paper on the role of triggers in conflict anticipation and prevention is meant to sensitise the reader to the processes of this development.

But if, from the foregoing analysis, 'conflict prevention' is an art with its own logic, rules and procedures about why, when, how, and what to target in terms of remedial measures, why, it may be asked, is intervention not being mounted when and where it is needed until it is too late? It certainly could not have been for lack of fore-warnings that the international community waited for Rwanda to explode. Abundant indicators pointed precisely to the imminent catastrophe. It could also not have been for lack of information with those in a position to help avert the danger. Too many powerful interests, lack of will, and so-called 'aid fatigue', rather, have been mentioned among the major factors responsible for timely preventive action not being taken if and when such an action becomes urgent. Hopefully, a conference such as this will help mobilise international public opinion to appreciate that it is cheaper to take preventive action than to wait for the explosion to take place, which requires taking on the consequences and costs of inaction, including dispatching and maintaining peacekeepers, allocating aid for complex emergencies and helping to 'rebuild war-torn societies'.

References

Adekanye, J. 'Bayo. 1995. "Structural Adjustment, Democratisation and Rising Ethnic Tensions in Africa", *Development and Change*, 26(2), 355–374.

Adekanye, J. 'Bayo. 1996a. "Rwanda/Burundi: 'Uni-Ethnic' Dominance and the Cycle of Armed Ethnic Formation", *Social Identities*, 2(1), 37–71.

Adekanye, J. 'Bayo. 1996b. "Gjeld, demokratisering og konflikt —Tilfellet Nigeria" (Debt, Democratisation and Conflict—The Nigerian Case), in P. Eklöf (ed.), *Fellesrådets Afrika-årbok 96/97 Tema: Gjeld, strukturtilpasning og konflikt* (Africa Yearbook 1996/97 Theme: Debt, Structural Adjustment, and Conflict). Oslo: Fellesrådet for det sörlige Afrika (Norwegian Council for Southern Africa).

Adekanye, J. 'Bayo. 1997a. "Dynamics of Ethnic Conflicts in Africa", in K. Volden, & D. Smith (eds.), *Causes of Conflicts in the Third World*. Oslo, Idegruppen/PRIO.

Adekanye, J. 'Bayo. 1997b. "Interactions of Ethnicity, Economy, and Configuration of Society in Separatist Movements in Africa", in T. Andresen, B. Bull, & K. Duvold (eds), *SEPARATISM: Culture Counts, Resources Decide*. Bergen: Chr. Michelsen Institute.

Deger, S. & S. Sen. 1991. *Arms and the Child: SIPRI Report for UNICEF on the Impact of Military Expenditure in Sub-Saharan Africa on the Survival, Protection and Development of Children*. Stockholm: SIPRI & New York: UNICEF.

Hansen, E. (ed.) 1987. *Africa: Perspectives on Peace and Development*. Tokyo: United Nations University & London: Zed.

UNDP. 1994. "New Dimensions of Human Security", *Human Development Report 1994*, 2:22–46. New York & Oxford: Oxford University Press.

Zartman, I.W. (ed.) 1995. *Collapsed States: The Disintegration and Restoration of Legitimate Authority*. London & Boulder, CO: Lynne Rienner.

The Structure of Conflict*

Mary Kaldor

Introduction

In the summer of 1993, I was in Sarajevo. It was impossible to leave because the Serbs were shelling the airport. So I spent my time doing what Sarajevans did. I went to the theatre, which was packed. We had to sit in the aisles. The play was performed by candlelight. It was a funny English play called *Run for your Wife* translated into Serbo-Croat. Drag queens, prostitutes, and policemen rushed across the stage and the audience rocked with laughter, reassuringly drowning out the sound of shelling. Afterwards, as a foreign visitor, I was invited to meet the theatre director, Haris Pasovic, an extraordinary man who spent the war years organising plays, concerts, film festivals, art exhibitions and seminars, determined to preserve Sarajevo's secular culture. He greeted me with the words: "Welcome to Sarajevo! Welcome to the twenty-first century! This is the end of history! Here you can see Europe's future!"

Was Haris Pasovic right? The wars taking place now in eastern Europe, Africa and other places can indeed be characterised as a new phenomenon, a twenty-first century phenomenon perhaps, distinct from what we are accustomed to think of as war. Large-scale organised violence between states is becoming an anachronism. In its place there is a new kind of violent conflict which is, as yet, difficult to categorise. But it needs to be analysed if we are to find new mechanisms for its prevention or resolution. The new conflicts are often described as internal conflicts or civil wars. Yet, although they are often very local, they cannot be classified as simply 'internal'; not only do they often involve neighbouring states, but they can only be understood in the context of the process we call globalisation—increasing global interconnectedness in economic, political and military domains. Interconnectedness should not be confused with integration. Globalisation is a contradictory process involving both integration and fragmentation; the point is that the lives of individual people are increasingly affected by distant events over which they may have little control.

---

* This chapter is a condensed version of the argument in my forthcoming book *New and Old Wars: Organised Violence in a Global Era*. Cambridge: Polity Press.

The global presence is very visible in most of these wars—foreign journalists, diaspora volunteers and a bewildering array of international agencies, including the United Nations, United Nations High Commission for Refugees, the International Committee of the Red Cross as well as many non-governmental organisations (NGOs). Indeed, the wars epitomise a kind of global/local divide that is characteristic of globalisation. On the one hand, there are members of the global class who travel frequently, communicate through telephone, fax, or e-mail, use credit cards and international currency and move freely using international IDs, protected by flak jackets and armoured cars. On the other hand, the vast majority of people affected by new wars are tied to the places they live by frontiers and roadblocks, and lack money. They live off humanitarian assistance and are vulnerable to shelling, sniper fire, looting and various atrocities.

To explain the new type of conflicts, I shall first analyse the structure of what might be called old conflicts, and then show how the new conflicts are different.

Old conflicts

What we are accustomed to think of as wars—what we might call old conflicts—emerged towards the end of the eighteenth century and were intimately connected with the emergence of the modern state, the process that Max Weber referred to as the monopolisation of legitimate organised violence, the notion that only the state has the authority to use physical coercion.

In earlier periods, there were private armies. When kings fought wars, they had to raise coalitions of armies from among the feudal barons, rather as the UN has to raise coalitions of national forces today when it mounts peacekeeping operations. The kings raised money from taxes or borrowed from the new bourgeoisie to pay for mercenary soldiers. But mercenaries were notoriously unreliable and posed a major problem in times of peace; if they were not paid, they tended to engage in looting and pillaging. So the use of mercenaries gave way to the establishment of standing armies, professional forces who wore uniforms and who introduced training, staff colleges and drill. Above all, standing armies helped change the notion of what constitutes legitimate war—a new set of secular rules which replaced the religious injunctions (*jus ad bello et jus in bellum*) of the Middle Ages. Later, towards the end of the nineteenth century, these rules began to be codified in international law. According to the Israeli military historian Martin Van Creveld:

> To distinguish war from crime, it was defined as something waged by sovereign states and by them alone. Soldiers were defined as personnel licensed to engage in armed violence on behalf of the state … To obtain and maintain their licenses, soldiers had to be carefully registered, marked and controlled to the exclusion of privateering. They were supposed to fight only in uniform, carrying their arms

'openly' and obeying a commander who could be held responsible for their actions. They were not supposed to resort to 'dastardly' methods, such as
violating truces, taking up arms again after they had been taken prisoner, and
the like. The civilian population was supposed to be left alone, 'military
necessity' permitting (1991:41).

In order to finance standing armies, taxation and borrowing had to be
regularised. Administrative reform was necessary to improve the efficiency
of tax collection and expenditure. The spread of law and order was also important to provide a secure basis for taxation and to build domestic political
legitimacy. A kind of implicit contract was established whereby the government protected territory from enemies abroad and guaranteed relative
peace at home, and the population paid taxes, accepted the rule of law, and
provided manpower for the armed forces. By the end of the eighteenth century, a whole series of binary distinctions had emerged which we take for
granted today:

- Between Public and Private, between the sphere of state and non-state
  activity.
- Between Internal and External, between what takes place within the territory of the state and what takes place outside.
- Between Economic and Political, between private economic activities
  and public state activities.
- Between Civil and Military, between domestic non-violent legal discourse and external violent struggle.
- Between the soldier (external) as legitimate bearer of arms and the non-
  combatant or criminal/terrorist.

Of course, the character of war has undergone many changes since the end
of the eighteenth century, as I show in Table 1 below. But the key characteristics of what I call 'old conflicts' are that war was the province of the state
and the state alone, and that wars were fought between states for the control
of territory. The decisive encounter of the war was battle, which Clausewitz
compared to cash payment in the marketplace. Clausewitz was the greatest
exponent of this type of war. He defined war as an 'act of violence designed
to compel our opponent to fulfill our will' (von Clausewitz, 1968:1). The assumption was that 'we' and 'our opponent' were states. Writing after the
experience of the Napoleonic wars, in which conscription was introduced
for the first time, Clausewitz elaborated what has become known as the
Trinitarian concept of war operating at three levels—the politicians, the generals, and the people. Clausewitz demonstrated the extremist logic of war at
each of these three levels: the inevitable tendency of war to escalate due to
the reasoning of politicians in their efforts to pursue state interest, the calcu-
lations of generals who need to disarm the enemy in order to prevent coun-

terattack, and the emotions mobilised among the people. According to Clausewitz, war always tends to extremes, limited only by what he called 'friction'—everyday difficulties of logistics, terrain, human error, and so on.

Table 1. *Evolution of 'Old Wars'*

	17th and 18th Centuries	19th Century	Early 20th Century	Late 20th Century
Type of polity	Absolutist state	Nation state	Coalitions of states; multi-national states; empires	Blocs
Goals of war	Reasons of state; dynastic conflict; consolidation of borders	National conflict	National and ideological conflict	Ideological conflict
Type of armed forces	Mercenary/ Professional/	Professional Conscript	Mass armies	Scientific-military elite/ Professional armies
Military tactics and technology	Use of firearms; defensive manoeuvres; sieges	Railway and telegraph; rapid mobilisation	Massive firepower; aircraft and tanks	Weapons of mass destruction
War economy	Regularisation of taxation and borrowing	Expansion of administration and bureaucracy	Mobilisation economy	Military -industrial complex

The extreme tendencies of this type of war can be traced through the evolution of old conflicts as shown in Table 1. The nineteenth century saw the introduction of conscription as well as new industrial technologies such as the railways and the telegraph, which greatly speeded up mobilisation, alongside the expansion of the role of the state. The increasing importance of mobilising national sentiment led to the growing use of propaganda. The twentieth century was marked by the emergence of total wars in which mass production and mass propaganda were harnessed to mass destruction. Indeed, the development of total wars meant that the boundaries established at the end of the eighteenth century began to break down. Total mobilisation eroded the boundaries between public and private, political and economic, military and civil. In the Second World War, there was a big increase in civilian casualties. The term 'genocide' entered legal parlance as a consequence of the Holocaust. What Martin Shaw calls 'implicit genocide' was also carried out by the Allies through mass bombardment (Shaw, forthcoming). The need for allies meant the transnationalisation of military forces and the erosion of the distinction between internal and external. Developments in military technology and the growth of destructiveness called into question the premise of Clausewitzean thought, that war is a rational instrument of state power. The logical endpoint of Clausewitz's extremist logic was nuclear weapons, which make all boundaries irrelevant. In the postwar period, the idea of this type of conflict was kept alive in the imagination through deterrence, extreme ideological conflict and through so-called 'spectator wars' like the Falklands/Malvinas War or the Gulf War; but actual old conflicts were already receding.

Of course, there were other wars. Some 5 million people died in wars in the postwar period. But because they did not fit the concept of war, because they were obscured by the central preoccupation of imagined East-West conflict, they were discounted, described as 'irregular' or 'low intensity' wars. However, it was these wars which provided the basis for the evolution of the new conflicts.

New conflicts

The central contrast with old conflicts is the erosion of the state—in particular, the erosion of the monopoly of legitimate organised violence. This is a process that results both from integration and fragmentation. On the one hand, the monopoly of legitimate organised violence is eroded as a consequence of integration—the increase in military interconnectedness. Nowadays, it is extremely difficult to wage war unilaterally against other states because of alliances, collective security arrangements, and various kinds of arms control agreements, as well as dependence on trade and technology and other kinds of military assistance. There are practical, moral and legal constraints against old conflicts. Even the United States, which is probably the only country not constrained in practical terms, would find it difficult to embark on a military adventure without some sort of multilateral sanction, as we saw recently in the debate about intervention in Iraq. The monopoly of legitimate organised violence is also eroded as a result of fragmentation, particularly, but not only, in situations where centralised states—former Communist or post-colonial states—introduce policies of deregulation, liberalisation, and structural adjustment. The process of fragmentation is almost exactly the reverse of the process through which modern states were established. Production declines, legitimacy is eroded and tax revenues decline both because of the decline of the economy and because of the growth of corruption. Spending on security forces declines and private units of organised violence begin to emerge—criminal gangs, private security firms, and paramilitary groups attached to political factions. Table 2 shows the evolution of new conflicts. In what follows, I describe the main elements of the structure of new conflicts.

Table 2. *Evolution of 'New Wars'*

	'Old Wars'	Guerrilla Warfare	Counter-insurgency	'Low-Intensity' War	'New Wars'
Political goals	National or ideological	Ideological	Ideological	Ideological	Identity politics
Type of forces	Centralised hierarchical regular units	Decentralised hierarchical irregular units	Centralised regular units versus guerrilla units	Decentralised irregular units	Dispersed decentralised coalition of paramilitary groups; warlords; regular units
Military strategy	Capture of territory by military means and overwhelming force; decisive battles	Capture of territory through political control of population; mixture of ideology and coercion	Destabilisation of population to undermine political control	Same as counter-insurgency	Population expulsion as means of population control
Military technology	Sophisticated weapons platforms: tanks; aircraft; missiles	Light weapons	Area destruction weapons, e.g. herbicides; landmines; etc.	Light weapons and area destruction	Light weapons, area destruction, communications
External support	Allies	Superpower patrons	Members of same ideological camp	Superpower patrons	Diaspora; neighbouring states
War economy	Centralised; totalising; autarkic	Local production; loot and plunder; financial support from patrons	Government finance	Patron finance; loot and plunder	'Globalised' war economy

Political goals

I describe the conflicts as wars and not as organised crime in order to em-phasise their political character. The main goal of the new conflicts is iden-tity politics. By identity politics, I mean the claim to power on the basis of identity, on a label—nation, religion, language, clan. In one sense, all wars involve identity—British against French, democrats against communists, and so on. But in old conflicts, identities were linked to geopolitical interest or to ideas about how society should be organised. In so far as there are ideas now, they tend to be nostalgic representations of the past. It is some-times argued that the new conflicts are throwbacks to the past, ancient hatreds that predate the colonial period or the period of communism. Cer-tainly, the parties to the new conflicts make use of powerful narratives that build on memory and tradition. Nevertheless, I share the view of scholars like Benedict Anderson or Ernest Gellner that these narratives are re-invented in a particular context, in this case, the discrediting of former ide-ologies of socialism or nation-building. In contrast to the politics of ideas, which tend to be integrative and inclusive, the politics of identity is fragmentative and exclusive, excluding all with a different label.

Two characteristics of identity politics that derive from contemporary developments should be mentioned. One is the transnational character of the new identity politics. Because of dramatic improvements in communications and travel, the role played by the diaspora is very important—Irish-Americans, Canadian Croats, Australian Greeks and Macedonians. Through ideas, money and technology, they can impose their fantasies of home on a very different reality. The other characteristic is the salience of the electronic media. The speed of mobilisation around identity politics is increased through television, radio and the circulation of videos. In rural areas, where the reading habit is underdeveloped, the 'magic' of radio and television is very powerful.

Types of forces

In contrast to the hierarchically organised, centralised forces that were characteristic of old conflicts, the new conflicts involve a range of different types of forces that compete and cooperate. These include:

- Regular forces or the remnants of regular forces. In some cases, regular forces are divided into different types of units—the army, the gendarmerie, the border police, the Presidential guard, and so on—which may begin to operate independently. In some cases, individual units that may not have been paid break away. In some cases the regular forces disintegrate and join other forces.

- Paramilitary units, usually organised around a single leader, sometimes attached to a political party, sometimes part of a criminal network. Arkan's Tigers and Seselj's Chetniks who operated in Bosnia on the Serbian side are good examples. Arkan was a leading figure in the Belgrade underground; he recruited the 'Tigers' from the fan club of the Belgrade football club, which he owned. Their reward was loot and pillage. Seselj was a radical nationalist; his 'Chetniks' were the military arm of the extreme political party which he still leads, the Serbian radical party. They were fanatic nationalists.

- Self-defence units, usually volunteer groups established to defend a particular area, often linked to local police forces. Thus the local police defended Tuzla in Bosnia-Herzegovina. In Rwanda, self-defence forces were established in some areas to prevent the massacre of Tutsis and were composed of both Tutsis and Hutus.

- Foreign mercenaries. These include British and French soldiers made redundant in the post-Cold War cuts, Mujahedeen—Islamic fighters, veterans of the Afghan war—and Russian officers serving on contract in the new armies of the post-Soviet states. A new phenomenon is private security firms operating under contract to governments or other groups. A particularly notorious example is the South African company Executive Outcomes, which protected diamond mines in Angola and Sierra Leone.

– Peacekeeping forces. These are multilateral regular forces.

Military strategy

It is possible to trace the evolution of military strategy through the various types of guerrilla warfare back to the revolutionary warfare articulated by Mao Tse Tung and Che Guevara, which developed as a way of getting around total wars. In guerrilla warfare, military forces were dispersed and decentralised but highly disciplined. A key tenet of revolutionary warfare was the avoidance of battles or direct engagement of the enemy; Mao insisted that the readiness to retreat was one of the main advantages of guerrillas. The aim of revolutionary warfare was to control territory through political rather than military means, by gaining the political support of the local population. The guerrilla had to be able to operate among the local population as the 'fish in the sea'. Eventually, the enemy would be worn down through political and military exhaustion.

Counter-insurgency involved the use of regular forces against guerrilla forces. Because of the difficulty of directly engaging the enemy and indeed of distinguishing the combatant from the non-combatant, counter-insurgency strategy aimed at undermining the political support of the guerrillas, of poisoning the sea so that it would no longer provide a habitat for the fish. Various destabilization techniques were used such as forcible resettlement (first developed by the French in Algeria) and area destruction using weapons such as napalm, land mines or herbicides (developed by the Americans in Vietnam). The 'low-intensity' conflicts of the 1980s—the Contras in Nicaragua or the Mujahedeen in Afghanistan—made use of similar techniques, but not with regular forces.

The new conflicts borrow from guerrilla warfare the notions of controlling territory through political rather than military means, and of avoiding direct engagement with the enemy. But political control depends on getting rid of everyone of a different label—the homogenisation of the local population. The aim is to sow 'fear and hatred' rather than to win 'hearts and minds'. To achieve this goal, the new wars borrow from counter-insurgency the techniques of destabilisation, ranging from mass murder through various forms of intimidation including physical intimidation such as torture and detention; psychological intimidation such as rape and destruction of cultural and religious monuments; and economic intimidation through sieges, blockades and roadblocks. Essentially, the new conflicts exhibit the very behavioural traits that were proscribed by the code of conduct that characterised the old conflicts.

The statistics of the new conflicts bear witness to the nature of military strategy. There has been an explosive increase in the numbers of refugees and displaced persons. According to one estimate, the number of refugees and displaced persons has increased from around 300,000 per conflict in 1969 to 1.3 million per conflict in 1992 (Weiner, 1996). Moreover, nowadays, most violence in wars is directed against civilians. Whereas at the turn of the century, the ratio of military casualties to civilian casualties in wars was eight-to-one, this ratio has been exactly reversed. Today, the ratio of military casualties to civilian casualties is one to eight.[1]

Military technology

The military technology used in the new wars is usually described as 'low-tech'. Although the weapons used are generally light and often simple is design, the term 'low-tech' is misleading since the technology is actually very advanced. There have been huge improvements in small arms in the last few decades so that machine-guns and rifles, for example, are much lighter, more accurate and easier to use; even children can use them. There have been similar developments in other types of weapons used, such as hand grenades and landmines. Modern communications are essential for coordinating disparate armed groups. In the war in Somalia, the clansmen used digital telephones that the Americans were unable to tap.

War economy

The economy of the new wars is almost the exact opposite of the total wars of the twentieth century. Those wars were totalising, centralising and autarkic. All resources were mobilised for the war effort. The new wars are decentralised; participation is low and unemployment is very high; dependence on outside resources is also extremely high. Figure 1 illustrates the resource flows in new wars. Production is largely destroyed, apart from a few valuable and often illegal commodities such as drugs—or, in the case of Angola and Sierra Leone, diamonds—and taxes are virtually non-existent. In this situation, there are two main sources of revenue for the various armed forces:

a)   What Mark Duffield (1994) calls 'asset transfer'. This includes loot, plunder and manipulation of the terms of trade through blockades and sieges so that people are forced to exchange assets (savings or foreign exchange received from remittances from abroad, cars, televisions, refrigerators, cattle, etc.) for necessities.

---

[1] For earlier figures, see Smith (1997); for the 1990s, see Kaldor (1997: Part 1).

b) External assistance. This includes aid from foreign governments, 'taxation' of humanitarian assistance, private assistance from the diaspora,
and revenue from illegal trade.

Figure 1. *Resource flows in post modern wars*

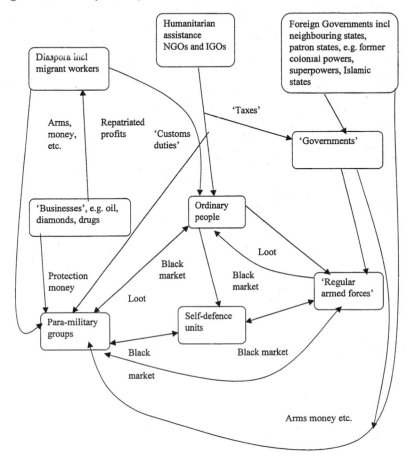

Different types of armed forces tend to be financed in different ways, although they increasingly resemble each other. Regular forces are financed
by governments, generally with resources received from foreign powers.
Paramilitary forces are financed through loot, plunder, diaspora support or
remittances from abroad. A typical pattern for the new private mercenary
armies is payment in rights to the valuable commodities they protect. All
types of forces tend to cream off humanitarian assistance and all tend to participate in the black market, though they fight on opposing sides.

All these sources of finance depend on continuing violence, so the different factions have a shared vested interest, albeit fragile, in war. This is

why some authors suggest that the motivation for these wars is economic.[2] But the point is rather that political and economic motives are increasingly intertwined. Wars can only be sustained on the basis of continuing sources of revenue, which in turn depend on continued war.

In a sense, the new wars could be described as a distorted social formation—a new set of coercive socioeconomic relations. This social formation has a tendency to spread through refugees, through various forms of illegal activity—trade, sanctions-busting, money laundering, etc—or through diaspora networks. It is possible to identify growing clusters of war-prone areas—the Balkans, the Caucasus, Central Asia, Central Africa, the Horn of Africa, and West Africa.

Conclusion

What does this analysis of new wars imply about the management of conflict? In the early 1990s, there were great hopes for humanitarian intervention. With the collapse of the Soviet Union, it was anticipated that organisations like the United Nations would enter a new internationalist era in which the need to defend human rights would override the insistence on state sovereignty. These hopes were dashed by the failure to prevent genocide in Rwanda, the humiliating withdrawal of US troops from Somalia and the shameful fall of the safe haven Srebrenica in Bosnia-Herzegovina. There have been many explanations for these disappointments—among others, the short-term imperatives of politicians, the lack of cohesiveness of the international community, the failure to allocate responsibility among different organisations. Many of these explanations have some merit. But probably the most important explanation was the failure to understand the character of these wars. There has been a tendency either to treat them as old wars, as wars fought between sides in which a solution can be found either through the victory of one side or through some political compromise; or else to treat them as incomprehensible, as anarchy. The first approach tends to end up legitimising the war factions, either through talks or support to one or the other side, which perpetuates the war. The second approach leads at best to the provision of humanitarian assistance, which helps to sustain the warring factions.

The implication of my analysis is that the key to any solution has to be the restoration of legitimacy based on an inclusive politics, to overcome the 'fear and hate'. In all of these wars, it is possible to identify what I call 'islands of civility' where local groups have defended an inclusive set of social arrangements. Examples include Tuzla in Bosnia-Herzegovina, where a non-nationalist municipality defended the town and maintained basic services, or north west Somaliland, where local elders negotiated a peace. Any

---

[2] See, for example, David Keen, 'When war itself is privatised', *Times Literary Supplement,* December 1995.

international effort to solve these wars has to build on these islands of civility politically, militarily and economically. Politically, the aim has to be to support and strengthen those groups and individuals who together constitute a potential forward-looking political project offering a real alternative to the politics of exclusive identity, and which provides a basis for the restoration of the rule of law and international norms of behaviour. Militarily, peacekeeping has to be rethought as international law enforcement, as the protection of civilians. If these wars are in practice a mixture of war, organised crime and human rights violations, the forces responsible for military security have to be reshaped as a mixture of military and police. Economically, reconstruction of local institutions and the legitimate tax base has to supplant both programmes of structural adjustment and humanitarian assistance. Since the social formation which is characteristic of the new wars is also to be found in pre-war and post-war situations, the aim has to be reconstruction of these distorted social relations.

But is such an approach feasible? And if not, was Haris Pasovic right? Are the new wars a twenty-first century phenomenon? Will these clusters of violence continue to spread? Is Sarajevo Europe's future? Many of the features of new wars that I have described are characteristic of the inner cities of Europe and North America. In the United States, private security officers outnumber police officers by two to one and right-wing paramilitary groups have been formed. The salience of identity politics is not just a phenomenon of the East and South. But I am not a pessimistic determinist either. We should be happy about the disappearance of old wars. I do think the barbarity of the two world wars is a thing of the past. But whether or not the new wars become a pervasive feature of the present cannot be predicted. It depends largely on our own actions, on whether it is possible to reconstruct legitimacy in the way I have briefly described, and on whether we can insist on the feasibility of an inclusive political project.

References

Duffield, M. 1994. "The Political Economy of Internal War: Asset Transfer, Complex Emergencies and International Aid", in J. Macrae and A. Zwi (eds), *War and Hunger: Rethinking International Responses*. London: Zed Press.

Kaldor, M. 1997. "Introduction", in M. Kaldor and B. Vashee (eds), *New Wars: Restructuring the Global Military Sector*. London: Pinter.

Kaldor, M. (Forthcoming). *New and Old Wars: Organised Violence in a Global Era*. Cambridge: Polity Press.

Shaw, M. (Forthcoming). "War and Globality: The Role and Character of War in Global Transition", in Ho-Won Jeong (ed.), *Peace and Conflict: A New Agenda*. Dartmouth Publishing.

Smith, D. 1997. *The State of War and Peace Atlas*. London: Penguin Books.

van Creveld. 1991. *The Transformation of War*. London: Macmillan

von Clausewitz, C. 1968 (first published 1832; translated 1908). *On War*. London: Pelican Books.

Weiner, M. 1996. "Bad Neighbours, Bad Neighbourhoods: An Inquiry into the Causes of Refugee Flows", *International Security*, Summer 1996, Vol. 21, No. 1

Arms and Conflicts in Africa: Myths and Realities of Proliferation and Disarmament

Siemon T. Wezeman

Introduction

There was a sigh of relief at the end of the Cold War. The constant threat of sudden war that had hung over our heads for so many decades had suddenly evaporated, and the tools that had maintained that threat were rapidly carried away to the scrap heap. Treaties were signed that reduced the arsenals of both quickly dissolving camps, and other treaties banning whole classes of weaponry could finally be agreed upon. Arms control seemed at last to promise peace and security for all.

Then, apparently out of nowhere, came alarming reports of a 'new' class of weapons that shattered that dream. Bloody conflicts raged in Rwanda, Somalia, Burundi and other faraway places; drug cartels reigned free; maniacs slew at will in Scotland, Tasmania and elsewhere; and crime became increasingly violent as ordinary criminals and the forces of the law all resorted to heavier and heavier firepower. The weapons used were not those usually on the agenda during arms control negotiations (nuclear, chemical, armour, aircraft or warships). The weapons that were doing more damage than weapons of mass destruction had ever done were rifles, pistols, machine guns and mortars—generally called 'small arms' or 'light weapons'. They are the simplest, cheapest and most readily available arms on this planet and it seemed as if anybody could get his or her hands on them.[1] It was as though the fabric of society was unravelling with this unlimited access to automatic weapons and world peace being threatened by international gun-runners and unscrupulous arms dealers. A cry went up for action, nationally and internationally.

While many important personalities have joined in the outcry, making public demands and promises, there is a lack of structured debate around the issue of disarmament. It is as though only a few have a grasp of the real issue. Or rather a grasp on the *real* issues, because the outcry and the debate generally confuse a number of very separate issues. The impression that

---

[1] But it is mostly men, not women, who use guns; the majority of gun owners, killers, soldiers and rebels are male.

firearms are spreading through society probably reflects reality in many countries. Unlike cars and television sets, firearms tend to have a long life, which leads to accumulation since new weapons are produced or imported while older weapons are still held; one could classify this phenomenon as 'gun pollution'. Despite this 'gun pollution', there is little evidence to support the idea that the proliferation of small arms today leads to more and bloodier conflicts than before. But the relative importance of small arms has increased, since most conflicts today are internal, disorganised affairs fought between government forces and rebels, rather than international wars fought in a 'disciplined' manner between armies.

It is quite clear that some societies are plagued by an abundance of firepower in the hands of criminals or 'unstable' persons. It is also clear that one has to ask if any purpose is served by allowing everybody to own deadly weapons and if this does not automatically lead to a more violent society. This is a national problem, to be solved by national discussions on the right to own weapons that result in national laws regulating weapon ownership. It is not useful to impose international laws on gun ownership, since there is no way to arrive at an internationally recognised 'rule' on the private ownership of weapons. In some societies the right to bear arms is part of a centuries-old tradition and has become a symbol of manhood and freedom. In others it is part of a sometimes very necessary tradition of hunting for food.

The issue of illegal trade or gun smuggling is on the other hand international, since borders are crossed. However, notwithstanding the recent growth of the 'black' or 'grey' arms market, there is evidence of only limited arms smuggling.

The third issue is the legal international transfer of weapons. It is here that international arms control has failed. The major powers (also the main producers of weapons) have failed to consider the negative implications of arms transfers. It is a fact that weapons can make the world unsafe, and that small arms tend to 'leak' to persons and organisations for whom they were never intended. This has made peacekeeping and preventive action more difficult and dangerous, and the availability of weapons provides opposition or government forces in many developing countries with a reason to bypass the democratic process and use arms to secure their political or military ends. Today's global arms market is certainly a lot smaller than it was ten years ago, but the international arms market remains important in the post-Cold War world. Despite the end of the Cold War the world has not become much safer for many people, as witnessed by the large number of wars fought over the last few years in Africa.[2] These wars have done massive harm to African societies and continue to hamper economic and social development.

---

[2] The term 'Africa' applies for the purposes of this paper only to sub-Saharan Africa. It does not include Egypt, Libya, Tunisia, Algeria and Morocco.

The vision usually associated with war is the use of weapons. This image has become more pronounced through the way in which wars are depicted in the media, especially television. Pictures are used to convey the message, and pictures of wars must depict death, carnage and weapons. For many this has led to the equation 'War = Weapons = War'. This has then been translated into a simple formula for reducing suffering and ending the fighting: eliminate the means by which war is waged—get rid of the weapons. Following this premise, combinations of restraint exercised among arms exporters and importers, the disarmament of society, improved border controls and the collection of data on trade in and stocks of weapons are considered to be the ways to go about eliminating these means of war.

This paper will present the possibilities of such programmes. However, it should be made clear at the outset that this author does not believe that just taking away the tools of war should be or even could be considered a solution to Africa's conflicts. Most of what follows is only meant to examine some ideas that have been put forward in the last few years; ideas which may be politically attractive for a number of reasons, but which in the end will not create a lasting solution to the death and suffering that result from African conflicts.

Conflicts and weapons in Africa

Most wars fought in Africa have been and are still civil wars. Government forces (army, police, paramilitary forces) are pitched against rebel forces (or sometimes against each other) in wars with political, cultural, economic or ethnic roots. Most African countries are also extremely poor and have only limited educated human resources. This combination of the civil war nature of African conflicts and lack of resources has specific implications for the way the wars are fought, the equipment used and the solutions that could end the conflicts.

Weapons used in African conflicts

Civil wars by nature tend to be guerrilla campaigns fought mainly with small arms or light weapons, weapons that can be carried by one or a small number of persons. They include hand grenades, mines, pistols and re-volvers, machine-pistols and submachine-guns, rifles (including assault rifles), machine-guns, anti-tank rockets, light mortars and some small guided anti-tank and anti-aircraft missiles.

Only occasionally do civil wars move up to the level of 'regular' or 'conventional' war, with more or less organised armies occupying territory and engaging in 'regular' combat with heavy weapons such as artillery, rocket batteries, tanks or aircraft. In Africa, Angola offers an example of a war that became 'regular' a long time ago, with the anti-government UNITA forces holding territory and operating heavy artillery and tanks.[3] The civil wars in Western Sahara and Sudan, and some of the conflicts in Somalia also occasionally follow a more or less 'regular' pattern. However, even in these 'regular' wars the use of major conventional weapons tends to be very limited, and for many African countries 'regular' war with major conventional weapons is out of the question even if they wanted to fight them. The average African country has only a handful of combat aircraft, helicopters, tanks or artillery, many of which are rusty and lacking spare parts. Money is not available for major shopping sprees to bolster the arsenals, and trained personnel are not available to maintain the equipment properly.[4] Most conflicts therefore follow the guerrilla model. Zaire, Rwanda, Burundi, Sierra Leone, Chad, Mali, Mozambique, Uganda, Senegal and Liberia are examples of recent African conflicts that are guerrilla wars fought with small arms.[5]

Many thousands of photographs and many kilometres of film show the weapons used in these conflicts. Experts can easily identify most of them. The picture that emerges is one of chaos. Both rebel and government forces are armed with a motley collection of weapons. Africa is a sort of Noah's Ark of small arms. Virtually every type of small arm ever made in the twentieth century has been used by one or more of the combatants.

Sources of weapons used in African conflicts

Identifying the types of weapons used in African conflicts may be easy. Tracing their origins has proved to be much more complicated, if not almost impossible. Some facts about the sources of weapons used in African conflicts are however very clear and undeniable.

With the exception of South Africa, none of the African states has ever had the capability to produce indigenously designed weapons. Most African countries do not even have the capability to produce weapons or other lethal military equipment under foreign licence. Because of the lack of indigenous arms production capacity, African wars are mainly fought with imported weapons.

It is possible to track down the main suppliers of major conventional weapons and platforms. These weapons systems are expensive and technically difficult to design and produce, which means that the number of possible producers and therefore the number of possible exporters are limited.

---

[3] UNITA: Uñiao Nacional para a Independencia Total de Angola.

[4] For example, when Kabila's forces started to move deeper into Zaire, the Zaire Air Force (on paper one of the stronger and better-equipped air forces in Africa) did not manage to stop or delay the rebels at all. A few planes dropped a few bombs; after that, they were never seen in action again. Rumour had it that most planes were unable to fly at all for lack of maintenance.

[5] This does not mean that no major weapons are used, or that use of heavy weapons is always unsuccessful. One of the main assets of the Sierra Leone government forces in their fight against the Revolutionary United Front (RUF) rebels was a couple of helicopters. Significantly, these were operated by a mercenary company, not by the Sierra Leone Air Force.

These systems are generally large and have in many cases very clear and public registration numbers, and are even named (e.g. ships and aircraft). Because of their price, their complexity and their size they do not lend themselves easily to use by sub-national groups, nor to smuggling or illicit storage. It is therefore not surprising that these are the weapons captured in the SIPRI[6] database on arms transfers, since enough information can be found in public sources to piece together a more or less comprehensive global picture of the trade in these major conventional weapons. In contrast, the movements of small weapons are not as easily tracked, their storage is uncomplicated and even a child could operate them after a few hours' training. As mentioned already, this category of small weapons is the most important in African conflicts and poses the biggest threat to peace in the region.

All this is fact. However, many questions remain unanswered, and here facts mix freely with estimates, guesswork, gossip, myth and fantasy. Is there a cache of weapons that moves from conflict to conflict? Are all Kalashnikovs Kalashnikovs? Is there an ordnance factory in Kenya actually producing ammunition? Were the FAL rifles seen in Liberia left over from shipments imported legally in the 1970s or were they recently imported illicitly?[7] All these and thousands of other questions remain unanswered.

There are no reliable statistics on the trade in small arms, nor is there solid data on stockpiles in the African countries. Estimates differ by factors of 10 to 100. There are also no exact details about who supplied what to whom and when. As mentioned, it is relatively easy to find out which weapons were used in a conflict, but it is almost impossible to find out how most of the identified weapons ended up in the hands of the combatants. One can point accusing fingers, but there is in most cases no clear information on the patterns of arms flows, either to African countries, between them or within them.

Stemming the flow of weapons in Africa

As mentioned already in the introduction, there is a move for eliminating the flows to and stocks of weapons in conflict areas, and especially vis à vis African countries. Programmes have been proposed to achieve this through a combination of measures, explored below.

Exporter restraints

Since nearly all weapons used in African conflicts are imported from abroad, it would seem logical to engage the exporter countries in the process of eliminating weapons from the African continent. One could envisage a partial or complete stop to legal deliveries of weapons to African countries, but

---

[6] SIPRI: Stockholm International Peace Research Institute.

[7] 'FAL' is a particular make of rifle.

such a ban would need to negotiate a few major hurdles and adjust exporter policies to an extent almost impossible to imagine.

Policies for exporting weapons

In the past, ideology—be it communist or anti-communist—was an important motive for arms transfers. This was true for transfers from the Soviet bloc to African countries such as Angola, Ethiopia and Somalia. This ideological motivation was particularly strong with the two main Cold War opponents, the USA and the Soviet Union. The European countries, on the other hand, have long based their exports on more economic motives and, especially in the case of some French transfers to Africa, visions of grandeur.

Today, the driving force behind arms transfers is invariably economic. The market is ruled by the profit motive. This is probably best exemplified by the 180-degree turns taken by the new Czechoslovak and South African governments in the early 1990s. After announcing that their respective countries would on moral grounds refrain from exporting weapons of any kind, both President Havel (*Defense News*, 1993:1) and President Mandela (Batchelor et al., 1998:128) quickly discovered the reality of economic stagnation and the fact that one of the most popular and viable export products of their countries was weaponry. Czechoslovakia promptly sold military jet trainers to (among other countries) Egypt and Bangladesh; South Africa is now actively promoting exports and was selling weapons to Rwanda almost the day the UN embargo was lifted.[8]

In several countries industrial, political and/or military lobbies have in the last few years argued for a relaxation of export regulations. The debate in Germany is a prime example. Even in Japan, traditionally an absolute non-exporter of weapons, some pressure has been put on the government to relax the rules in order to keep the national defence industry alive.

Economic gains from arms exports do not necessarily mean making a profit on the sale of the weapons themselves. Arms exports are often coupled with other exports that could be more lucrative. It is not entirely clear to what extent the refusal to export arms is detrimental to gaining other orders, but there are some cases where a clear connection has been made between arms exports and contracts for other items. After all, the transfer of weapons from one country to another can be seen by the recipient country as the strongest sign of political support from the exporter, and as legitimising the recipient's regime.

---

[8] South Africa even 'forgot' its promise to supply complete data on exports to the UN Register of Conventional Arms (UNROCA). Before the change of government in 1994, South Africa responded to the UNROCA with a note saying that it would comply as soon as the UN arms embargo was lifted. After it was lifted South Africa's first report to the UNROCA did mention exports, and even gave exact designations of weapons exported. But the report did not detail either the number or the buyer (only noting that 'confidentiality clauses' in the contracts precluded publication of further details). Thus, it defeated the purpose of the UNROCA.

The main new feature of the arms trade today it that it is the buyers, the arms importers, who call the tune. They have become less dependent on single suppliers. Whereas in the past buying Soviet weapons almost automatically meant extreme problems in getting any weapons or other sensitive equipment from the US or Europe, today alignment to one of the former Cold War blocs bears no stigma, and there is fierce commercial competition between former bloc members. Prices are being undercut, and incentives being promised in the form of offsets, political agreements or economic aid. The result is that the client is increasingly becoming the king of the market.[9]

Codes of conduct and international 'guidelines'

There has been awareness among several groups of countries (including the European Union, Organisation for Security and Cooperation in Europe, and the five permanent members of the UN Security Council) that there can be negative consequences to unlimited transfers of arms. Consequently these groups produced a series of guidelines, also called codes of conduct, for the 'proper' ways of exporting weapons. While they differ slightly, these sets of guidelines agree on a number of criteria on which arms transfer policies should be based. Export policies should take into account:

- International agreements limiting arms transfers (embargoes, bans on specific types of equipment).
- The human rights situation in the recipient country (massive violations should not be 'rewarded' with arms transfers).
- The existence of conflicts in the recipient country (conflicts should not be exacerbated by arms transfers).
- The preservation of regional peace and security (regional balances should not be upset).
- The respect shown by the recipient country for international law (countries supporting terrorism or otherwise not fulfilling international commitments should not receive arms).
- The risk of arms being diverted from their original destination or purpose (recipient countries have to live up to their 'end-user' declarations).
- The security of other friendly states (arms transfers should not endanger the security of other states friendly or allied to the supplier country).
- The technical and economic capacity of the recipient country (financial or human resources of the recipient countries should not be unduly burdened by arms imports).

---

[9] Probably the best proof for this new order is the US decision to revoke a 20-year-old ban on selling advanced combat aircraft to Latin American countries, after several potential clients started eyeing Russian and European alternatives. While Latin America is not a very important market for the US aerospace industry, this was nevertheless enough of a threat for them to lobby for a relaxation of the ban.

While on paper these guidelines look like a praiseworthy attempt to come to terms with the fact that arms transfers, morals, foreign policy and development policy have not been exactly in line in the past, the reality is that these guidelines are just that: guidelines, not rules, and as such carry limited force.

Feasibility of exporter restraints

Are exporter restraints feasible at all? While many countries' national arms export regulations are as strict or even stricter than the above-mentioned guidelines, there are many ways to circumvent these rules. One of the most common is to define a conflict as something else, usually as an 'internal security matter'. Thereafter, a number of arguments can be used to legitimise further delivery of weapons:

- Arguing that the weapons are basically not useful in the 'internal security' situation, and are thus only for defence against outside aggression. (Probably the most commonly used argument.)
- Defending the transfers as serving the legitimate right and even duty of a sovereign state to enforce law and order in the country without foreign interference (pointing out that the weapons delivered merely do that).
- Bringing up overriding 'national security' imperatives of the supplying country to ignore an existing conflict or other factor that would have prevented delivery.

In the African case, the argument that weapons need to be supplied in order to build or maintain a credible African peacekeeping force has been used to override the 'rules'.[10] In other cases, weapons are simply classified as non-weapons (as with many helicopters, patrol vessels and smaller trainer aircraft), and any negative influence on human rights or national and international security is bluntly denied.

A completely different approach is to sell the licence to produce a weapon to a company in another country, from where the weapon will then be exported to third countries. Exports are regulated by the laws of the country where the actual production takes place, not by the laws of the country where the weapon was designed (even if it supplies many key components, if not whole kits, for the weapon).

Export regulation is a political decision of independent countries and their governments. The problem with conventional weapons is that unlike nuclear and chemical weapons, they are generally not seen as 'bad'. Their export is therefore not greatly stigmatised. Certainly, the 'holy' national

---

[10] For example, the Netherlands tried to gain Parliamentary approval for the transfer of 50 Leopard 1V main battle tanks to Botswana, when at the same time the Dutch armed forces specifically requested lightly-armed, wheeled armoured vehicles because they found the more heavily-armed tracked vehicles unsuitable for peacekeeping operations.

right of self-defence (enshrined in the UN Charter, and often used as a valid ground for export licences) is more consistently respected than are some other rights that might suffer from the arms trade.

While it is true that some countries force export regulations and controls on others by applying all sorts of pressure, it is generally accepted that the arms trade is a legitimate trade not significantly different from other areas of commerce. Export regulations and policies are a result of a government's evaluation of economic benefits, national security, public opinion, international security and labour policies. In some cases, they are influenced by bribery and blackmail.

The problem with arms exports is largely not the question of whether a country should or should not export certain weapons to certain countries; the root of the problem is in the way export policy is made. Generally, policy is made by pressure groups inside and outside governments. They seek to convince other groups through the age-old tactics of providing select information and producing impressive but vague rules, definitions and information.

Arms export is a hot issue in many civilised countries, largely due to the direct influence that arms have on life and death. While nearly all exports to a country with a non-democratic regime indirectly help that regime to maintain its hold on society, arms exports do not have such a discreet influence. They are meant for those government institutions that are seen on the street, keeping the government in the saddle. For the public, it is easy to understand—because they are seen every day on television and in the newspapers—that weapons do suppress, producing a moral dilemma for the viewer or reader. The whole public debate on arms exports is therefore an extremely sensitive and moral one. And there is nothing wrong with that; policy cannot and should not be made completely objectively.

It is up to the public to elect their governments and thereby choose their policies. However, it is up to the government to serve the public that elects and pays for it. It is here that certain discrepancies crop up between stated policy and reality. The only solution is to put the question before the public, and the only way to do so is through complete openness and transparency on 'hot' issues. A number of suggestions have been made in recent years to increase this transparency and force politicians to take a stand on subjects related to arms exports.

Despite a national consensus in many democratic exporter countries, it is still problematic to identify the countries that were responsible for arms transfers in the past, and especially those that could be responsible for transfers in the future, and have them agree to restraints. Since virtually all countries in the world possess just the class of weapons that has proven its usefulness in African conflicts—small arms—the whole world should agree to adhere to restraints.

Would exporter restraints matter?

If and when exporters do agree on some formula resulting in a stop to arms exports to Africa, a second question would arise: Would it matter?

The answer is again largely negative. An export stoppage seems a bit like locking the stable after the horse has bolted. There are now no major flows of weapons from other continents into Africa. West and East European countries, the US, China, Israel, North Korea and several other nations have over the last decade stuffed Africa with enough small arms to 'survive' a temporary export stoppage. As mentioned earlier, one problem with small arms is their durability. While combat aircraft and vehicles may last 20 years before they are completely outdated and two decades more before the last remnants fall apart, rifles last a century or more with only limited maintenance and remain useful instruments of civil war. An export stoppage of arms to Africa, even if agreed on and adhered to by all possible exporters in the world, would not take away the problem of the large stocks of weapons already available domestically in many African countries, or illegally available from neighbours on a continent where borders are mere lines on the map. The problem of weapons in Africa is therefore more an African problem.

But an export stoppage would be at best a political gesture signalling dissatisfaction with the internal situation in a country (as with the EU embargo against Nigeria). It would also help to increase confidence among states (by refusing to supply weapons to the extent that the balance in the region could be disturbed).

Importer restraints

For the same reasons that an export stoppage would not have any significant effects on the supply of small arms in Africa, a cessation of imports would not make much difference either. The weapons are already there, and if a government finds it necessary to import more, there are many ways and excuses to circumvent statements or agreements. Importer restraint will never go so far as to leave government forces without the means to maintain law and order as defined by the ruling powers. Again, this is at best a signal of political will, intended not to pacify internal opposition but to lower tensions with neighbouring states.

Increased border controls

African countries are generally large. Borders in Africa are long and in many cases do not follow natural obstacles. Cross-border contacts are numerous, especially in those cases where people on either side are ethnically related. Border controls are largely insignificant; in some cases they are virtually non-existent. Usually, a handful of customs officers backed up by a few policemen or soldiers are responsible for controlling hundreds if not thousands of kilometres of border. It comes as no surprise that illicit cross-border trade or smuggling is as rampant as the weak economic circumstances permit. This also means that there are no major barriers to prevent weapons from crossing the border illicitly. In normal circumstances that would not pose a huge problem, but with the availability of major stocks of weapons left over from wars in several African countries, it is. There is evidence, for example, that weapons from Angola, Ethiopia, Somalia and Mozambique have found their way across borders to Zaire, Congo and several other 'hot spots' on the continent. In some cases, it was as if the same batch of weapons moved from conflict to conflict to conflict, not at all deterred by intervening borders.

While the theory of the moving batch of weapons is likely to be an exaggeration, it is quite clear that the lack of border controls has made it easy for opposition groups to acquire weapons from other African sources and smuggle them to their own countries. In some cases, this is particularly easy because neighbouring countries covertly or openly support armed oppositions and allow rebels to establish bases in their territory.

Increased border controls and international cooperation in enforcing them would be the only means to stop this illicit arms trade. However, taking into account the situation on most of the African borders, it seems that this goal would be extremely difficult to realise. Most borders are just too long and too porous to be policed effectively. In addition, the amount of weaponry necessary to destabilise a country and sustain a violent conflict in African conditions is usually very small. A few hundred to a few thousand weapons would do the trick. All of these weapons would be small and easily concealed; the ammunition could be measured in truckloads rather than shiploads. To intercept such trade would require a massive investment in border patrols, with very few economic benefits.

The effects of improved border controls

Again, the question arises: Would improved border controls have an impact? The answer could well be yes. Preventing the illicit trade would take away many of the means for armed opposition. But it can only be done at the cost of massive investment in border controls, and most African countries do not have the financial means to do so.

There is also the question of the desirability of establishing such controls. From the viewpoint of a government under siege or under possible threat from an armed opposition, it would be desirable to cut off the flow of weapons to all but the official armed forces. But border controls could be in the wrong hands. The German Democratic Republic had strong border controls and so has North Korea; but has that made anybody happy? What if, for example, Burundi guards its borders as tightly as North Korea's, with consent from neighbouring countries? Would that help resolve the conflict or just leave the Hutus at the mercy of the Tutsi government? And would the EU or the UN provide financial support to establish such border controls?

Disarmament of society

Exporter and importer restraints and border controls are ways to keep weapons out of a country, but in most African countries there are already stocks of weapons available, either legally or illegally. While many disagree about the exact numbers of weapons that are already in Africa, it is clear that the disarmament of society should be the focus of any programme trying to control the proliferation of weapons. However, such disarmament is a major undertaking fraught with numerous problems, as proven during disarmament programmes in Mali, Angola, Mozambique, El Salvador and Bosnia.

There is first of all the very real and practical problem of identifying and collecting all the weapons. Especially with easily-concealed small arms, it is extremely difficult to determine if all weapons have been handed in. Even in well-organised societies with strict laws on firearms, strong enforcement agencies and histories that have not left them with major stocks of weapons from recent wars, illegal weapons exist in quantities that would enable any opposition group in an average African country to challenge government forces with good chances of success. While the collection of a few thousand rifles in Mali or Mozambique may be trumpeted as a major accomplishment, the question always remains: How many weapons are still in circulation?

While one could live with the fact that some weapons may still be around, a second problem is much more important. Disarmament may be effective in removing the means to wage war, but it does not resolve the conflict. While it may be argued that it might force a negotiated settlement, this option is in many cases no more than a fantasy, embraced happily by some because disarmament is practically feasible and actually ends war as it is pictured by most media.

The risk is that a programme of disarmament of society will merely ensure that the sanctioned government's armed forces is the only possible armed force in a country. This risk is a reasonable one in a countries where there are robust democratic means of venting disenchantment with government policies and measures, and where economic and cultural problems can be solved or at least addressed in a peaceful way. This type of government or society does not, however, exist in most African countries. Many of Africa's governments are military or civilian dictatorships, many African rulers came to power through undemocratic means, and economic and especially cultural (ethnic, religious) problems are exclusively dealt with by suppression. African countries have been left with the heritage of colonisation. Their borders have been drawn on maps in Berlin, Paris or London and have nothing to do with the realities of population, tradition or even geography. This legacy has left African countries with a population that is often a mix of different religious or tribal cultures. African countries have often complained about this, but have ignored the possibility that this mix could lead to valid reasons for internal discontent.

Disarmament, strict border controls and strict laws on the possession of weapons may leave many opposition groups in Africa without any means to defend themselves against governments that are not willing to relinquish even a bit of their power. Contradictorily, many governments in Africa have their roots in armed opposition movements against colonial powers or against earlier dictatorships. One would expect such governments to under-stand the problems strict controls can cause if they are not accompanied by measures to democratise government and involve the whole population in it. However, these very governments know that weapons helped them to gain power in a struggle; they do not want new insurgents to take up arms against them.

Transparency

At the end of 1991 the United Nations passed Resolution 46/36 L, entitled 'Transparency in Armaments'. In the spirit of the Resolution, states volun-tarily submit annual information on the export and import of seven speci-fied types of conventional weapons. It was hoped that such transparency would facilitate international security. On January 1, 1992, the United Nations Register of Conventional Arms was established to collect and record this data.

Between 1993 and 1997 approximately 90 governments participated every year in the Register either by submitting data on their exports and im-ports of arms for the preceding year, or by sending a *note verbale* containing information related to arms imports and exports, national laws on firearms or statements about their inability or unwillingness to participate.

In the African situation the relevance of informing neighbours about arms imports is minimal. The existing inventories of major conventional weapons, usually quite limited, do not threaten to destabilise the continent, nor would the import of a few armoured vehicles or aircraft lead to in-creased tension between African countries. This is probably one of the main reasons why African countries have been conspicuously absent from the UN Register.

Transparency as envisaged in the UN Register is purely a means to in-crease confidence among states, not *within* states. However, the information supplied to the UN also increases the amount of information available to groups and organisations outside government circles. Such groups can use this information to question arms exports or imports. If data is available on the import of all weapons, including those small arms that are important for internal security, non-governmental groups might feel more secure in the knowledge that the military means to suppress them are not (yet) available. After all, the idea underlying the UN Register is to provide early warning signals about potentially destabilising accumulations of weapons. While the

UN Register is focused on relations between countries, there is no problem in translating the idea for use in relations between groups within a country. In addition, the concept is not dependent on parliamentary democracy. There is actually no mechanism through which discrepancies in reporting or suspected destabilisation can be addressed. It is up to individual countries to interpret the data and act on it. Non-governmental groups could use the system of confidence-building in the same way nations do: by not opting for a 'worst case scenario' because data on the degree of threat is missing.

Conclusion

Implementing the measures of restraint, disarmament and control as described above may succeed in removing many of the tools of war, but they cannot deal with the most fundamental problem of war: the root causes. The best that can be hoped from a lowering of the level of militarisation would be a general lessening of tensions and greater mutual trust between the warring parties, possibly enticing them to enter a process of negotiation instead of seeking a solution through violence.

From a governmental point of view, the worst that could happen would be a one-sided disarmament by government forces, weakening the position of the government and thereby enticing opposition forces to abandon all non-violent approaches to ending conflict in favour of a military victory.

Another, probably even worse, scenario would give a government whose legitimacy could be shaky to the extreme (a dictatorship) the means to cut off arms supplies to an opposition with very legitimate reason to use force to overthrow the government. One could describe the situation almost as a plot to keep an internationally recognised— but from a democratic viewpoint illegitimate—government in power with the help of foreign governments who refuse to supply arms to the legitimate opposition or even to help control the borders to prevent illicit arms transfers. This would leave the government as the only sanctioned armed force, unlikely to be successfully challenged even by a powerful opposition.

None of the described 'solutions' (exporter restraint, importer restraint, border control or disarmament) can stand on its own. It seemed as if this was understood many years ago but again and again, projects, proposals and recommendations crop up that look only at the weapons angle of conflicts. Taking away the means to wage conflict may seem relatively easy. It may in the short term even lead to less casualties of war in Africa, and may also be something the public and the politicians can grasp and understand. To be effective in the long term, however, solutions focusing on arms control can only be part of a much broader and more complicated solution. Such a solution would attack the roots of the conflict, not just the means. It would involve channelling economic aid to projects of direct benefit to the general population and the training and schooling of government officials, military personnel, political parties and opposition movements.

That would probably be the easy part. There would also have to be some possibly painful adjustments of policy in the developed countries. While the carrot-and-stick policy has been attacked from all sides, developed countries should ask themselves the question: 'What do *we* stand for in this world?' If 'we' have a policy of 'one person, one vote' democracy, if 'we' have basic standards of human rights to be maintained, then 'we' cannot be satisfied with asking for or supporting just a programme of disarmament. Not even as a start, 'because we have to start somewhere'. To solve the conflicts that plague Africa, 'we' have to demand much more from many African governments than a removal of the means of waging war. It would be proper first to start by establishing some of the population's confidence in the economy and in political security and peace before embarking on a programme to eliminate all illicit weapons in Africa. If 'we' still want to support the disarmament of African society, 'we' should also acknowledge the need to provide security, especially to those groups with legitimate reason to oppose governments in power. If 'we' disarm the public, 'we' should ensure that they do not become victims of a criminal government. In civilised countries, there is a trusted police force to ensure public safety. But in Africa, the security of the public will have to be the responsibility of any agency that decides to disarm society.

References

Batchelor, P. and S. Willet. 1998. *Disarmament and Defence Industrial Adjustment in South Africa.* Oxford: SIPRI/Oxford University Press.

Czech Revive Arms Industry, *Exports. Defence News,* Vol. 8, No. 24, 21–27 June 1993, p. 1.

Promoting the Rule of Law in Post-Conflict Societies*

Rama Mani

Introduction

One of the most significant challenges facing common security and civil society in Africa today is that of dealing with the many African societies emerging—or poised to emerge—from violent conflict. More than half the world's ongoing or recently terminated conflicts are in Africa. War and conflict in African countries have cost 10 million households their livelihoods, created 5 to 10 million war orphans, generated 25 million refugees or internally displaced people, and left a lasting legacy of 20 million unexploded landmines.[1]

Post-conflict situations are often characterised by residual hostilities and the potential to slide back into recurrent violence and chaos. A return to violence often has devastating and irreversible consequences for the society concerned and for international security at large. Angola is a bitter reminder of the consequences of ignoring brief windows of opportunity to build peace and dissipate the potential for violence that follows the end of conflict.

In its search for ways to build a durable peace in societies emerging from conflict, the international community has turned to the concept of *the rule of law*. The rule of law, with its tacit promise of stability and order, has

---

* This paper is based in part on a one-day seminar organised as part of the preparations for the 1997 annual meeting of the Common Security Forum, on the subject of promoting the rule of law in post-conflict societies. The seminar was held on 26 September 1997 at the Harvard Center for Population and Development Studies, and jointly organised with the Centre for History and Economics at King's College, Cambridge. An eminent group of legal and human rights practitioners and scholars debated some of the questions raised above, drawing on their diverse experiences in promoting the rule of law in Africa, Asia and Central America. Chatham House rules were applied at the seminar, therefore remarks are not attributed to specific individuals in this paper. Seminar participants: Sudhir Anand, Sissela Bok, Antonia Chayes, Julia Harrington, Todd Howland, Neil Kritz, Melissa Lane, Jennifer Leaning, Rama Mani, Ian Martin, Frank O'Donnell, Bill O'Neill, James Ross, Peter Rosenblum, Emma Rothschild, Henry Steiner, Nancy Dorsinville, Woo Lee and Manabi Majumdar. See Harvard Seminar (1997). The paper also draws on research conducted at the University of Cambridge, and interviews and primary research conducted in the United States in September and October 1997 by the author. The author acknowledges gratefully the comments of Samantha Gibson. The Nordic Africa Institute and the Swedish Ministry of Foreign Affairs provided valuable support.

[1] Cleaver, K., "Foreword", in Coletta, 1996:xiii.

become a commonplace with a diverse range of actors involved in post-conflict peace-building and reconstruction. These actors include several agencies and departments of the United Nations, the World Bank, major bilateral donor agencies like the United States Agency for International Development (USAID), non-governmental organisations like Amnesty International, and regional organisations such as the Organisation for Security and Co-operation in Europe (OSCE) and the Organisation of American States (OAS). The term 'international community'[2] is used throughout this paper to refer to this amalgam of international organisations, as well as to the governments which play a leading role in particular conflicts.[3]

Rule of law programmes in some shape or form have become a cornerstone of most attempts to build peace in post-conflict societies. These programmes are in place in countries as diverse as Rwanda, Mozambique, Haiti, El Salvador and Cambodia, where conflicts and peace processes have taken entirely different forms. In some cases, such as in El Salvador and Guatemala, the negotiated peace agreements called for some institutional reforms in the rule of law, underlining how central legal reforms are to the peace-building process.

The main thinking behind this approach is simple enough: law is a prerequisite for peace, security and stability; a society without law will inevitably be a society without peace. While the rule of law seems the obvious answer, confusion and controversy persist about the meaning of the rule of law, and therefore about how it should be translated into action in post-conflict societies. No two rule of law programmes are alike. The various rule of law programmes in place today include a wide range of activities including legal training, redrafting constitutions, passing and enacting legislation, promoting commercial law, funding civic education, rebuilding court houses and promoting human rights. These programmes reflect the diverse and often contradictory agendas and interests of donor organisations—sometimes to the detriment of the needs and interests of the local war-torn community they were designed to serve. Not surprisingly then, most rule of law programmes have been riddled with obstacles and marked by a lack of co-ordination between the various actors involved.

It is therefore legitimate to ask what the 'rule of law' really means. What have been the successes of the international community in this task, and could performance be enhanced? What are optimal strategies for building the rule of law in societies emerging from conflict? If the rule of law is to

---

[2] The term 'international community' is not very precise, but is used here for simplicity. For a discussion of the term, see Vantage Conference (1997:6–7). A more complete list of the actors involved in post-conflict societies is provided later in this paper.

[3] For example, in Cambodia, the 'international community' would have included the members of the Association of South East Asian Nations (ASEAN), the permanent members of the UN Security Council and Japan, who all played a leading role in the peace process and its immediate follow-up. The nucleus of primary actors varies with each situation.

serve the function of preventing renewed conflict and building peace, one must begin with an understanding of its meaning, its scope and its application in post-conflict countries. Interference with the core institutions of a society and with the attitudes of its people are extraordinary undertakings, and yet they have become standard in rule of law programmes and are often done in a 'matter-of-fact' way, without due concern for the seriousness of the operation. This paper thus seeks to answer two sets of questions. First, what does the rule of law mean and what is its relevance to post-conflict societies? Second, what difficulties do international actors commonly face when attempting to promote the rule of law in post-conflict societies and how might they be overcome? The objective of the paper is to contribute to debates about how to improve performance in promoting the rule of law in post-conflict African societies.

The concept of the rule of law

The 'rule of law' has been portrayed as a political ideal, a legal institution, the centrepiece of any viable political system, the enemy of democracy, a current reality and a distant aspiration.[4] Its origin can be traced back to Aristotle, with his well-known injunction that the rule of law was preferable to the rule of man.[5] Despite its renewed popularity in recent academic debate and in international practice, persistent confusion about its meaning and scope affects the practice of building rule of law in post-conflict societies.

The definitional controversy is partly attributable to a divide in legal thinking between natural law and positive law over whether law is or should be moral. Natural lawyers tend to insist that law must be moral, and that unjust law simply is not law.[6] Legal positivists stress formal criteria rather than the content of law, so that even a bad or iniquitous law is nevertheless a law if it fulfils the criteria of legality.[7] This difference in opinion is reflected today in two opposing conceptions of the rule of law, the minimalist and the maximalist.[8]

The minimalist view separates the rule of law from its moral content, and restricts the concept to its historical role and basic function. Rule of law doctrine developed as a response to the threat of the abuse of power

---

[4] For a view of rule of law as inimical to democracy, see esp. Hutchinson and Monahan (1987:91–123), "Democracy and the Rule of Law".

[5] Aristotle (1981), Book III, xv–xvi.

[6] The main principles of natural law were first laid out by St. Thomas Aquinas in *Summa Theologia*, Part II, "Treatise on Law".

[7] For a defence of the positivist position and a debate over the two views, see H.L.A. Hart (1992), Chapter IX, "Law and Morals".

[8] 'Minimalist' and 'maximalist' are the author's own terms to represent this dichotomy of views, but others have made similar observations. Dworkin distinguishes between what he calls the 'rule book' and the 'rights' conceptions of the rule of law, which correspond in some ways to the minimalist and maximalist views portrayed here (Dworkin, 1985:9–32).

(especially by the state), and as protection from the arbitrary rule of man. Its basic meaning is government that is subject to and operates within the law, and a situation where the individual is protected from the state. It consists at a minimum of clear and widely known rules that are objectively applied, and of a functioning judiciary and justice system which guarantee individuals a certain degree of freedom if they know and follow the rules.[9] One minimalist conception is to take the rule of law to mean literally what it says: that people should obey the law and be ruled by it.[10] In its minimalist sense, the rule of law could be consistent with a wide variety of political systems in addition to liberal democracy. It could, for example, be consistent with a theocratic or monarchic state that follows certain regular procedures. Minimalist proponents would suggest that this minimalist version of the rule of law exists in some form in almost all human societies.[11]

The maximalist view is closer to the natural law position. In this view the rule of law is a *chapeau* encompassing structural, procedural and substantive elements. For maximalists, the rule of law embraces democracy and good governance on the one hand and human rights on the other. It establishes principles to constrain the power of government and it obliges the government to adhere to prescribed and publicly known rules. The maximalist position holds that the rule of law has the potential to be both universal and universally applicable. It is not seen as a particularly Western concept or a product of the common law system, as it espouses universal values and is expressed in universally replicable institutions and procedures.

Some maximalist definitions extend the rule of law doctrine still further to cover economic and social rights in addition to civil and political rights. The International Commission of Jurists (ICJ), established in 1955 to promote the rule of law, equates the rule of law concept with 'the legal protection of human rights'. It defines the rule of law as:

> a dynamic concept ... which should be employed not only to safeguard and advance the civil and political rights of the individual in a free society, but also to

---

[9] One development of the minimalist view was the concept of the *Rechtstaat* or the state of law, particularly in nineteenth century continental Europe. The concept of the *Rechtstaat* gave primacy to administrative control in its bid to eliminate arbitrariness. A state following iniquitous law could, nevertheless, be a state of law. For this reason, maximalist proponents of the rule of law see the *Rechtstaat* as an inadequate, even distorted, expression of rule of law doctrine. See e.g. R. Flathman and G. Gaus in Shapiro (1994), "Public Reason and the Rule of Law". A range of rule of law proponents, including A.V. Dicey, et al. (1959), reject *Rechtstaat* as an expression of the rule of law.

[10] For this view, see Raz (1979:210–228), "The Rule of Law and Its Virtue". Raz seeks to demolish the myth of the 'overriding importance' of the rule of law and its association with a myriad other political ideas.

[11] It should be noted that contemporary legal theory (including legal realism, critical legal studies and sociological jurisprudence) casts doubt on the concept of the rule of law even in this minimalist sense. These theories oppose formal conceptions and prefer elastic and realistic notions of a rule of law and legality.

establish social, economic, educational and cultural conditions under which his legitimate aspirations and dignity may be realised.[12]

Equation of the rule of law with human rights is widely contested. Some human rights activists support—or at least accept—the concept of the rule of law, and acknowledge that its institutions are necessary for the guarantee of human rights. Others feel that rule of law terminology obfuscates human rights objectives, and they dislike any association between the two.[13]

In practice, rule of law and human rights terminology is often used interchangeably. There is admittedly some correlation between the two. Both rule of law and human rights doctrines arose (though at different times) as responses to the threat of state abuse of power, in defence of citizens' rights and security. Several of the procedural elements of human rights covenants are central parts of the rule of law, such as the right to fair trial and freedom from arbitrary arrest. Further, the guarantee of human rights requires the effective functioning of the institutions of the rule of law. Nevertheless, there are areas of the two doctrines which do not overlap, and the differences between the two should not be overlooked.

Differences in approach to the definition and scope of the rule of law have led to varying articulations of the requirements for its establishment. A recent articulation of the rule of law which incorporates the main elements of most existing definitions, both minimalist and maximalist, was provided by the OSCE. A document the OSCE adopted in 1990 lists an extensive catalogue of requirements for the rule of law, which include: a representative government with an accountable executive; a government acting in compliance with the constitution and the law; clear separation of powers between the state and political parties; an independent judiciary and bar association; a civilian-controlled military and police; public procedure in the adoption of legislation; public knowledge of administrative and other laws; and effective and known means of redress available to citizens subject to administrative decisions. The OSCE document also includes the main human rights provisions in its list of rule of law conditions.[14]

The OSCE catalogue of conditions for the rule of law is quite appropriate for post-conflict countries and is used as the working definition of the term in this paper. As will be demonstrated, however, this is not necessarily

---

[12] ICJ (1981:25). This definition was adopted by ICJ at the New Delhi Congress of Jurists in 1959.

[13] Human rights experts participating in the rule of law seminar at Harvard in 1997 had divided views on this issue.

[14] The OSCE document was cited at the Harvard seminar by Neil Kritz of the US Institute of Peace. The OSCE, though a European body, has a relatively heterogeneous membership of 55 states.

a definition that is accepted by or acted upon by all actors in this field, for 'the rule of law still means many things to many people'.[15]

Actors, activities and areas involved in rule of law promotion

As noted above, a wide and diverse range of actors have become involved in promoting the rule of law in countries emerging from conflict. They include several agencies and departments of the United Nations (UN), the office of the UN Commission for Human Rights (UNCHR), the UN Crime Prevention and Criminal Justice Division (CPCJD), the UN Development Program (UNDP), the Department of Peacekeeping Operations (DPKO), and the Department of Political Affairs (DPA). Several regional organisations have adopted rule of law programmes in their work in post-conflict countries as well, including the OSCE, the North Atlantic Treaty Organisation (NATO), the European Union (EU), the Organisation of American States (OAS) and the Organisation of African Unity (OAU). International financial institutions are also involved in certain (mainly commercial and economic) aspects of the rule of law, including the World Bank and the Inter-American Development Bank (IADB). Another set of actors are the bilateral donor agencies such as the United States Agency for International Development (USAID) and the Canadian International Development Agency (CIDA). A number of international non-governmental organisations (NGOs) have also become engaged in promoting or advocating the promotion of the rule of law, such as the International Human Rights Law Group, Amnesty International, Human Rights Watch and the Washington Office on Latin America. This list is not exhaustive, but is representative of the variety of organisations involved.[16]

Rule of law programmes have been undertaken in almost all the countries which have recently emerged from conflict, especially since 1990.[17] These countries include El Salvador, Mozambique, Haiti, Ethiopia, Rwanda and Cambodia. The international actors involved tend to vary by country and by region. In Haiti, for example, USAID is a major player and North American-based organisations like CIDA, IADB and the OAS are active as well.

The programmes undertaken under the umbrella of the rule of law are diverse and wide-ranging. The main elements, which will be elaborated upon later, include establishing or strengthening the judiciary, reforming the police and improving the prison system. Rule of law programmes may in-

---

[15] A participant at the Harvard seminar expressed this view.

[16] A similar list of international actors involved in this area can be found in Vantage Conference (1997:6–7).

[17] This does not imply that rule of law programmes did not exist before. USAID for example had rule of law programmes in several Central American countries in the 1980s. Rule of law programmes have also been implemented in many former Soviet Bloc countries.

clude training judges and lawyers, supporting human rights education, building courthouses and providing equipment for the justice ministry. By way of illustration, international assistance to the judicial system in Rwanda has included training programmes for magistrates and judicial police run by a Belgian NGO, Citizens Network; financial assistance for the salaries of Justice Ministry personnel from the EU, Belgium, Germany, the Netherlands and Canada; US$1 million worth of supplies and equipment for the justice system provided by the US; and repair of court facilities funded by Norway and Switzerland.[18]

Programmes such as those listed above are also sometimes referred to as judicial or justice system programmes, legal reform programmes, or administration of justice programmes. In this paper, the generic term 'rule of law' programmes is used to cover this gamut of operations related to the restoration of the rule of law as defined earlier.

Is promoting the rule of law an international responsibility?

A primary question is whether the international community has a responsibility to promote the rule of law. (In this case, the question is posed in the context of post-conflict societies.) In strictly legal terms, the answer is in the negative. There is no responsibility under international law or treaty obligations for countries to promote the rule of law, particularly internationally. Nevertheless, a responsibility to do so could be derived indirectly.

Article 1.3 of the United Nations Charter states, 'the purpose of the UN is to achieve international co-operation … in promoting and encouraging respect for Human Rights'.[19] The human rights conventions[20] also ascribe clear rights to citizens, which signatory states are expected to respect. Some conventions go further toward the creation of an international responsibility. For example, the Genocide Convention, ratified by two-thirds of UN member states, clearly states: 'The contracting parties confirm genocide, whether committed in time of peace or in time of war, is a crime under international law which they undertake to prevent and punish.[21]

---

[18] "Promoting Human Rights and Building a Fair Judicial System", in Kumar et al. (1996:75).

[19] *Charter of the United Nations and Statue of the International Court of Justice* (New York: United Nations Department of Public Information) undated, p. 3. Signed 26 June 1945. Came into force 24 October, 1945.

[20] *viz*. The International Covenant on Economic, Social and Cultural Rights (ICESCR) (adopted 16 December 1966, came into force 3 January 1966) and the International Covenant on Civil and Political Rights (ICCPR) (adopted on 16 December 1966, came into force 23 March 1976). For texts, see United Nations (1988:7–38).

[21] Article I, "Convention of the Prevention and Punishment of the Crime of Genocide", in *Human Rights* op. cit. p. 143. Approved for signature and ratification 9 December 1948. Came into force 12 January, 1951. As of September 1994, 114 countries had ratified the convention.

Therefore, it can be argued that there is a collective responsibility on states under international law to promote and protect human rights.[22] If this argument is accepted, it follows that states are also obliged to promote and protect the institutions which guarantee the respect of human rights. This directly implies the institutions necessary to maintain the rule of law, such as the judiciary and police. This derivation of an international legal responsibility of states to promote the rule of law underlines the link to human rights doctrine mentioned earlier. Recent experience suggests that the international community recognises such a responsibility and, in many cases, has undertaken rule of law programmes in post-conflict societies as a result.[23]

Beyond legal obligations and altruistic motives of peace building and conflict prevention, a factor underlying international attention to this aspect of post-conflict peace building is that of international *moral* responsibility, deriving from historical and current conduct.[24] Destabilisation policies of the major powers on both sides of the Iron Curtain during the Cold War often employed strategies which directly or indirectly contributed to the breakdown of the rule of law, particularly in developing countries. Elements of these strategies included disrupting elections; supporting dictators; sponsoring terrorists, warlords and militia; corrupting government and court officials; and assassinating opponents.[25] Ironically, it is sometimes those same major powers that are involved today in espousing and promoting the rule of law in post-conflict societies.[26]

Historical legacy and its associated moral burden, particularly in Africa, can be drawn further back, to the colonial period.[27] Some powerful countries continue to undermine the promotion of the rule of law even today within and outside Africa, whether wilfully or unwittingly. One example is Haiti, where the US has inadvertently or deliberately hampered the work of the Truth Commission and the process of addressing past injustices. Yet, at

---

[22] While it cannot be explained here in detail, it should be pointed out that this legal obligation would fall on non-signatories as well as signatories of the relevant international treaties. According to customary international law, a general practice such as a widely ratified international treaty is accepted as international law. See e.g. Brownlie (1990:4–11).

[23] Several other factors have also influenced the current focus on the rule of law: the emphasis on democratisation since the end of the Cold War, the so-called 'CNN factor', and the recent increase in public attention paid to conflicts and humanitarian crises.

[24] Several notable scholars have deliberated on the question of moral responsibility and international justice. See e.g. Hoffman (1996:141–187), "Problems of International Justice"; and Brian Opeskin, "The Moral Foundations of Foreign Aid", *World Development*, Vol. 24, No. 1, 1996. pp. 21–44.

[25] The issue of destabilisation was discussed in the Harvard seminar. There is a substantial body of literature written during and after the Cold War on destabilisation policies. Two recent analyses include Chomsky (1991) and Shalom (1993).

[26] Targets of such destabilisation policies have included: Afghanistan, Rwanda, (former) Zaire, Angola, and much of Central and Latin America.

[27] An extreme but fairly typical example of the colonial legacy is the alleged Belgian role in inculcating or fostering ethnic divisions between the Tutsi and Hutu in Rwanda.

the same time, US agencies are engaged in promoting the administration of justice in that country.[28] Another illustrative case is France's *Operation Turquoise* in Rwanda, where the French government's avowed humanitarianism during its intervention in the genocide of the Tutsi stood in contradiction to its long-term military and financial support for the previous (genocidal) Hutu government.[29] It bears mentioning that states have a moral duty not only to promote the rule of law within (post-conflict) states, but also to respect the rule of law in international conduct.

Common elements of rule of law strategies in post-conflict societies

Field experiences in rule of law promotion in a variety of post-conflict developing countries suggest a few common elements in rule of law programmes for post-conflict societies. Three core elements are common to most programmes and are sometimes referred to as the 'tripod' of the justice system: the judiciary, the police, and the prison system.[30] A fourth element (suggested at the Harvard seminar) is administrative law.

The first element in promoting the rule of law is establishing an independent judiciary, which fulfils the criteria of legality. Ideally, the role and function of courts is to serve as a forum for peaceful resolution of disputes and to render some sense of justice. However, in the aftermath of divisive conflicts, courts should not be overburdened with too many cases or made responsible for disputes which may not be amenable to judicial resolution. Care should be taken not to politicise an institution that is supposed to be blind to politics. In some cases, when domestic courts are weak, it may be necessary to separate the handling of exceptional crimes of the past from the daily business of the courts. An illustrative case is El Salvador, where the UN Truth Commission specifically stated that the persons it identified by name as human rights abusers should not be tried in national courts, because El Salvador's justice system at that time did not meet the minimum requirements for rendering justice fairly and reliably to the accused.[31]

Law enforcement and criminal justice require an efficient and functioning police force and prison system, as these are indispensable to the functioning of the justice system. The police and prison system (and their relevance to human rights and justice) have often been ignored in international

---

[28] See, e.g. Human Rights Watch (1996). This report documents US interference in the search for justice—notably, the CIA's illegal confiscation of key documents required by the Truth Commission in Haiti, and the US government's refusal to extradite from the US a key Haitian official charged with abuses. These activities are common knowledge to experts working in Haiti. USAID is the predominant player in sponsoring rule of law programmes in Haiti.

[29] For two detailed analyses of the genocide see Prunier (1995) and African Rights (1995).

[30] See Vantage Conference (1997:4). At the Vantage Conference, reforming the judicial system and reckoning with war criminals were regarded as part of the same process. In contrast, participants at the Harvard seminar (1997) called for a clear distinction between these two tasks.

[31] Johnstone (1995:35–39).

assistance programmes, but are beginning to receive more attention. A primary dilemma facing many transitional countries is whether to remove the old discredited police force while training a new one (but face the potential for rising crime and insecurity in the short term) or whether to maintain the discredited force which the population distrusts for its role in perpetrating injustices rather than safeguarding justice. Haiti's recent experience illustrates the need to vet and purge discredited elements of the police and military.[32] Namibia presents a relatively successful case of the creation of a revamped and relatively credible police force in a racially polarised post-conflict society, and might have lessons with wider applicability for Africa.[33]

Though it tends to be overlooked in many rule of law programmes, administrative laws influence many aspects of the daily lives of citizens and condition their attitude to the rule of law. Yet, very often, administrative laws are enacted by decree, rather than through open and public procedures, thus entrusting great power and authority to un-elected administrative bureaucrats. It is necessary, therefore, for administrative laws to be considered as an important element in post-conflict rule of law promotion.

Even if a rule of law programme were to incorporate the four elements named above, it might fail if it were implemented without accounting for the unique circumstances that are specific to each post-conflict society. In each country certain political, social and historical factors define the post-conflict context, establish its constraints and, consequently, influence the course of rule of law promotion. The most salient factors are dealing with the past, the political context, and the society and local culture. These contextual factors need to be taken into account early on when designing and implementing strategies for restoring the rule of law.

Dealing with the past

'The past *is* the present', it was observed in post-genocide Rwanda, signalling why addressing the past is such an important, albeit sensitive, issue in most post-conflict societies.[34] In many countries, despite the signing of peace agreements, the past continues to impinge on the present and, therefore, directly influences restoration of the rule of law. Sometimes the wounds of the past can take decades to be addressed and to heal. In many European countries, Nazi war criminals are still being identified and prosecuted today for crimes they committed over 50 years ago.

---

[32] See Neild (1995) and (1996).

[33] For an analysis of this process, see e.g., Laurie Nathan, "Human Rights, Reconciliation and Conflict in Independent Namibia: The Foundation of the Namibian Army and Police Force", in Kumar Rupesinghe (1992:152–168). I am also grateful to Ambassador Martin Andjaba, Permanent Representative of the Republic of Namibia to the United Nations, for his comments on the rule of law and peace-building in Namibia. (Private interview, New York, 3 October 1997.)

[34] This observation was made at the Harvard seminar.

Justice cannot be rendered to victims of past abuses if the rule of law is not operational (for example, arrest, imprisonment and trial of the accused). Nor can the rule of law be restored unless the trust of the population is regained through attempts to render justice for the past. Moreover, accounting for the past gives a new dynamic to the rule of law by signalling that all guilty parties will be treated alike and that all are henceforth equal before the law. Dealing with past abuses can be seen in this respect as a first test for the rule of law in post-conflict societies. Though the process of addressing the past is distinct from the process of restoring the rule of law in the present and future, the two processes are interdependent, and can be mutually reinforcing if conducted concurrently.

There is clearly no single best way for post-conflict societies to address past abuses.[35] A variety of approaches including truth commissions, trials, non-military sanctions, compensation and silence have been tried in various situations. Numerous factors other than the mandate of the law have conditioned and determined societies' responses to past abuses. In Mozambique, for instance, despite the degree and scale of atrocities perpetrated during the conflict, the political leadership decided to amnesty all combatants in the conflict on both sides and not to establish any mechanism to address the past.[36] In contrast, in Rwanda both the national and the international community considered it unthinkable to condone the crime of genocide.

In order for the population in the war-torn society to have a sense of ownership of the process of addressing the past, the process ideally should be conducted in a manner that suits the needs and wishes of people in the society in question, and not according to international dictates. In part it is the attitude of the government in question that influences the way the past is handled. For example, whereas in Rwanda and South Africa the governments were keen to confront the past, in Cambodia and Bosnia they clearly opposed any reckoning with the past. It is not always easy, therefore, to ascertain or to act upon the wishes of 'the people'.

If it is also to serve as a reinforcement for the rule of law, the process of redressing the past should be conducted where possible within the country, in domestic institutions, and should not be internationalised without good reason. International assistance can be useful in reinforcing the institutional capacity of the society to address the past within its boundaries. In Ethiopia, for example, the transitional government exercised its independence by de-

---

[35] The seminal work on this subject is Kritz ed. (1995).

[36] According to the Permanent Representative of Mozambique to the United Nations, the primary political motivation for the decisions to amnesty all combatants and have no systematic reckoning for the past was the desire to move on, promote reconciliation and build peace. (Personal interview with Ambassador Carlos dos Santos, New York, 30 September 1997.) Research conducted by Priscilla Hayner, a leading independent researcher on truth commissions, suggests that Mozambicans found a unique and culturally-specific method of dealing with the past by 'healing' war criminals and cleansing them of their sins. (Personal interview, New York, 3 October 1997.)

ciding to try those accused of human rights abuses during the Mengistu regime in national Ethiopian courts. However, the government asked for substantial international assistance to finance the process and received funding from several donors.[37]

The political context

Perhaps the most decisive factor emerging from a survey of the experiences in promoting the rule of law in several post-conflict countries is the importance of the local political context. This context places constraints on the processes of legal reform and the broader project of peace-building. The nature of the conflict and the way it was resolved influence the post-conflict situation. Moreover, the nature of the regime in power after the conflict (and its relationship with international actors and with its own population) often determines the outcome of efforts to reinstate the rule of law.

Civil society can provide a countervailing force to an oppressive or irresponsible government. However, it is the political context—that is, the will of the political leadership—that largely determines how much political space civil society is allowed. It has been noted that in Haiti, the political vacuum and lack of government leadership (pernicious in itself) left space for the emergence of strong indigenous NGOs and allowed external actors to work closely with them. By contrast, in Rwanda, the new government over time circumscribed NGOs' autonomy and limited the possibilities for international actors to engage civil society in their work.

Experience demonstrates how important it is that international actors take into account the local political context, and (where necessary and appropriate) apply political pressure on the leadership. In Cambodia, when the political climate deteriorated following the 1993 elections, international actors focused their rule of law efforts on the grassroots level, and failed to heed warning signs in the formal political sphere.[38] Hun Sen's coup in the spring of 1997 aborted almost entirely international efforts to promote the rule of law.

Society and culture

An essential starting point for the proper establishment of the rule of law is the society itself: its people and its culture. There are two points which require consideration here. The first is the need to engage the meaningful participation of the population in the process of building the rule of law. The second is to consider carefully local history and culture. The formal and in-

---

[37] The Ethiopian case was presented by a participant at the Harvard seminar. Donors included the US and Nordic countries.

[38] Cambodia was discussed at the Harvard seminar. The internationally-assisted elections and the elected government's subsequent distancing from the international community is analysed in Heininger (1994).

formal legal traditions of the society are particularly important and need to be built upon when a rule of law strategy is devised.

In several post-conflict countries there has been a tendency for outside experts hired by international agencies to fly in and propose or impose legal programmes with relatively little consultation with the local population, and with limited knowledge of the society's history, culture, needs and attitudes towards the justice system. For example, when they designed legal reform packages in Cambodia, several international legal experts treated the country as a *tabula rasa* without a pre-existing legal culture. This approach greatly offended and alienated Cambodians, who subsequently demonstrated that they did have their own legal traditions.[39]

The rule of law is a *culture*. Particularly after it has been absent or abused during long conflicts, this culture requires careful regeneration, which can only be done with the full involvement, ownership and investment of the local population in the process. Moreover, it can only be successful if it builds upon the existing traditions, history and culture of the society, and is not an alien legal system.

The observations made above regarding both the political context and the society and culture reinforce the necessity of pursuing simultaneously both top-down and bottom-up approaches in promoting the rule of law—that is, of working at once with the political elite and the grassroots.[40] Several international actors, particularly some UN agencies and NGOs, recognise the importance of working with grassroots and community groups to entrench the culture of the rule of law and have set up several training and education programmes for the civilian population (for example in Haiti and Rwanda).

The media and the military can play important roles in rule of law programmes. While it is not possible to elaborate here on these two factors, the necessity of cultivating an educated and co-operative media and a supportive military must be considered in the context of rule of law promotion (particularly when an international military peacekeeping mission is present).[41]

---

[39] This example was brought up at the seminar, and reflects the general attitude taken in Cambodia. Individual lawyers (such as the person who shared this example at the seminar) may disagree.

[40] This point was made repeatedly at the Harvard seminar.

[41] At the Harvard seminar both these points were discussed at length. Elements of the Bosnian media have frustrated attempts at justice by lionising persons of their ethnicity as soon as they were identified as war criminals. At a recent conference organised by the United States Institute of Peace, prosecutors on both sides of the ethnic divide recognised that winning over the media was their shared objective in the pursuit of justice. In the case of Rwanda, seminar participants commented that a regrettable compromise (struck between the UN and the Tutsi government in Rwanda when negotiating UNIMIR's—United Nations Assistance Mission to Rwanda—return to Rwanda) had been the shutting down of the radio station run by UNIMIR during the first mandate. The UN radio station had been one of the only outlets for relatively non-partisan voices and its closure was a lost opportunity for promoting reconciliation. These examples

Shortcomings in international practice and the potential for improvement

International efforts to date in promoting the rule of law in post-conflict societies have not been entirely successful. They have faced obstacles which were sometimes beyond their control, and sometimes of their own making.

The first set of difficulties encountered by international actors involved in promoting the rule of law are those caused by lack of credibility and political will. In Rwanda, the international community's (in particular the UN Security Council's) inability to prevent the genocide deeply discredited the international community in the eyes of many Rwandans. This loss of credibility was exacerbated by the failure of the International Tribunal for Rwanda under its first prosecutor, and made it very difficult for the UN Human Rights Field Operation in Rwanda and other international actors to gain the trust of the Rwandan government and people.

Genuine political will to restore the rule of law is required not only of the post-conflict government itself, but of the donor countries and agencies as well. Cambodia and Bosnia are often cited as cases of governments which were not interested in restoring the rule of law or redressing past abuses, and it is obvious that this lack of will obstructs the process for both domestic and international actors. In some cases, one or more intervening donor states have also lacked the political will to see the rule of law restored and justice rendered for the past. The US in Haiti is a case in point.[42] The lack of political will can greatly hamper the work of all international actors on the ground, however well-planned their programmes or good their intentions.

A second set of problems which is also beyond the control of individual actors on the ground is the marginalisation of human rights in the post-conflict reconstruction agenda.[43] The human rights framework and its objectives are sometimes obscured or undermined in the process of restoring the rule of law. Though the Human Rights High Commissioner (HRHC) has been assigned a pivotal role by the General Assembly in promoting the rule of law in post-conflict situations, in reality the office of the HCHR (previously the UN Centre for Human Rights) is still a relatively small player in rule of law promotion, as it lacks the resources of the larger players like USAID. Consequently, missions conducted under the purview of the HCHR are

---

highlight the importance of cultivating well-trained media and encouraging freedom of the press. Regarding the role of the military: while some participants commented on how starkly the military mentality and approach to problems differed from the civilian approach, others remarked that recent years had seen rapprochement between the two. The US army, for example, was credited for its distinctly rule of law approach—lending credence to the jest that the US army has a lawyer in each platoon. There was general agreement at the seminar that the military could be a critical variable in the promotion of the rule of law; and given its increasingly frequent presence in transitional situations, its vast potential and resources should be recognised.

[42] Another example cited at the Harvard seminar was of the recent massacres in East Zaire: one participant suggested that neither the Tutsi government in Rwanda, the US government, nor the new government of Laurent Kabila were interested in seeing the truth emerge.

[43] This concern was expressed by a participant at the Harvard seminar.

under-resourced and weak, as observed in the Rwandan human rights field operation. Therefore, they have difficulty fulfilling their ambitious mandates.

A third set of problems is to some extent the consequence of the rule of law programmes and their agents. Perhaps the biggest weakness is the lack of harmony between programmes and the absence of co-ordination between the many actors involved in rule of law promotion.[44] A range of problems are observed in common in the operations undertaken by the UN and regional organisations, bilateral agencies and NGOs. They include low levels of competence of some personnel; pay scales sometimes incommensurate with responsibility; and weak knowledge of the local legal system, culture and language.[45] The inadequacy of the legal training of lawyers engaged in rule of law promotion is also a concern. Even highly regarded law schools offer few courses in comparative law or in the legal traditions of developing countries. Consequently, lawyers are often not adequately equipped to address post-conflict situations, particularly when confronted with legal systems different from their own.[46]

Rule of law promotion also faces the common problem of a resource shortage, which weakens the potential of actors who might otherwise be more effective. The Organisation of African Unity (OAU) is an important regional actor, but it has very little funding available for rule of law promotion. Before the recent return to violence in Sierra Leone, the OAU brokered a quite ambitious peace agreement with significant human rights and rule of law components. The agreement was then handed over to the African Commission on People's and Human Rights to be operationalised and implemented. However, the OAU could provide scant resources for implementation of this agenda.[47]

The short and chequered career of the international community in post-conflict rule of law promotion might suggest to some that international actors should withdraw from this arena altogether. However, despite shortfalls, many rule of law programmes are beneficial and have potential for improvement. The case of Rwanda suggests that in some instances the high degree of hostility and suspicion that characterises most post-conflict situations makes an international presence both desirable and necessary, however weak its reputation or ineffective its performance.[48]

---

[44] This concern was expressed by a participant at the Harvard seminar.

[45] Only one person on the Rwandan mission spoke KinyaRwanda. (Harvard seminar discussion.)

[46] An illustrative case mentioned at the seminar was the bitter competition between American and French lawyers over the model of the legal system to be established in Romania and Cambodia. (Though neither side could articulate the differences between their systems or their relative merits.)

[47] This point was emphasised at the Harvard seminar.

[48] This point was emphasised at the Harvard seminar.

There is indeed vast opportunity for improving upon past performance. A perceptible change in thinking about conflict and post-conflict situations has permeated to the highest levels of the UN system. There is an understanding that post-conflict peace-building must address not only the symptoms of conflict but also its root causes, and these issues are increasingly being negotiated and written into peace agreements to ensure that they will be adequately addressed thereafter.[49]

The Track Two Reforms announced by the new UN Secretary-General in July 1997, particularly those proposing a new National Development Assistance Framework, can also be seen as a sign of hope. This proposal is intended to improve co-ordination among various UN actions and to integrate human rights into the UN's development assistance framework. These reforms, together with the higher profile recently accorded the High Commissioner for Human Rights, may help to ensure an international response in post-conflict societies that better integrates human rights and the rule of law.

The Ethiopian experience provides lessons for how rule of law programmes could improve. Ethiopia's transitional government established a Special Prosecutor's Office to address the past. A programme was set up to accumulate evidence in order to try those detained for alleged human rights abuses, and to systematically create a historical record of the past. However, despite substantial funding from the international community and a large team of trained Ethiopian investigators and international legal consultants, the programme eventually collapsed. Its main problems were the lack of a clear framework and guidelines, absence of an evaluation mechanism to keep the process on track and weak accountability and transparency on the part of the donors.

The weaknesses of the experiment in Ethiopia highlight some basic requirements for effective design and implementation of rule of law programmes. These include a clear and transparent framework determined by a wide consultative process; clear guidelines and specific human rights objectives, which are agreed upon by both donors and recipients and are openly articulated; and an evaluation mechanism that is agreed upon and put in place from the beginning.[50]

---

[49] The recent peace agreements in Guatemala provide evidence of this new thinking (at least on paper), as they go far beyond traditional peace agreement elements such as ceasefires by attempting to address the root causes of the conflict. This constructive and realistic attitude towards peace-building and rule of law was reflected by high-ranking UN officials in the Department of Political Affairs who were involved in Central American, Bosnian and African peace negotiations. (Personal interviews in New York with Alvaro de Soto (9 September 1997); Francesc Vendrell (29 September 1997); and B. Ramcharan (3 October 1997).)

[50] The Ethiopian example and suggestions on how to improve rule of law programmes were put forward by a Harvard seminar participant.

Conclusion: Integrating peace, law and justice in post-conflict societies

This paper has attempted to clarify what the rule of law means in the context of post-conflict societies. It has demonstrated the versatility and complexity of current international efforts to promote the rule of law in these societies. It identified the main elements of rule of law promotion programmes as well as the contextual factors that affect the process of establishing the rule of law in post-conflict societies. The paper has also identified the shortcomings of international efforts to promote the rule of law in practice and made some suggestions about how these efforts might be improved.

The paper highlighted some of the issues that influence the international community's efforts to promote rule of law in the aftermath of conflict, which will require further reflection. They include the need to clarify the definition, scope and goals of the rule of law; the need to take into account the political context and, therefore, to work both with political elites and the grassroots communities; the need to facilitate the post-conflict society's efforts to address the past on its own terms; the importance of the society's participation; and the value of building on the society's own history, culture and legal tradition when promoting the rule of law.

The road to restoring the rule of law and promoting respect for human rights in war-ravaged countries in Africa and elsewhere will be, inevitably, a challenging one. While the sheer number of rule of law programmes in operation might suggest that programmes of this kind are now 'normal', promoting the rule of law in a fragile post-conflict scenario is a matter of deadly seriousness, and should be recognised as an extraordinary political undertaking. The international community must act now and act well, for the cost of failure is too high and painful to consider.

References

African Rights. 1995. Rwanda, *Death, Despair and Defiance*. London: African Rights.

√ Aristotle. 1981 (revised edition). *The Politics*. Harmondsworth, Middlesex: Penguin.

√ Brownlie, I. 1990. *Principles of International Public Law*. Oxford: Clarendon Press.

Chomsky, N. 1991. *Deterring Democracy*. London: Vintage.

Coletta, N., M. Kostner and I. Wiederhofer. 1996. *Case Studies in War-to-Peace Transitions: The Demobilisation and Reintegration of Ex-Combatants in Ethiopia, Namibia and Uganda*. Washington, DC: World Bank.

√ Dicey, A.V., et al. 1959. *An Introduction to the Study of the Law of the Constitution*. Houndsmill, Basingstoke: Macmillan. 10th edition. 1st edition 1885.

√ Dworkin, R. 1985. "Political Judges and the Rule of Law", in *A Matter of Principle*. Cambridge, Mass: Harvard University Press.

√ Hart, H.L.A. 1992. *The Concept of Law*. Oxford: Clarendon Press. Revised edition. 1st edition 1961.

Harvard Seminar. 1997. *Promoting the Rule of Law in Post-Conflict Societies*. Cambridge: Centre for History and Economics.

Heininger, J. 1994. *Peacekeeping in Transition: The United Nations in Cambodia*. New York: The Twentieth Century Fund Press.

Hoffman, S. 1981. *Duties beyond Borders: On the Limits and Possibilities of Ethical International Politics.* Syracuse: Syracuse University Press.

Human Rights Watch. 1996 Vol. 8, No. 7(B). *Haiti, Thirst for Justice: A Decade of Impunity in Haiti.* New York: Human Rights Watch.

Hutchinson, A. and P. Monahan (eds). 1987. *The Rule of Law: Ideal or Ideology?* Toronto: Carswell.

ICJ (International Commission of Jurists). 1981. *Development, Human Rights and the Rule of Law.* Oxford: Pergamon Press.

Johnstone, I. 1995. *Rights and Reconciliation: UN Strategies in El Salvador.* International Peace Academy, Occasional Paper Series. London: Lynne Rienner Publishers.

Kritz, N. (ed.) 1995. *Transitional Justice.* Washington, DC: US Institute for Peace.

Kumar, K. et al. 1996. *Rebuilding Post-War Rwanda. Study 4 of The International Response to Conflict and Genocide: Lessons from the Rwanda Experience.* Copenhagen: Steering Committee of the Joint Evaluation of Emergency Assistance to Rwanda.

Neild, R. 1995. *Policing Haiti: Preliminary Assessment of the New Civilian Security Force.* Washington, DC: The Washington Office on Latin America.

Neild, R. 1996. *The Haitian National Police.* Washington, DC: The Washington Office on Latin America.

Post-Conflict Justice: The Role of the International Community. 1997. Report of a Vantage Conference in Queenstown, MD, April 4–6 1997. Muscatine, Iowa: Stanley Foundation.

Prunier, G. 1995. *The Rwanda Crisis: History of a Genocide.* New York: Columbia University Press.

Raz, J. 1979. *The Authority of Law: Essays on Law and Morality.* Oxford: Clarendon.

Rupesinghe, K. (ed.) 1992. *Internal Conflict and Governance.* Basingstoke: Macmillan Press.

Shalom, S. R. 1993. *Imperial Alibis: Rationalising U.S. Intervention after the Cold War.* Boston: South End Press.

Shapiro, I. (ed.) 1994. *The Rule of Law.* London: New York University Press.

United Nations. 1988. *Human Rights: A Compilation of International Instruments.* New York: United Nations.

Vantage Conference. 1997. *Post-Conflict Justice: The Role of the International Community.* Report of a Vantage Conference in Queenstown, MD, April 4–6 1997. Muscatine, Iowa: Stanley Foundation.

Aid and Politics in Malawi and Kenya: Political Conditionality and Donor Support to the 'Human Rights, Democracy and Governance' Sector

Samantha Gibson

Introduction

Since the end of the Cold War, donor countries have increasingly linked foreign aid to democratic reforms. Political conditionality is the most conspicuous symptom of this trend, and Kenya and Malawi provide two of the most dramatic examples of recent donor interventions. In the early 1990s, largely because of concerns about political repression and human rights violations, bilateral donors suspended aid to both countries and made resumption of aid conditional on political reforms. At the same time, donors began to make grants intended to promote democracy and human rights. How have these donor interventions affected domestic politics in Kenya and Malawi?

This chapter is divided into four sections. The first section demonstrates that although objections have been raised to donors' increasing use of political conditionality, *not* suspending aid also has substantial implications for domestic politics. The cases of pre-1990 Kenya and Malawi demonstrate that aid influenced the nature of domestic politics well before donors imposed explicit political conditionalities on both countries.

The next two sections consider how this new aid agenda has affected the process of political liberalisation in both countries. By suspending aid, donors forced the issue of reform to the top of governments' agendas—something domestic actors had been unable to do alone. Donors then followed aid bilateral suspension with extensive funding for the democracy and governance (DG) sector, supporting a group of civil society organisations that engage in civic education, human rights advocacy and other activities intended to further the process of democratic consolidation.

Section four stresses the decisive role that political conditionality played in the introduction of multiparty politics in Kenya and Malawi (despite donors' insistence that they were only advocating an environment more tolerant of human rights and political pluralism, not advocating a specific system of government). However, donors' subsequent efforts to assist the process of democratic consolidation through support to civil society have so far had only limited impact.

Finally, donors' direct and indirect interventions in the domestic politics of African countries raise critical questions about North-South partnerships. The chapter closes by posing questions about donor accountability, the role of governance and the state in development, and the nature of civil society in Africa.

Aid and politics in Kenya and Malawi before political conditionality

Economic conditionality was a common feature of development assistance programmes throughout the 1980s, but the imposition of explicit conditions relating to the domestic politics of aid-recipient states was considered taboo until quite recently. Multilateral donors were (and still are) prohibited by their constitutions from commenting on member states' domestic political affairs. Bilateral donors generally avoided overt involvement in the internal politics of recipient countries, partly because of sensitivity to the newly-independent states' hard-won sovereignty, and partly because the cold war security interests of many of the larger donors prevailed over competing human rights interests.[1]

However, donors' historical reluctance to comment on the domestic politics of African countries does not suggest that they have ever played a neutral role in the internal politics of aid-recipient countries. As much as suspension of aid conveys donor disapproval of a regime, a steady flow of aid to a rights-abusing regime conveys a powerful message of support and approval of that government's activities. Some critiques of political conditionality overlook the fact that the mere presence of foreign aid will have either direct or indirect influence on internal politics, whether aid is conditioned or not. As the Kenya and Malawi cases described below demonstrate, development aid in both countries was used by the incumbent governments for partisan political ends throughout the period before conditionality was introduced. What is new about political conditionality is not that aid is affecting domestic politics—it always has. What *is* new about political conditionality is that now it can no longer be assumed that donors will continue to provide unconditional support to allied regimes, regardless of their human rights violations or oppressive politics.

The extension of development assistance in the form of non-humanitarian project or programme aid is more than simply an expression of goodwill from a rich country to a poor one. Development assistance to a repressive

---

[1] In this paper I imply that 'donors' are a somewhat homogenous group, primarily because space does not allow detailed accounts of individual donor policy in both Kenya and Malawi during all three periods under discussion. Within the group of bilateral donors there is clearly a considerable diversity in terms of the size of the programmes they establish in recipient countries, the countries in which they choose to work and the extent to which they raise political concerns with partner governments. Despite this diversity, in the Kenya and Malawi cases there was a general pattern among the majority of bilateral donors, with important exceptions that would be given due consideration in more lengthy papers.

regime also brings with it a message of outside recognition and implied approval of the recipient regime, and provides financial assistance that can be used to strengthen a government's near-monopoly on political and economic power. On the other hand, suspension of aid can destabilise a recipient regime, or change the government's perceptions of the costs of resisting domestic demand for political reforms. There is no question that foreign aid influences domestic politics in recipient countries, although in some countries donors have more influence than in others. What is a question, however, is with which actors in recipient states the donors choose to collaborate, and to what ends they use this influence.

For many years, both Kenya and Malawi enjoyed the favour of the major multilateral and bilateral donors. Their strategic locations and ideological affinity with Western powers, as well as pervasive poverty, attracted substantial aid programmes. Until 1989, Kenya was a top aid-recipient in sub-Saharan Africa (World Bank, 1989) and was widely considered an African success story, particularly when compared with its neighbours. Malawi was rewarded by the US and UK in particular for President Banda's willingness to maintain relations with South Africa, to provide support to Renamo and to host Mozambican refugees. Multilateral donors rewarded Malawi's good debt repayment record with aid. Large bilateral donors and the European Union were also generous. Throughout the first 25 years of independence, project aid consistently supplied over 85 per cent of the development budgets in both countries, and programme aid covered as much as 50 per cent of recurrent expenditures during periods of economic decline.[2]

How did this largely unconditional aid affect domestic politics in Kenya and Malawi? Both governments used project aid for partisan ends. Nearly all infrastructure development in Kenya and Malawi has been provided by project aid from both bilateral and multilateral donors. This assistance has provided the state with resources in the form of roads, schools, energy projects and other major infrastructure with which it can support the patronage networks necessary to maintain power and suppress or marginalise dissent.[3] As a result, it is nearly impossible for these large-scale projects to have a neutral effect on partisan politics.

---

[2] Kenya: Waller, 1995. Malawi: July 1996 interviews in the Central Bank and Ministry of Economic Planning and Development. Project aid is generally tied to a specific infrastructure project like roads, dams, radio towers or schools. Programme aid (also called non-project assistance or balance of payments support) is aid in the form of hard currency, deposited in the central bank of the recipient country. It was intended to help finance imports that became otherwise unaffordable during the structural adjustment years, and comprises about half the aid-receipt of most African countries. (Project aid is the other half.) Programme aid is often tied to a particular sector (e.g., importing medicines or computers for the health sector), but is in practice quite fungible and can essentially be used by the government as a cash deposit in a bank account.

[3] For further discussion of rents, aid and political power, see: Clapham, 1996, Sandbrook, 1993, Bates, 1989.

Project aid

Project aid intended to promote the overall level of social or economic development has been manipulated to favour certain political constituencies. Recipient regimes have used aid to promote partisan political ends by implementing aid projects in locations with a strong record of supporting the president or ruling party, and withholding it from those which do not. Examples of both practices can be found in Kenya where, since the early 1980s, President Moi and his closest advisors have exercised increasingly centralised and personal control over political decisions and resource allocation in Kenya (Barkan, 1991; Widner, 1992). Interviews with former Finance and Planning Ministry officials revealed that the President's personal influence on development policy extends down to the level of specific (donor-funded) infrastructure projects. A study of the only two ministries that publish details of their project expenditure demonstrates that the pattern of projects undertaken by the ministries of health and transport over the 1970s and 1980s shifted from President Kenyatta's favoured regions in Central Province to the Rift Valley and Western Provinces, President Moi's political stronghold.[4]

As easily as recipient regimes can use funds to promote the interests of their allies, they can also exploit centralised decision-making processes in order to ensure that groups seen as enemies of the regime do not benefit from donor-funded projects. For instance, in 1994, a bilateral donor offered to fund a badly needed water project in Kisumu, western Kenya, and Finance Ministry officials approved the project—but the project was ultimately vetoed by the Office of the President because the city was considered an 'opposition zone' due to the recent election of a non-KANU mayor.[5]

Project aid to Kenya has also been used for partisan political ends during election campaigns. During a recent parliamentary by-election in western Kenya, donor-supplied road building equipment was parked on the shoulder of a dilapidated road, and the local KANU official announced that if the ruling party's candidate won, the equipment would be used to improve the local road—but if he lost, the equipment would disappear (*ibid.*).[6]

In Malawi, foreign aid was used in different ways, but with a similar intent. In speeches broadcast repeatedly on national radio, President Kamuzu Banda regularly referred to 'Kamuzu's hospitals' and 'Kamuzu's roads,' implying that the services existed only because of Banda's personal largesse (Feidler, 1996). In fact, Malawi's development budget (including the health and transport sectors that administer 'Kamuzu's hospitals' and 'Kamuzu's

---

[4] Chege and Barkan, 1989; study of the health and transport ministries.

[5] The Kenya Africa National Union (KANU) was the only legal political party in Kenya in 1982–1991. Information from confidential interview with former aid desk officer in the Kenyan Ministry of Finance, March 1996.

[6] The opposition candidate won, and the equipment disappeared shortly after election day.

roads') has been nearly entirely aid-funded since independence, and projects of any size cannot be undertaken without donor support. From the late 1960s to late 1993, President Banda and his Malawi Congress Party (MCP) required that every Malawian produce an MCP membership card to enter hospitals or markets, both of which were largely donor funded. Because their religion forbade them from joining political parties, Jehova's Witnesses were denied access to public services of this kind under President Banda's rule. In these subtle but important ways, development assistance is used by repressive regimes to bolster their hold on power while marginalising or eliminating opposing voices.

Non-project aid

Project aid was not the only way that donor assistance indirectly influenced domestic politics in aid-recipient countries during the years before the 'democracy agenda' surfaced. Recipient regimes derived significant *symbolic* benefit (as well as financial support) from their relationship with donors. Even relatively casual remarks made by aid officials could be used by a president or a ruling party to imply international approval of his rule. In speeches broadcast repeatedly on national radio, President Banda quoted a senior World Bank official's remark that Malawi was a 'star performer'. Front-page newspaper photos of President Moi accepting oversized million-dollar cheques from donor agency officials could only send a signal to supporters and opposition alike that the international community supported the regime.

Not surprisingly, aid to security forces was particularly useful to regimes like Moi's and Banda's that viewed the suppression of internal dissent as a high policy priority. Much aid in the form of police and military training proffered to repressive regimes not only serves to strengthen what can be arbitrary and violent domestic forces, but also implies overt or at least tacit accord with the regime's repressive activities (whether or not that is the donor's intent). Since 1991, donors have periodically denounced the human rights violations perpetrated by police and security forces in Kenya under Moi, and in Malawi under Banda. What tends to go unnoticed, though, is that for decades the very same donors provided unqualified support to the same forces.[7]

Thus, international aid flows helped the repressive, centralised, patronage-based Moi and Banda regimes strengthen and maintain their monopoly on political power. They did this through strategically placed (donor-funded) projects, through the symbolic approval conferred by the uncondi-

---

[7] Aid to security and police forces is a particularly difficult issue about which to generalise. Some donors were quite careful about keeping aid as far from the Kenyan and Malawian police as possible. Also, there are several examples of aid programmes that support responsible community policing practice.

tional renewal of aid, through the use of donor-funded equipment for election campaigns, and (at times) suppression of the opposition. In addition to the political benefits derived from project aid described above, a steady stream of balance of payments support provided a relatively flexible and highly fungible source of cash to the central government. This aid-funded expenditure helped to soften the fiscal blow of declining export earnings throughout the 1980s, and partially mitigated potential political unrest (Holmquist, Weaver and Ford, 1994:99).

The new donor agenda: Human rights and democracy

By 1989–1990, Kenya's and Malawi's status as darlings of the donor community was under threat. Although the authoritarian practices of the Moi and Banda regimes had been indirectly supported by foreign aid for many years, suddenly the countries were no longer perceived as 'ornaments', but were now considered 'eyesores' (Gibbon, 1995:7). A number of factors combined to make donors reconsider their previously cordial relationships with the Moi and Banda regimes. The end of the Cold War, the ascendance of an increasingly influential international human rights movement, the emergence of indigenous reform movements, increasing donor disillusionment with what was seen as a pervasive rent-seeking culture among politicians and pressure from home to cut aid expenditure all contributed to donors' increasing criticism of internal political processes in aid-recipient countries. This was particularly the case for countries such as Kenya and Malawi, which had well-known human rights problems, were heavily reliant upon foreign aid and were no longer part of the West's roster of key strategic allies. In this changed aid climate, donors began to argue that more pluralistic and competitive political systems would make errant governments more transparent and accountable, thus better policy makers. Diplomats stationed in Nairobi and Lilongwe began—many for the first time—to raise the issues of human rights and political pluralism with the host governments.

Consultative group meetings

Initially these concerns were raised with the governments of Kenya and Malawi only through official diplomatic channels and on an individual, ad hoc basis. However, by late 1991 donors, frustrated by the lack of impact that diplomatic dialogue had on the Moi and Banda regimes, joined together to intensify the pressure for reforms.

This collective pressure was placed on Kenya and Malawi through the medium of the Consultative Group (CG) meetings. The major aid forum for many African countries, CGs include top representatives from every donor agency as well as a high-level delegation from the aid-recipient country, usually led by the Minister of Finance. It is at these World Bank-chaired meetings that poor countries state their needs and donors make aid pledges for the following several years. While heated discussions about economic reforms were commonplace at these CGs throughout the 1980s and until 1991, politics were off limits in formal aid negotiations such as these.

Donors' presentations at the CGs convened for Kenya in November 1991 and Malawi in May 1992 were, however, explicitly political. In these meetings, aid to both countries was for the first time explicitly linked to 'democratisation' and improved respect for human rights. Although the level of oppression in Kenya and Malawi in 1991 and 1992 was no more severe than it had been at any time in the past ten years, it was at that point that donors combined forces and used political conditionality as a tool to promote political change.

In both cases, there was remarkable co-ordination between nearly all bilateral donors. In Kenya, all except the French agreed to jointly suspend aid worth $350m as a result of their concerns over the Government of Kenya's intolerance of political pluralism, government corruption, slowness to implement economic reforms and widespread human rights abuses.[8] In Malawi, every bilateral donor agreed to suspend all non-humanitarian aid (totalling $US27m) due to the seriousness of human rights violations perpetrated under Banda's leadership. The donors' collective press statements noted that if the situation improved, the aid packages might be reinstated when the political situation was reviewed in six months—but that nothing was certain.

Donors cut aid and the multiparty era begins

Right up until the time that aid sanctions were imposed in Malawi and Kenya, there was little reason to believe that either Moi or Banda were planning to introduce any kind of political reforms or address the international community's growing concerns about human rights. In fact, quite the opposite was the case. Both governments used harsh sedition and treason laws to detain or confine 'confusionists' who attempted to cover controversial political issues in the press, those who were in favour of a multiparty system of government, or those who otherwise threatened the regimes' increasingly authoritarian rule. In Malawi, any number of acts could be construed as 'disrespectful to His Excellency Ngwazi Dr Hastings Kamuzu Banda', and the offender sentenced to serve a prison term. For women, forms of 'disrespect' punishable by imprisonment included falling ill on the day they were due to dance in honour of the President on his tour of the district. For men, even starting a small business could land them in jail. After all, the President's businesses (within the Press Group of companies) accounted for

---

[8] The IMF and World Bank also suspended aid to Kenya in 1991, but this suspension was due to slippage on economic conditions.

one third of Malawi's GDP, and any enterprise a person started could be considered to be entering into competition with the Kamuzu himself.

Membership in the ruling Malawi Congress Party was a requirement to gain access to public services as well as civil service jobs. Access to the broadcast media by those who were critical of the ruling regime was (and still is) highly restricted. Newspapers or magazines that were not wholly supportive of the government were confiscated and printing presses were destroyed. In addition, party and state security forces were used to intimidate and harass those considered to be enemies of the state or party, including human rights activists.

The donors' terms of suspension in 1991 and 1992 were quite general. They did not address any of the governments' human rights or democracy problems in particular, nor specifically prescribe a multiparty system. Indeed, the donors were careful to avoid mention of multipartyism, instead demanding 'greater tolerance for political pluralism' and 'fundamental reforms in the way the government deals with basic human rights'.[9] Although the donors explicitly avoided raising the issue of multiparty politics as a key reform issue, decision-makers in the governments of Kenya and Malawi interpreted the donors' broad demands for 'greater openness' as a code for multiparty politics, and determined among themselves that aid would not be reinstated unless the single party system was scrapped. Government officials serving at that time noted their domestic political practices had never incited the wrath of the donors before the multiparty movement started in other parts of Africa and Central and Eastern Europe—therefore, they concluded, multipartyism must be what the donors were getting at, even if they did not say so in as many words.[10]

The Kenyan government's response to aid suspension was immediate; within a week President Moi announced that Kenya was no longer a single party state, and that multiparty elections would be held within the year. The decision appeared to have come directly from the Office of the President, since neither parliament nor the party were consulted. After a chaotic registration and campaign period, flawed multiparty elections were held in December 1992, and the majority of the suspended aid was reinstated at the CG meeting of March 1993. Overall aid flows to Kenya returned to normal, with a few donors scaling down.[11] Since introducing multiparty politics, the

---

[9] CG press statements, November 1991 and May 1992.

[10] Interviews with former bureaucrats and Ministers of Information, Foreign Affairs, and State, Nairobi and Lilongwe, 1996.

[11] Although most donors have resumed normal aid relations with the Government, several donors have attempted to divert aid funds from the central government. The Americans are a particularly dramatic case: 90 per cent of the United States' Kenyan aid is now channelled through civil society organisations and US-based NGOs (US Agency for International Development, internal documents, 1994). Some German aid is now provided directly to the Nairobi City Council (rather than the central government), which is opposition-controlled (Waller, 1995:118). German programme aid was suspended in 1993/4, but project aid continued (Bass,

government and the ruling party has continued to harass the opposition, to use state resources to intimidate the independent press and to create civil disturbances, and has generally resisted reform at every turn—but most donors agree that state-driven political oppression in Kenya from 1992 has been marginally less severe than it was under the single-party regime and do not anticipate significant reversals in the trajectory toward greater political openness.

The Malawian government's initial response to the political conditionalities imposed in the 1992 CG was slower than Kenya's. It was several months before the President announced a referendum on the question of whether or not a multiparty system should be adopted, but other donor-specified reforms were introduced in the meantime. The Red Cross was brought in to inspect some prisons and Malawians were no longer forced to buy party membership cards in order to enter markets, ride buses, or enter hospitals. However remarkable these 'concessions', aid was still not released. When the referendum was finally announced in October of 1992, donors mobilised funds and monitors for the campaign and voting exercises. The multiparty supporters won the referendum and the voting day was pronounced sufficiently free and fair by both the winning and losing sides of the referendum as well as the international community. Aid to Malawi was resumed a year and a half after it was suspended.[12] Major constitutional reforms were undertaken, press freedoms flourished (although access to radio for the opposition is a chronic problem), amnesty was declared for all prisoners on death row. In multiparty elections six months later, the MCP and President Banda were voted out of office and power was peacefully transferred to a new government.

The examples of Kenya and Malawi reveal several ways in which donors influence recipient country politics, both by default and by design. In the first instances, when no overtly political conditions were attached to aid, donors indirectly contributed to repressive internal politics, in *de facto* rather than *de jure* terms. Presidents and ruling parties can use development aid to strengthen patronage networks, reinforce party control of the electorate, and derive symbolic value from the international community's unwillingness to distance themselves from repressive policies. In the second instance, when political conditions were attached to aid by a tightly co-ordinated group of donors, multiparty elections and somewhat improved human rights practices were forced onto the governments' agendas.

1994:15). The Danes suspended a portion of their aid in 1990 primarily because of concerns about corruption (Bass, 1994; Steffenson interview 1996). Norway cut aid by 20 per cent in 1991 in protest over the Government of Kenya's detention of a political prisoner. The GOK responded by severing diplomatic relations (Bass, 1994:9).

[12] There was one exception. At the December 1993 CG Denmark stated that its aid would be withheld until there was a new government in Malawi.

Procedural vs. substantive democracy: The problem of democratic consolidation

Soon after aid to Kenya and Malawi was suspended, it was clear that political conditionality had some effect on liberalising domestic politics at the level of procedural democracy—in these cases, the introduction of multi-party politics—but had little effect at the level of substantive democracy.[13] The process of democratic consolidation is meant to be a period when an initial move away from authoritarianism to procedural democracy is then expanded to include the qualities of substantive democracy, including diverse and autonomous civil society organisations, responsible and independent media, a broad base of political participation, representative and effective political parties and an independent judiciary. Democratic consolidation implies the 'dispersal of political power' to local government, the judiciary, parliament, and civil society and development of a 'social consensus on democratic political values' (Sandbrook, 1993:91).

Many donors—the US and Sweden most conspicuously—recognised the limitations of negative, punitive incentives like conditionality and soon developed positive inducements to further political reform and work related to the consolidation of democracy in Kenya and Malawi. Beginning at roughly the same time as aid was suspended, donors began to shift their democracy and human rights promotion efforts largely to institutions in civil society, with some projects targeted at government bodies like the courts and parliament. What kind of civil society groups have donors funded, and have these efforts contributed to democratic consolidation in Kenya and Malawi?

Political aid to civil society

Civil society has been defined in many ways. As Pelczynski notes, 'few social and political concepts have travelled so far in their life and changed their meaning so much.'[14] For this chapter, I will use the broad characterisation favoured by mainstream political scientists writing in the late 1980s and early 1990s. In this characterisation, civil society is the realm of associations and activities that exist between the household or family level and the state.[15] Churches, labour unions, professional associations, co-operatives, the press and other groups that are (mostly) independent of the state are the most commonly identified actors within civil society. This section of the chapter illustrates the recent dramatic increase in the variety and number of

---

[13] Procedural (also known as 'formal') democracy applies to the formal rules that govern elections and provide for citizens' basic civil and political rights—legalising opposition parties, allowing for freedom of association and expression. Substantive democracy goes beyond rules and laws, to include a pluralistic and independent civil and plural *society* that facilitates the participation of all classes in political life. Holmquist, Weaver and Ford 1994 use 'democracy of content' to describe a similar concept. See also Fatton, 1995 and Gibbon, 1993.

[14] Quoted in Bratton 1994.

[15] See also Putnam, 1993, Harbeson, 1994, Bratton, 1994, Barkan 1997, Bermeo, 1997, Gibbon, 1993.

donor-funded 'democracy and governance' (DG) groups within civil society in Kenya and Malawi and shows that this type of intervention, despite its scale, has so far had only a relatively limited impact on the process of democratic consolidation.

Donors invest in civil society and the DG sector

In addition to imposing political conditionalities on some governments they deem undemocratic, many donors have also begun to dedicate relatively small but rapidly increasing proportions of their aid budgets to what has become known as the 'democracy and governance (DG) sector'. The DG sector encompasses human rights NGOs, 'good governance' groups, policy think tanks, legal aid services, constitutional reform groups, societies for the advancement of women and minorities, election monitoring and civic education bodies, and a host of other organisations associated with political reform and human rights. In Malawi and Kenya, donor aid to trade unions and the independent press also falls in this category.[16]

The flow of aid to 'pro-democracy' NGOs and other civil society groups in Malawi and Kenya began around 1992–1993, just after political conditionality was imposed in both countries. Before this time, very few donors were involved in grant-making to this sector in Africa, but since then, budget allocations for DG projects has grown faster than almost any other sector of aid budgets. For instance, US funding for DG activities in Africa now rivals expenditure on AIDS (Harbeson, 1995). In geographical terms, the bulk of DG expenditure has shifted from Latin America in the late 1980s to Africa in the 1990s, which received a 57 per cent share of donors' global expenditure on the DG sector in 1993/94, and was projected to increased still further (Robinson, 1996:22).

Five to 12 per cent of overall OECD development assistance expenditure is now dedicated to the DG sector (Barkan, forthcoming), but the percentage tends to be higher in those countries where donors have made democratic consolidation a priority.[17] For most donors, Malawi and Kenya are among this group of priority countries. DG projects also tend to be relatively less expensive than traditional capital-intensive or technical assistance-intensive projects. Thus, even what might appear to be a relatively low total expenditure on the DG sector finances a considerable *number* of individual grants, projects, and community activities.

---

[16] For this paper, the discussion is limited to DG organisations in civil society, although some grant-making in this sector is earmarked for government bodies and political parties.

[17] It is difficult to know the *exact* percentage of any one donor's aid budget spent on the DG sector. Until 1996, the Development Assistance Committee of the OECD did not require that individual donors report DG activities as a separate category; a human rights project would sometimes be recorded under 'governance', sometimes under 'capacity building', etc.

Donor dependency: Are donors creating the DG sector in Kenya and Malawi?

Most bilateral donors are now investing in the DG sector in Africa.[18] But are the donors actually *creating* this sector? A recent survey of Nairobi's DG sector showed that there were more than 120 DG groups working in Kenya at the end of 1996—of which the vast majority were based in Nairobi. Only a few of these existed before 1993, and only nine of the 120 do any local fundraising.[19] Malawi's DG sector is slightly younger and much smaller than Kenya's, but the urban-based, donor-dependent trends are consistent with the Kenyan experience. Of the eight DG groups active in Malawi in 1996, all were dependent upon foreign donors for funds.[20]

The dependency of the DG sector on external finance is partially the product of the ready availability of donor funds for this sector, and partially due to the constraints on local sources of funding. Although the government of Malawi no longer discourages people from forming independent organisations, the vast majority of people are simply too poor to give money to a DG organisation. Kenya has a more prosperous middle class and a better-established tradition of charitable giving than Malawi. But many Kenyans fear giving to the sector because security forces still regularly harass groups and individuals the government sees as a challenge—including people involved with certain DG groups. Clearly, there are formidable obstacles to the DG sector achieving financial independence from external donors. Foreign aid will likely be the dominant source of funding for DG groups for the foreseeable future. A handful of these groups did exist before donor funding, and a few have memberships upon which to draw limited resources, but the great majority would not survive if donors were to withdraw from the sector.

What DG organisations do

The most active and well-funded organisations within the DG sector tend to have tense relationships with the government. This is particularly true in the Kenyan case, where the government regards independent civil society organisations with such extreme suspicion that the government's NGO registration unit was established as part of the Internal Security Division of the Office of the President. Donors wholly fund many organisations whose activities the Kenyan government considers subversive, including: the Centre for Law and Research International which, with Danish funding, pub-

---

[18] Japan is a notable exception.

[19] Andreassen, Maina and Ngunyi, 1996. Even before the emergence of the DG sector, Kenyan and Malawian NGOs have relied upon foreign aid for more than 90 per cent of their funds. (Fowler, 1993 (Kenya), Faiti, 1995 (Malawi)).

[20] Interviews with Shyley Kondowe of the Malawi Institute for Democratic and Economic Affairs, and Gillian Flies of the National Democratic Institute, Lilongwe 1996.

lished a detailed report on corruption in Kenyan society;[21] and the Kenya Human Rights Commission, which issues quarterly reports on the local human rights situation, provides information to donors and the international press about rights violations in Kenya, researches prison conditions, and organises demonstrations protesting police brutality. The Association of Free and Independent Press defends its members against government interference in their reporting, and the public interest law group *Kituo cha Sheria* took the government to court over squatter's rights.[22] All of these groups are funded by international donors, which generally cover both core operating costs and programme costs.

In Malawi, the Public Affairs Committee (PAC) is one of the most prominent and best-funded DG group in the country. It started out in 1992 as a 'pressure group' calling for dialogue with the government, greater political openness and improvements in human rights. The group was launched when Malawi's Catholic bishops read aloud a pastoral letter appealing to the government for attention to the growing economic inequality and political intolerance in the country. At the time, the letter was considered so outrageous by the Malawi Congress Party that its central committee determined that the people who eventually founded PAC (most of whom were church leaders) should be killed.[23]

Not all DG groups in Malawi and Kenya confront the government or its policies as directly as the groups noted above. A growing number conduct seminars or workshops with 'civic education' themes. These activities are meant to educate citizens about their rights, the constitution, what they can expect of their political representatives, and how *'matipati'* (multiparty) politics is different from the old one-party system. Because these civic education groups are at most only a few years old, it is too soon to assess their effect on the manner and extent in which people participate in the political process. There is no evidence in either country that these workshops have been associated with mass political mobilisation, yet violent disruption of several civic education meetings by the KANU youth wing and closure of meetings by local government administrators suggests that the Moi regime is suspicious of their agenda.[24] In contrast, since coming to office in 1993, the new Malawi government has neither supported nor interfered with civic education undertaken by NGOs.

---

[21] The report was banned in Kenya and subsequently published in Denmark (with Danida support).

[22] Kituo's offices were firebombed three times as a result of this action.

[23] Taped proceedings of this 1992 meeting were leaked to the BBC World Service, and international concern for the fate of the bishops kept the MCP from carrying out their plans.

[24] Kenya News, 12 June 1997. Features Africa Network.

The DG sector and democratic consolidation

The process of democratic consolidation in Africa is not yet well understood. Much more research has been undertaken in Latin America, where the process of transition from military rule to democracy has been underway since the early 1980s. This research stresses that the evolution of substantive democracies—rather than simply democracies of procedure—tends be driven by several factors. Social movements with a mass membership (often facilitated by the Church), a mobilised peasantry or well-organised labour force, a sector of the elite or middle class supportive of reform, a reliable and independent media, and mature political parties are all cited as important elements of consolidations in the Latin American region.[25] Few of these conditions exist in Kenya and Malawi, and DG aid is unlikely to create them.

There are many reasons for the inability of DG aid to transform the context in which democracy develops. Aid to the DG sector in Kenya and Malawi today is focused almost entirely on organisations located in urban areas. Legal aid organisations and human rights NGOs tend to be located in capital cities (not in the rural areas, where human rights violations are often a serious problem), and independent newspapers are expensive and are not distributed in the remote rural areas where most people live. Many civic education groups do not find their way out of the capital city and into the countryside, where rural people (more than city dwellers) are likely to be neglected by their elected representatives, intimidated by provincial administrators or suffer from poor public services. Peasants and the urban poor tend not to identify with a particular political party or social movement, and few of the DG organisations active in Malawi and Kenya have endeavoured to support efforts to organise these marginalised people. Civic education programmes run by church groups may turn out to be an exception to the tendency of DG groups toward urban bias, because most traditional churches have an existing grassroots network of personnel and infrastructure.

Not only do organisations supported by DG aid tend to be urban-based, but there is no indication that these groups will necessarily represent democratic ideals in terms of their internal structure, the constituency they claim to represent or promote, or their focus of activities. There is nothing unique about civil society *per se* that ensures groups within it will be inherently more peaceful, consultative, 'neutral' or 'democratic' than state organs. Oversight of a large volume of small grants has proved to be a considerable burden on already busy donor agency personnel in Lilongwe and Nairobi, and many have understandably found it difficult to assess the wide range of issues that should be considered when making grants to DG organisations.

---

[25] For further discussion, see Stepan, 1988 and Schmitter, O'Donnell and Whitehead, 1986.

Many of the DG proposals received by donor agency staff are creative, low-cost attempts at improving human rights practices or voter awareness; but what might seem reasonable on paper may not turn out to be what the donor had hoped. A proposal for a radio spot on human rights in a vernacular language might seem a good idea in the form of a two-page proposal, but may evolve into a 30-second condemnation of the dominant ethnic group's treatment of a particular minority. Rarely can DG organisations truthfully claim to be wholly non-partisan. In a recent case in Kenya, one donor, when confronted with funding proposals by two voter education bodies—one a branch of the ruling party's former women's wing, and one an organisation chaired by the wife of an opposition party presidential candidate—resolved the problem by giving *each* group a Land Rover. Many programme officers expressed frustration that they did not have time to conduct sufficient background research on the civil society groups they provided with DG funding.

It is too soon to judge the extent to which aid to the DG sector has or has not been effective in its collective aim of securing democratic consolidation. However, the character of the DG sector in Malawi and Kenya thus far raises some doubts about whether the activities donors have supported will support these countries moving from the first steps of procedural democracy toward more substantive democracy—although they may contribute on the margins.

Summary and conclusions

Donors to Africa have had direct and indirect influence on domestic politics since the origins of development aid in the 1960s. In the Kenyan and Malawian cases, aid indirectly strengthened the increasingly authoritarian rule of both Presidents and their parties. Shortly after the Cold War ended, donors distanced themselves from the Moi and Banda regimes by suspending aid and imposing political conditionalities, forcing the introduction of multiparty politics. During the multiparty era, the donor community has fully funded the DG sector in civil society.

No matter what approach is adopted, no form of development assistance is free of political implications. Whether donors continue aid to repressive regimes or suspend it, whether they target funds at governments or at civil society, development assistance is politically charged. Donors' potential for influence is only intensified in weak economies. Foreign aid comprises just over 10 per cent of most sub-Saharan African countries' GDP, and runs as high as 92 per cent in war-torn Mozambique. For better or for worse, donor influence in internal political affairs will persist for as long as economic growth and development evade the continent.

Donors' influence on domestic politics during the period of non-conditionality and political conditionality was fairly clear. In the period when donors were lending unconditional support to Banda's and Moi's authoritarian regimes, foreign aid indirectly impeded democracy and contributed to a repressive political environment in Malawi and Kenya. When donors imposed political conditionalities on aid in 1991 and 1992, they used aid as a lever to force the transition to a more pluralistic political climate. What is less clear is what effect donors' interventions in civil society and the DG sector will have on politics in Kenya and Malawi.

This chapter has set out the three primary ways in which donors have influenced (and attempted to influence) politics in Kenya and Malawi since independence. The cases are meant to provide background material for more critical—and hopefully constructive—debates about donors' increasingly interventionist role in African politics. Several questions emerging from the case studies echo themes raised in the Partnership Africa papers of 1996.[26]

If donors are to truly engage with Africans as partners in a common enterprise, and with Africans as 'subjects, not objects' of development,[27] with whom should donors seek to cooperate? Who are 'Africans?' Are they represented by the state, or civil society? After many years of unconditional aid to repressive, unrepresentative governments, donors suspended aid to regimes they deemed unaccountable to their citizens. But are largely urban civil society groups of the sort favoured by DG aid any more representative or accountable than the states the same donors sanctioned in 1991 and 1992? As the cases of Kenya and Malawi suggest, there are no easy answers to these questions.

What *is* clear is that unconditional aid, political conditionality, and aid to the DG sector in Kenya and Malawi all fell short of an ideal development partnership between donors and the African poor. Freed of the constraints of the Cold War, donors, recipient states, and civil society in North and South alike are well poised to take this opportunity to reflect upon and reformulate the idea of partnership with Africa.

References

Andreassen, B.A., W. Maina and M. Ngunyi. 1996. *Supporting Human Rights in Times of Democratic Transition: External Aid to the DG Sector in Kenya.* The Norwegian Institute of Human Rights Oslo/ NBI, Oct 1996 (mimeograph).

Bass, H. 1994. "The Human Rights Dimension of Germany's Development Aid: Two Examples (Kenya, China)", *Berichte und Analysen Dritte Welt*, Vol. 6, Issue 1.

Barkan, J. 1991. "The Rise and Fall of a Governance Realm in Kenya", in G. Hyden and M. Bratton (eds), *Governance in Africa*. Boulder: Lynne Rienner.

Barkan, J. 1997. "Can Established Democracies Nurture Democracy Abroad? Lessons from Africa", in A. Hadenius (ed.), *Democracy's Victory and Crisis*. Nobel Symposium No. 93. Cambridge: Cambridge University Press.

---

[26] Papers prepared for the Swedish Foreign Ministry's 'Partnership Africa' initiative held in 1996–1997. See, for example, Kifle, et al., 1997.

[27] "Introduction" to *A New Partnership for African Development: Issues and Parameters*. Kifle, Olukoshi, Wohlgemuth (eds), 1997.

Bates, R. 1989. *Beyond the Miracle of the Market: The Political Economy of Agrarian Development in Kenya*. Cambridge: Cambridge University Press.

Bermeo, N. 1997. Civil Society, Good Government and Neo-Liberal Reforms, in Faundez, J. (ed.), *Good Government and Law: Legal and Institutional Reform in Developing Countries*. London: Macmillan.

Bratton, M. 1994. "Civil Society and Political Transitions in Africa", in J. Harbeson, N. Chazan, D. Rothschild (eds), *Civil Society and the State in Africa*. Boulder: Lynne Rienner.

Bayart, J. F. 1986. "Civil Society in Africa", in P. Chabal (ed.), *Political Domination in Africa*. Cambridge: Cambridge University Press.

Chege, M. and J. Barkan. 1989. "Decentralising the State: District Focus and the Politics of Reallocation in Kenya", *Journal of Modern African Studies*, Vol. 27, pp. 431–453.

Clapham, C. 1996. *Africa and the International System: The Politics of State Survival*. Cambridge Studies in International Relations, 50. Cambridge: Cambridge University Press.

Faiti, D. 1995. *National NGO Co-ordination: Experiences from the Council for NGOs in Malawi*. Master's thesis, University of Wales Centre for Development Studies.

Fatton, D. 1995. "Africa in the Age of Democratization: The Civic Limitations of Civil Society", *African Studies Review*, Vol. 37, pp. 67–101.

Feidler, K. 1996. "Power at the Receiving End: The Jehovah's Witnesses' Experience in One-Party Malawi", in K. Ross (ed.), *God, People and Power in Malawi*. Blantyre: Kachere Press.

Fowler, A. 1993. *Non-Governmental Organisations and the Promotion of Democracy in Kenya*. PhD Dissertation in Development Studies, University of Sussex.

Gibbon, P. 1993. "'Civil society' and political change, with special reference to 'developmentalist' states." Paper presented to workshop on "Experiences of Political Liberalisation in Africa, Centre for Development Research", Copenhagen, June 1993.

Gibbon, P. 1995. *Markets, Civil Society and Democracy in Kenya*. Uppsala: Nordic Africa Institute.

Harbeson, J. 1994. "Civil Society and Political Renaissance in Africa", in N. Chazan, J. Harbeson, D. Rothschild (eds), *Civil Society and the State in Africa*. Boulder: Lynne Rienner.

Harbeson, J. 1995. "Non-Governmental Organisations and the Promotion of Democracy in Kenya", *African Voices*, Vol. 4 (USAID newsletter).

Holmquist, F.W., F.S. Weaver and M.D. Ford. 1994. "The Structural Development of Kenya's Political Economy", *African Studies Review*, Vol. 37, No. 1, pp. 69–106.

Kifle, H., A. Olukoshi, L. Wohlgemuth (eds) 1997. *A New Partnership for African Development: Issues and Parameters*. Uppsala: Nordic Africa Institute.

Ndegwa, S. May 1993. *NGOs as Pluralizing Agents in Civil Society in Kenya*. Working Paper 491, Institute for Development Studies, University of Nairobi, Kenya.

Ndegwa, S. 1996. *The Two Faces of Civil Society: NGOs and Politics in Africa*. West Hartford, CT: Kumarian Press.

Putnam, R. 1993. *Making Democracy Work: Civic Traditions in Modern Italy*. Princeton: Princeton University Press.

Robinson, P. 1996. "Democratization: Understanding the Relationship between Regime Change and the Culture of Politics", *African Studies Review*, Vol. 37, No. 1, pp. 39–68.

Sandbrook, R. 1993. *The Politics of Africa's Economic Recovery*. Cambridge: Cambridge University Press.

Schmitter, P., G. O'Donnell and L. Whitehead. 1986. *Transitions From Authoritarian Rule: Comparative Perspectives*. Baltimore: Johns Hopkins University Press.

Stepan, A. 1988. *Rethinking Military Politics: Brazil and the Southern Cone*. Princeton: Princeton University Press.

Waller, P. 1995. "Aid and Conditionality: The Case of Germany, with Particular Reference to Kenya", in O. Stokke (ed.), *Aid and Political Conditionality*. London: Frank Cass.

Widner, J. 1992. *The Rise of a Party-State in Kenya: From Harambee to Nyayo*. Berkeley: UC Press.

World Bank. 1989. *World Development Report*. Oxford University Press.

The Interaction between State and Civil Society in Southern Africa: Prospects for Peace and Security

Patrick Molutsi

Introduction

The experience of post-colonial state-society relations in Africa shows that peace and security are matters not to be left to the state alone. In sub-Saharan Africa in general and southern Africa in particular, the state became the enemy of its own citizens and therefore a major threat to both national and personal security. Several other players must be brought to the fore in order to keep peace and ensure general security in society. Civil society—defined for our purposes as a network of organised, self-governing and autonomous organisations operating at the national, regional and international levels—has a major role to play in the maintenance of peace and security. Security, defined in broad terms not merely as the protection of national borders or the prevention of inter-state conflict, but more importantly as the absence of violence and conflict at the intra-state, community, family and individual levels, is a multi-dimensional and all-inclusive process. It is the other side of peace, which has been thus defined by the United Nations Educational Scientific and Cultural Organisation (UNESCO):

> [...] peace is not merely the absence of war [...] (but also) interdependence and co-operation to foster economic and social development, disarmament, arms control and limitation, human rights, the strengthening of democratic institutions, protection of the environment and the improvement of the quality of life, for all are indispensable elements for the establishment of peaceful and more secure democratic societies.[1]

Security is also about democracy and development. Many sources of conflict and violence are directly related to poverty and to material and moral deprivation. Undemocratic states often unleash violence on the very people they are obliged to protect. Civil society, too, can be disruptive and violent

---

[1] Quoted in Ibbo Mandaza, *Southern Africa Monthly Political and Economic Series* (SAPEM), Vol. 6, No. 2, July 1996. SAPEM is a monthly manuscript published by SAPES Books, Harare, Zimbabwe.

in those cases where, due to competition over limited resources, citizens start identifying with the parochial social identities of region, ethnic group or gender. The tendency of the army to fight the very people it was armed to protect is often higher in poverty-stricken societies, as the case of Mozambique vividly illustrates.

This chapter focuses on the interaction between state and civil society in the maintenance of peace and security in southern Africa. Starting from UNESCO's definition, the analysis takes the position that security is a collective effort of states and citizens, and the regional and international community. Efforts towards achieving peace at each of these levels constitute an important precondition for human security in general and (most importantly) at the individual level. Furthermore, security is not merely the absence of war but the creation of conditions conducive to the sustenance of a healthy and peaceful life. Civil society-state relations is but one of the many dimensions of peace and security in southern Africa. Other sections of this book have addressed the related issues of governance, control of small arms, health and education, etc. This introduction is followed by five sections: an introduction, current democratic changes in southern Africa, a discussion of the relationship between state and civil society and a conclusion.

Democratic trends in southern Africa: Prospects for the promotion of peace and security

A few years ago Adam Przeworski and his colleagues published an essay entitled 'What Makes Democracies Endure?' (Przeworski et al., 1996:39–55). They identified affluence, growth (with moderate inflation), declining inequality, a favourable international climate and parliamentary institutions as some of the requirements for the sustenance of democracy. These 'pre-conditions' for democracy are debatable and will remain so as long as empirical evidence is elusive. However, the same question should be appropriate for the security debate today. The key question is: What preconditions are required for long-term security and peace in the world in general and in southern Africa in particular? Some scholars believe that the current political movements in eastern Europe and Africa which are ushering in what Huntington (1996:3–13) described as the 'Third Wave of Democratisation' will constitute major forces for maintenance of peace. Particularly, two propositions hold true. First, in eastern Europe and sub-Saharan Africa, violence has largely been engineered by the state against its own citizens. Second, democracies do not normally go to war with each other. If both propositions are correct, then indeed democratisation is an important step towards peace. Southern Africa is on the right track towards peace, despite the persistence of major hurdles relating to grassroots violence, crime, army and police indiscipline, poverty, inequality and weak democratic institutions.

The political complexion of southern Africa has changed drastically since 1989. The protracted struggles staged by democratic forces from both within and without the region and individual countries, as well as solidarity support and the pressure of sanctions from the international community (including governments and civil society organisations) had forced hitherto invincible regimes in Zambia, Namibia, Malawi and South Africa to submit to democratic governance by 1994. In Zambia and Lesotho the democratic elections of 1991 and 1993 ushered in popularly elected governments. In Namibia, the South West Africa People's Organisation (SWAPO) won a convincing majority in 1989 to lead a new democratic government. In Malawi, too, the forces of opposition that had been organising against all odds brought down President Banda's one-party regime in 1994. Changes, particularly in South Africa, impelled peace settlements in Mozambique and Angola. Hence, although many of these governments remain fragile, they all represent a new democratic trend towards good governance in southern Africa. At the end of 1998, of the 14 countries which constitute the Southern African Development Community (SADC), only two—The Democratic Republic of Congo (DRC) and Swaziland—were yet to accept a pluralistic political system as the mode of governance. However, even Swaziland is an embattled state. Throughout 1998, democratic forces led by banned opposition parties and the trade union movement put considerable pressure on it to introduce democracy. The King has since called for a referendum on whether to follow the democratic trend in the region.

At the state level, southern Africa has committed itself to democratic governance. Multi-party constitutions and elections operate in most countries of the region, though with varying degrees of acceptability and success. Governments have taken progressive steps to create democratic structures, increase the power of local government and promote local participation by the population. At the regional level, new structures of peace and economic integration have been set up. SADC is gaining momentum as an economic grouping of states in the region. After apartheid ended in 1994, governments transformed the former Frontline States structure into a regional Peace and Security Organ under the chairmanship of President Robert Mugabe of Zimbabwe. There is a general understanding that intra-state conflict should be controlled or resolved peacefully. Southern Africa has played a vital role in ending the potentially explosive conflict between Botswana and Namibia over Sedudu Island in the Chobe River. The leaders of southern Africa demonstrated their unity of purpose on the issue of intra-state conflict when they rejected the *coup d'etat* in Lesotho in 1994 and reinstated the beleaguered government of Prime Minister Ntsu Mokhehle. They reiterated their determination to maintain peace in the region when they sent peacekeeping forces to both Lesotho and the DRC in 1998. While costly wars continue in the DRC and Angola (and are certainly drawing the whole region into a new conflict situation), it is noteworthy that there is some semblance of unity among the leadership of the region when it comes to fighting dictatorships.[2]

The above notwithstanding, by the end of 1998, 50 per cent of SADC member states—Angola, Botswana, the DRC, Lesotho, Namibia, South Africa and Zimbabwe—were directly involved in conflict situations in which enormous amounts of resources were expended. Botswana and South Africa were involved in SADC peacekeeping efforts in Lesotho. Angola, Namibia and Zimbabwe were involved in the civil war in the DRC. Coupled with the renewal of conflict between the government of Angola and its traditional opponent UNITA (Unity for the Total Liberation of Angola) in mid-1998, these engagements are slowly threatening to engulf the whole region in serious conflict. In these conflicts, some sections of civil society are directly involved through their opposition to the state. In both Lesotho and the DRC, opposition forces have enlisted the support of some non-governmental organisations.

Despite this rather bleak picture, the conditions for peace exist in southern Africa. Institutions have been created to promote peace and security at the national and regional levels. However, the strength of these democratic governments and their commitment to participatory democracy in the maintenance of peace and security and the consolidation of democracy and development remain open to question.

The democratic conditions prevalent in southern Africa today were created largely by the struggles of the organisations of civil society—trade unions, human rights bodies, women's organisations, the church, community-based organisations and the opposition parties. Without civil society activity, the pace of change would have been quite different. Indeed, without the pressure exerted and boycotts undertaken by these organisations in Zambia, Lesotho, Malawi and South Africa, it is doubtful whether change would have occurred at all. The critical question, then, concerns the role of civil society in the current political discourse in southern Africa. There is always the danger that Havel observed in eastern Europe:

> We could applaud our achievements and lapse into a state of lethargy while awaiting the results of all the changes. At most, we could engage in minor repairs to the state or make sure that it functions without major complications. (1996:12)

Civil society organisations in most of post independence sub-Saharan Africa allowed themselves to be de-politicised (Mamdani, 1991). This political dislocation of civil society helped create conditions for dictatorship and the rise of the one-party state in most of the sub-Saharan region in the 1960s and 1970s (*ibid.*). The present situation requires civil society to '[...] reflect on the

---

[2] This understanding was reached in the SADC Meeting held in Durban, South Africa, September 1998.

meaning of all the changes that [it] has introduced, on the goals [it] seeks to achieve, and on the future steps that need to be taken.' (Havel, 1996:12)

In reflecting on the achievements so far, civil society and citizens in general need to understand the nature of the state in southern Africa. Very often, this concept is taken for granted. Perhaps as Migdal (1988) observed, this is because the state has became a central and omnipresent phenomenon in every citizen's life, regardless of where they live within its territorial boundaries. As he put it, after independence:

> The state organisation became the focal point for hopes of achieving broad goals of human dignity, prosperity, and equity; it was to be the chisel in the hands of the new sculptors. This new state, it was believed, could create a very different social order, a unified channel for people's passions that until now had run in countless streams. (Migdal, 1988:4)

In southern Africa, the new euphoria about the state is still as high as it was elsewhere in the 1960s. The attainment of majority rule in South Africa and the defeat of dictatorships in most other countries of the region are no doubt exciting developments. However, it is already evident—only five years after the watershed year of 1994—that citizens' expectations of the state are inflated. Not only do states in southern Africa differ in their capabilities and resources, but some also have emerged from the ashes of devastating and violent internal wars. These wars have rendered them weak and incapable of achieving peace and development without massive contributions from internal and external state resources.

State-society relations in an historical perspective

In the period between 1930 and 1990 in southern Africa, state-society relations were largely characterised by unprecedented hostility and violence. The state became a violent institution. The racist states of the 1970s and 1980s in South Africa, Zimbabwe and Namibia were clearly against their own people. Several citizens were forced to leave their countries, others were imprisoned and millions more were deported to highly policed settlements where their movements were controlled by armed men and collaborative semi-dictators in the form of traditional chiefs or, in the case of South Africa and Namibia, Bantustan 'presidents'. The racist state not only used brute force on its citizens but also, by denying development and imposing land-alienation, it created permanently impoverished and insecure communities for whom crime and violence became a part of normal life.

Ironically, this experience was not restricted to white minority regimes. In Malawi, Mozambique and Angola, the state unleashed violence of unprecedented proportions against real or perceived opponents. Chingono, referring to the war in Mozambique, analysed state violence on citizens as follows:

> To argue that the state has played a role in the production of chaos, anarchy and violence, and in this case in Mozambique, is not novel. It is commonplace knowledge, especially in Mozambique, that Renamo anti-state insurgency and what Wilson calls, 'cults of violence and counter-violence' were largely attempts to challenge and subvert the state's monopoly of violence. In other words, as elsewhere in the world, state violence generated violence [...] (1996:6)

The post-colonial state in southern Africa has also been ambivalent in its relationship with its society. While claiming to be democratic and committed to development, it became suspicious of and deeply opposed to the development of a strong opposition in the form of political parties, civil society structures and individual citizens themselves. In Malawi, Tanzania and Zambia, for instance, the creation of the one-party state was but a culmination of protracted struggles against the opposition. Such states ended up in a situation similar to that of the racist society cited above. The second type of post-colonial state in the southern African region was that found in countries such as Botswana and Mauritius. Here, a modicum of democratic governance obtained: a multi-party system was in place; the opposition (though restricted in its activities), was allowed to function openly; trade unions and women's, church and human rights organisations were also permitted to function.

In Angola and Mozambique, the relatively fragile state found it necessary to incorporate the organs of civil society. These states used civil society organisations as part of the forces fighting against one section of the population. The trade unions and women's organisations in both countries were members of the central committee of the ruling party and could not question state actions against their fellow citizens on behalf of either Renamo (Mozambique National Resistance) or UNITA.

Clear patterns and lessons emerge from this description of state-society relations in southern Africa in recent decades. In the first instance, a picture of a repressive, suppressive and violent state emerges. This state instilled fear and mistrust, which created the conditions for the rise of a vibrant and in some respects equally violent civil society. The latter, as we show below, was to become instrumental in bringing about democratic change in many countries of the region. However, in the process of controlling society, the state in southern Africa not only armed itself to the teeth but also impoverished the people, thereby creating a long-term dependence on the state. The social, political and economic insecurity of the peoples of southern Africa rendered their civil society organisations weak partners in the peace movement.

Since 1994, the new democratic state has warmed to civil society. As noted earlier, the introduction of democratic constitutions and regular democratic elections in most countries have created the broad conditions for peace. In 1998, 12 of the 14 SADC member states were multiparty democracies. At least all of them had an opposition (though often very weak and inconsequential) represented in parliament. Several states have also established independent watchdog institutions that, in addition to traditional institutions (such as the offices of the auditor-general and attorney-general) included independent electoral commissions, independent media boards, ombudsmen, etc. But has the state in southern Africa become truly democratic in the post-1994 era? This question must be addressed in order to assess whether progress has been made in establishing peace in the region.

Democracy and development in southern Africa: The basis for peace

The basis for peace and security in southern Africa is clearly dependent on democracy and development. Scarce state resources should be diverted from military uses to education, health and social development. This is a challenge of establishing democracies grounded on truly functioning institutions and a participatory culture. However, they are challenges that the present state, institutionally fragile, economically impoverished and politically insecure, may not be equal to on its own, despite claims to the contrary. A recent study of governance and human development showed that more than half of the SADC countries are facing serious economic problems—high budget deficits, trade imbalances and over 15 per cent of GDP devoted to debt servicing (SAPES, 1998). The countries included the DRC, Lesotho, Namibia, Malawi, Mozambique, Tanzania, Zambia and Zimbabwe. Across the region, an average of 40 per cent of the population are below the poverty line, unemployment ranges between 30 per cent and 40 per cent, and levels of annual economic growth average below 3 per cent (*ibid.*). In the newly-independent countries of Zimbabwe, Namibia and South Africa, where people's expectations are very high, the thorny issue of land redistribution was reflected in Gini coefficients of well over 0.65.

The state's insecurity is directly related to its inability to bring about democracy and development. This in part explains its relative unfriendliness to individual citizens and civil society organisations. In Zimbabwe, state-society relations in the last two years have worsened due to increased inflation and general economic decline. The trade union movement staged a devastating national strike in December 1997 which left much property destroyed and business interests intimidated. A series of other strikes ensued between August and November of 1998, following the government's decision to send an army contingent to war in the DRC (*The Zimbabwe Herald*, 1998). In Zambia, too, state-civil society relations have become increasingly difficult due to the adoption of structural adjustment programmes and the subsequent privatisation of public enterprises.

The modern state has become a central organ of the social, political and economic life of all societies. As Migdal noted, although there are strong and weak states, on the whole the state's influence in modern society is pervasive (1988). Even the most remote settlement and community feels the state's influence in the form of development projects—schools, health facilities, roads, clean water, etc. However, the presence of the state is also often felt through fear; fear of repressive and violent state organs like hostile tax collectors, police, and armed forces on search operations or fighting 'rebels'.

Developing a strong democratic culture

The prospects for sustained peace and security in Southern Africa are now better than ever before. As noted earlier, many states in the region have committed themselves to democratic governance and the institutional framework required does exist. At the regional level, too, there is a high degree of rapprochement between states, resulting in better understanding and co-operation on matters of national and regional interest. However, three issues require further consideration and monitoring at the state level if peace and security for the population are to be secured. These are: protection of democratic institutions; reduction of state power; and opening up official structures to involve other stakeholders (including civil society organisations) in the creation of peace and security at all levels.

Protection of democratic institutions

Peace, as already implied by our discussion so far, is closely associated with democratic governance. Without democracy it is difficult to imagine peace. Where there is no peace, security is threatened. These are the lessons from the history of southern Africa under the oppressive regimes of the past. However, in some respects the hard-earned democratic institutions remain fragile and unprotected. It is becoming increasingly evident that constitutions are subject to manipulation by those in power. The experiences of Lesotho, Namibia and Zambia are cases in point. However, even peaceful manipulations such as the change of the term of office of President from two periods of five years each to three periods of five years each in Namibia is cause for concern. Perhaps there is need not only to insist on referenda before constitutions are changed, but also to insist on a time period of, say, 15 years before any changes can be considered. This might help to consolidate institutions, though it might also be a recipe for states of emergency or military coups d'état. Civil society itself should realise that democracy requires constant monitoring. It is not sufficient to struggle for positive political change and then return to being a spectator, as it appears to have been the case in Zambia.

Reducing state power

Related to the point above is the general trend of a strong state in southern Africa. The ruling parties in Botswana, Namibia, Lesotho, South Africa, Tanzania, Zambia and Zimbabwe control overwhelming majorities in parliament. The opposition is weak and marginal to the decision-making processes. This results in weak parliaments dominated by the executive. Perhaps, as Barkan and Reynolds (1995) have suggested, the solution lies in introducing proportional representation, as opposed to the first-past-the post electoral system currently dominant in the region. But some of the numerous functions of the state also need to be transferred to local government, non-governmental organisations and the private sector in order to reduce the dominance of the state in social life.

Opening up state structures

The preceding analysis clearly points to the need for more stakeholders in the governance process. Southern Africa has a rich network of civil society structures in the form of trade unions, women's organisations, human rights bodies, research and training institutions and church organisations. All these are growing in strength and experience. They may still lack the funds and personnel to reach the levels of their counterparts in the developed world, but they are showing signs of progress. Their problem remains that of exclusion due to the ambivalence of the state. Yet, as pointed out earlier, the nature of violence and threats to peace in southern Africa are such that without the involvement of these organisations, the state alone cannot achieve much peace.

Conclusion

The interaction between the state and civil society in southern Africa on matters related to peace and security is limited. Excessive involvement of the state in the economic, social and political spheres as well as its mistrust of civil society stultifies the latter's participation. On the whole, however, prospects for peace and security in the region are good. The central challenge that remains is the consolidation of democracy through human development. Poverty, inequality and general economic problems are major factors that must be taken into consideration in the development of better state-civil society relations. More reforms, especially at the level of the state, are also required. Civil society also needs to press for more participation in development and peace efforts.

References

Barkan, S. and A. Reynolds. 1995. "Constitutional Engineering in Southern Africa", *Journal of Democracy*, April 1995, Vol. 6, No. 1.

Chege, M. 1995. "Between African Extremes", *Journal of Democracy*, 6:1, January 1995.

Chingono, M. 1996. *The State, Violence and Development: The Political Economy of War in Mozambique, 1975–1992*. Vermont, USA: Avebury, Ashgate Publishing Limited.

Darnoff, S. 1996. "Democratic Electioneering in Southern Africa: The Contrasting Cases of Botswana and Zimbabwe", *Göteborg Studies in Politics*, 45.

Fukuyama, F. 1995. "The Primacy of Culture", *Journal of Democracy*, 6:1, January 1995.

Havel, V. 1996. "Civil Society after Communism", *Journal of Democracy*, 7:1, January 1996.

Holm, J. & P. Molutsi, (eds) *1989. Democracy in Botswana.* Ohio, USA: Ohio University Press.

Huntington, S. 1996. "Democracy for the Long Haul", *Journal of Democracy,* April 1996, Vol. 7, No. 2.

Lee, M.C. & G. Nzongola-Ntalaja (eds) 1997. *The State and Democracy in Africa.* Harare, Zimbabwe: AAPS Books.

Gyimah-Boadi, E. 1960. "Civil Society in Africa", *Journal of Democracy,* 7:4, April 1996.

Mamdani, M. 1991. "Democratisation in Sub-Saharan Africa". Unpublished paper presented at "CODESRIA Conference on Democratisation in Africa", Dakar, Senegal.

Mandaza, I. 1997. *Race and Class in South Africa.* Harare: SAPES Books.

Migdal, J. 1988. *Strong Societies and Weak States: State-Society Relations and State Capabilities in the Third World.* Princeton, NJ: Princeton University Press.

Molomo, M.G. 1995. "Civil Society in Botswana: Theoretical and Conceptual Issues", in G. Somolekae (ed.), *Proceedings of a Workshop on Civil Society and Elections in Botswana.* Democracy Research Project, University of Botswana, Gaborone, 1997.

Molutsi, P. 1995. "The Structure of Civil Society in Botswana", in G. Somolekae (ed.), *Proceedings of a Workshop on Civil Society and Elections in Botswana.* Democracy Research Project, University of Botswana, Gaborone, 1997.

Nordis, G. 1992. "Nationalism and Democracy: Comments", *Journal of Democracy,* 3:4, October 1992.

Przeworski, A. 1993. *Democracy and the Market: Political and Economic Reforms in Eastern Europe and Latin America.* New York: Cambridge University Press.

Przeworski, A., et al. 1996. "What Makes Democracies Endure?", *Journal of Democracy,* January 1996, Vol. 7, No. 1.

Reynolds, A. 1995. "The Case for Proportionality", *Journal of Democracy,* 6:4, October 1995.

Somolekae, G. (ed.) 1995. *Proceedings of a Workshop on Civil Society and Elections in Botswana.* Democracy Research Project, University of Botswana, Gaborone, 1997.

SAPES/UNDP/SADC. 1998. *SADC Regional Human Development Report 1998: Governance and Human Development in Southern Africa.* Southern African Regional Institute for Policy Studies of SAPES, Harare, 1998.

Cosmopolitan Patriots*

Kwame Anthony Appiah

My father was a Ghanaian patriot. He once published a column in the *Pioneer*, our local newspaper in Kumasi, under the headline 'Is Ghana worth dying for?' and I know that his heart's answer was yes.[1] But he also loved Asante, the region of Ghana where he and I both grew up, a kingdom absorbed within a British colony and, then, a region of a new multi-ethnic republic, a once-kingdom that he and his father also both loved and served. And, like so many African nationalists of his class and generation, he always loved an enchanting abstraction they called Africa.

When he died, my sisters and I found a note he had drafted and never quite finished, last words of love and wisdom for his children. After a summary reminder of our double ancestry—in Ghana and in England—he wrote: 'Remember that you are citizens of the world'. And he went on to tell us that this meant that—wherever we chose to live, and, as citizens of the world, we could surely choose to live anywhere—we should make sure we left that place 'better than you found it'. 'Deep inside of me', he went on, 'is a great love for mankind and an abiding desire to see mankind, under God, fulfil its highest destiny'.

The favorite slander of the narrow nationalist against us cosmopolitans is that we are rootless: what my father believed in, however, was a rooted cosmopolitanism, or, if you like, a cosmopolitan patriotism. Like Gertrude Stein, he thought there was no point in roots if you couldn't take them with you. 'America is my country and Paris is my hometown', Stein said.[2] My father would have understood her.

We cosmopolitans face a familiar litany of objections. Some, for example, have complained that our cosmopolitanism must be parasitic: where,

---

* This article has already appeared in *Critical Inquiry*, Vol. 23, Spring 1997, University of Chicago Press. We thank them for their permission to reproduce it here.

[1] This question was first put to him by J.B. Danquah, leader of the major opposition party in Nkrumah's Ghana, in 1962. See Joseph Appiah, *Joe Appiah: The Autobiography of an African Patriot* (New York, 1990) p. 266. My father's column is reprinted in Joseph Appiah, *Antiochus Lives Again: (Political Essays of Joe Appiah)* ed. Ivor Agyeman-Duah. (Kumasi, Ghana: I. Agyeman-Duah, 1992).

[2] Gertrude Stein, "An American and France" (1936) in *What Are Masterpieces?* (Los Angeles, 1940), p. 61.

they ask, could Stein have gotten her roots in a fully cosmopolitan world? Where, in other words, would all the diversity we cosmopolitans celebrate come from in a world where there were only cosmopolitans?

The answer is straightforward: the cosmopolitan patriot can entertain the possibility of a world in which *everyone* is a rooted cosmopolitan, attached to a home of one's own, with its own cultural particularities, but taking pleasure from the presence of other, different places that are home to other, different, people. The cosmopolitan also imagines that in such a world not everyone will find it best to stay in their natal patria, so that the circulation of people among different localities will involve not only cultural tourism (which the cosmopolitan admits to enjoying) but migration, nomadism, diaspora. In the past, these processes have too often been the result of forces we should deplore; the old migrants were often refugees and older diasporas often began in an involuntary exile. But what can be hateful if coerced, can be celebrated when it flows from the free decisions of individuals or of groups.

In a world of cosmopolitan patriots, people would accept the citizen's responsibility to nurture the culture and the politics of their homes. Many would, no doubt, spend their lives in the places that shaped them; and that is one of the reasons local cultural practices would be sustained and transmitted. But many would move; and that would mean that cultural practices would travel also (as they have always travelled). The result would be a world in which each local form of human life was the result of long-term and persistent processes of cultural hybridization: a world, in that respect, much like the world we live in now.

Behind the objection that cosmopolitanism is parasitic there is, in any case, an anxiety we should dispel: an uneasiness caused by an exaggerated estimate of the rate of disappearance of cultural heterogeneity. In the global system of cultural exchanges there are, indeed, somewhat asymmetrical processes of homogenization going on, and there are forms of human life disappearing. Neither of these phenomena is particularly new, but their range and speed probably is. Nevertheless, as forms of culture disappear, new forms are created, and they are created locally, which means they have exactly the regional inflections that the cosmopolitan celebrates. The disappearance of old cultural forms is consistent with a rich variety of forms of human life, just because new cultural forms, which differ from each other, are being created all the time as well.

Cosmopolitanism and patriotism, unlike nationalism, are both sentiments more than ideologies. Different political ideologies can be made consistent with both of them. Some cosmopolitan patriots are conservative and religious; others are secularizers of a socialist bent. Christian cosmopolitanism is as old as the merger with the Roman empire, through which Stoicism came to be a dominant shaping force in Christian ethics. (On my father's bedside were Cicero and the Bible. Only someone ignorant of the history of the church would see this as an expression of divided loyalties.) But I am a liberal, and both cosmopolitanism and patriotism, as sentiments, can seem to be hard to accommodate to liberal principles.

Patriotism often challenges liberalism. Liberals who propose a state that does not take sides in the debates among its citizens' various conceptions of the good life are held to be unable to value a state that celebrates itself, and modern self-described patriots, here in America, at least, often desire a public education and a public culture that stoke the fires of the national ego. Patriots also seem especially sensitive these days to slights to the national honor, to skepticism about a celebratory nationalist historiography; in short, to the critical reflection on the state that we liberals, with our instrumental conception of it, are bound to engage in. No liberal should say, 'My country, right or wrong' because liberalism involves a set of political principles that a state can fail to realize; and the liberal will have no special loyalty to an illiberal state, not least because liberals value people over collectivities.

This patriotic objection to liberalism can also be made, however, to Catholicism, to Islam, to almost any religious view; indeed, to any view, including humanism, that claims a higher moral authority than one's own particular political community. And the answer to it is to affirm, first, that someone who loves principle can also love country, family, friends; and, second, that a true patriot holds the state and the community within which they live to certain standards and have moral aspirations for them, and that those aspirations may be liberal.

The cosmopolitan challenge to liberalism begins with the claim that liberals have been too preoccupied with morality *within* the nation-state. John Rawls's *A Theory of Justice*, which began the modern reformulation of philosophical liberalism, left the questions of international morality to be dealt with later: how to develop the Rawlsian picture in an international direction is a current preoccupation of professional political philosophy. The cosmopolitan is likely to argue that this order of priorities is all wrong.[3]

It is all very well to argue for, fight for, liberalism in one country—your own; but if that country, in its international operations, supports (or even tolerates) illiberal regimes elsewhere, then it fails, the cosmopolitan will argue, because it does not sufficiently weigh the lives of human beings as such. Liberals take it to be self-evident that we are all created equal, that we each bear certain inalienable rights, and then seem almost immediately to become preoccupied with looking after the rights of the local branch of the species, forgetting—this is a cosmopolitan critique—that their rights matter

---

[3] Like most philosophers who have thought about justice recently, I have learned a great deal from reading Rawls. This essay obviously draws sustenance from his work and the discussions it has generated; indeed, his *A Theory of Justice* (Cambridge, Mass., 1971) was the most important book I read the summer I was deciding whether or not to be a philosopher! I find it hard, however, to relate the position I am taking here explicitly to what I understand of his current views; and so, much as I would have liked to do so, I have found it best not to take them on.

as human rights and thus matter only if the rights of foreign humans matter, too.[4]

This is surely more of an objection to the practice of liberalism than to its theory; (and, as I shall argue later, cosmopolitans have a reason for caring about states, too). At the heart of the liberal picture of humanity is the idea of the equal dignity of all persons: liberalism grows with an increasing appreciation of the inadequacy of an older picture in which dignity is the possession of an elite. Not every premodern society made its elite hereditary, as the eunuchs who ran the Ottoman empire would have attested. But it is only in the modern age that the idea has grown that every one of us begins life with an equal entitlement to respect, an entitlement that we may, perhaps, lose through misbehavior but that remains with us otherwise for all our lives.

This idea of the equal dignity of all persons can be cashed out in different ways, but it undergirds the attachment to a democracy of unlimited franchise; the renunciation of sexism and racism and heterosexism; the respect for the autonomy of individuals, which resists the state's desire to fit us to someone else's conception of what is good for us; and the notion of human rights—rights possessed by human beings as such—that is at the heart of liberal theory.

It would be wrong however to conflate cosmopolitanism and humanism because cosmopolitanism is not just the feeling that everybody matters. For the cosmopolitan also celebrates the fact that there are *different* local human ways of being; humanism, by contrast, is consistent with the desire for global homogeneity. Humanism can be made compatible with cosmopolitan sentiments, but it can also live with a deadening urge to uniformity.

A liberal cosmopolitanism, of the sort I am defending, might put its point like this: we value the variety of human forms of social and cultural life; we do not want everybody to become part of a homogeneous global culture; and we know that this means that there will be local differences (both within and between states) in moral climate as well. As long as these differences meet certain general ethical constraints—as long, in particular, as political institutions respect the basic human rights—we are happy to let them be.

Part of what the equal dignity of all persons means for the liberal is that we respect people's autonomous decisions for themselves, even when they are decisions we judge mistaken—or simply choices we would not make for ourselves. This is a liberal principle that fits well with the cosmopolitan feeling that human cultural difference is actively desirable. The requirement that the state respect the basic human rights is, as a result, very demanding.

---

[4] We liberals *don't* all agree on where the rights come from. I favor an 'antirealist' view in which human rights are embodied in legal arrangements within and between states rather than one in which they somehow antecedently exist or are grounded in human nature or divine ordinance.

It rules out states that aim to constrain people beyond what is necessary to enable a common life. Voluntary associations that are the product of autonomous affiliations may demand a very great deal of people, as long as they retain the right of exit (a right that it is one of the state's proper purposes to sustain). Thus I can bind myself with a vow of obedience, as long as I retain my autonomy: as long as, that is, if I finally decide that I can no longer obey, whoever I have bound myself to is obliged to release me. Broad freedom of contract—and the state's enforcement of contracts freely made—is rightly seen as a liberal practice, giving force to the autonomous decisions of free individuals; but not every contract can be enforced by a state that respects autonomy—in particular, contracts to give up one's autonomy.[5]

In short, where the state's actions enable the exercise of autonomous decision, my sort of liberal will cheer it on. Cosmopolitanism can also live happily with this liberal individualism. The cosmopolitan ideal—take your roots with you—is one in which people are free to choose the local forms of human life within which they will live.

Patriotism, as communitarians have spent much time reminding us recently, is about the responsibilities as well as the privileges of citizenship. But it is also and above all, as I have been suggesting, not so much a matter of action—of practical morality—as of sentiment; if there is one emotion that the very word brings to mind it is surely pride. When the national anthem plays, when the national team wins, when the national army prevails, there is that shiver down the spine, the electric excitement, the thrill of being on the winning side. But the patriot is surely also the first to suffer their country's shame; patriots suffers when their country elects the wrong leaders or when those leaders prevaricate, bluster, pantomime, betray 'our' principles. Patriotism, is about what the nineteenth-century Liberian scholar-diplomat Edward Blyden once so memorably called 'the poetry of politics', which is the feeling of 'people with whom we are connected'.[6] It is the connection and the sentiment that matter, and there is no reason to suppose that everybody in this complex, ever-mutating world will find their affinities and their passions focussed on a single place.

My father's example demonstrates for me, more clearly than any abstract argument, the possibilities that the enemies of cosmopolitanism deny.

---

[5] A (lifetime) vow of obedience—even if, because I receive something in return for my vow, it may look like a legal contract—should be enforced only if enforcing it is consistent with respecting the autonomy of the person who made the vow. There are difficult issues here. On the one hand, moral persons are historically extended in time, and treating someone as a single moral person requires holding one's later 'stages' responsible for the commitments of earlier 'stages.' On the other, there are moral limits on what people can bind their later selves to do: and one relevant limit is that we may not bind our later selves to abstain from rational ethical reflection. (An enforceable lifetime vow of obedience looks awfully like a contract to enslave oneself, which would presumably be unconstitutional in the United States. But it turns out to be quite hard to say what's wrong with offering 'freely' to be a slave in return for some benefit, if you believe in freedom of contract.)

[6] Edward W. Blyden, *Christianity, Islam, and the Negro Race* (London, 1887), pp. 226, 227.

We cosmopolitans *can* be patriots, loving our homelands (not only the states where we were born but the states where we grew up and the states where we live); our loyalty to human kind—so vast, so abstract, a unity—does *not* deprive us of the capacity to care for lives nearer by.

But my father's example makes me suspicious of the purportedly cosmopolitan argument against patriotism (my father's Ghanaian patriotism, which I want to defend) that alleges that nationality is, in the words of a fine essay of Martha Nussbaum's, 'a morally irrelevant characteristic'. Nussbaum argues that in 'conceding that a morally arbitrary boundary such as the boundary of the nation has a deep and formative role in our deliberations, we seem to be depriving ourselves of any principled way of arguing to citizens that they should in fact join hands' across the 'boundaries of ethnicity and class and gender and race'.[7]

I can say what I think is wrong here only if I insist on the distinction between state and nation.[8] Their conflation is a perfectly natural one for a modern person—even after Rwanda, Sri Lanka, Amritsar, Bosnia, Azerbajan. But the yoking of nation and state in the Enlightenment was intended to bring the arbitrary boundaries of states into conformity with the 'natural' boundaries of nations; the idea that the boundaries of one could be arbitrary, while the boundaries of the other were not, is easy enough to grasp, once we are reminded of it.

Not that I want to endorse this essentially Herderian way of thinking: nations never preexist states.[9] A nation—here is a loose and unphilosophical definition—is an 'imagined community' of culture: or ancestry running beyond the scale of the face-to-face and seeking political expression for itself.[10] But all the nations I can think of that are not coterminous with states are the legacy of older state arrangements— as Asante is in what has become Ghana; as are the Serbian and Croatian nations in what used to be Yugoslavia.

I want, in fact, to distinguish the nation and the state to make a point entirely opposite to Herder's, namely, that if anything is morally arbitrary it is not the state, but the nation. Since human beings live in political orders narrower than the species, and since it is within those political orders that questions of public right and wrong are largely argued out and decided, the fact of being a fellow-citizen—someone who is a member of the same order—is not morally arbitrary at all. That is why the cosmopolitan critique of liberal-

---

[7] Martha Nussbaum, "Patriotism and Cosmopolitanism", *Boston Review*, Oct–Nov 1994, p. 3.

[8] The tendency in the anglophone world to sentimentalize the state by calling it the nation is so consistent that if, earlier, I had referred to the state team or the state anthem, this would have made these entities seem cold, hard, and alien.

[9] For discussion of Herder's views, see my *In My Father's House: Africa in the Philosophy of Culture* (New York, 1992), Chap. 1.

[10] The expression 'imagined community' was given currency by Benedict Anderson's *Imagined Communities: Reflections on the Origin and Spread of Nationalism* (London, 1983).

ism's focus on the state is exaggerated. It is exactly because the cultural variability that cosmopolitanism celebrates has come to depend on the existence of a plurality of states that we need to take states seriously.

The nation, on the other hand, *is* arbitrary, but not in a sense that means we can discard it in our moral reflections. It is arbitrary in the root sense of that term because it is, in the *Oxford English Dictionary*'s lapidary formulation, 'dependent upon will or pleasure'.[11] Nations often matter more to people than states: mono-ethnic Serbia makes more sense to some than multicultural Bosnia; a Hutu (or a Tutsi) Rwanda makes more sense to others than a peaceful shared citizenship of Tutsi and Hutu; only when Britain or France became nations as well as states did ordinary citizens come to care much about being French or British.[12] But notice that the reason nations matter is that they matter to *people*. Nations matter morally, when they do, in other words, for the same reason that football and opera matter: as things desired by autonomous agents, whose autonomous desires we ought to acknowledge and take account of, even if we cannot always accede to them.

States, on the other hand, matter morally intrinsically. They matter not because people care about them but because they regulate our lives through forms of coercion that will always require moral justification. State institutions matter because they are both necessary to so many modern human purposes and because they have so great a potential for abuse. As Hobbes famously saw, the state, to do its job, has to have a monopoly of certain forms of authorized coercion, and the exercise of that authority cries out for (but often does not deserve) justification even in places, like so many postcolonial societies, where many people have no positive feeling for the state at all.

There is, then, no need for the cosmopolitan to claim that the state is morally arbitrary in the way that I have suggested the nation is. There are many reasons to think that living in political communities narrower than the species is better for us than would be our engulfment in a single world-state: a cosmopolis of which we cosmopolitans would be not figurative but literal citizens. It is, in fact, precisely this celebration of cultural variety—within states as well as between them—that distinguishes the cosmopolitan from some of the other heirs of Enlightenment humanism.

It is because humans live best on a smaller scale that we should defend not just the state but the county, the town, the street, the business, the craft, the profession, the family *as* communities, as circles among the many circles narrower than the human horizon that are appropriate spheres of moral concern. We should, in short, as cosmopolitans, defend the right of others to live in democratic states, with rich possibilities of association within and

---

[11] Oxford English Dictionary, s.v. 'arbitrary'.

[12] See, for example, Linda Colley, *Britons: Forging the Nation, 1707–1837* (New Haven, Conn. 1992).

across their borders; states of which they can be patriotic citizens. And, as cosmopolitans, we can claim that right for ourselves.

The fundamental thought of the cosmopolitanism I defend is that the freedom to create oneself—the freedom that liberalism celebrates—requires a range of socially transmitted options from which to invent what we have come to call our identities. Our families and schools, our churches and temples, our professional associations and clubs, provide two essential elements in the toolkit of self-creation: first, they provide ready-made identities—son, lover, husband, doctor, teacher, Methodist, worker, Moslem, Yankee fan, mensch—whose shapes are constituted by norms and expectations, stereotypes and demands, rights and obligations; second, they give us a language in which to think about these identities and with which we may shape new ones.

Let me offer an example to give concreteness to these abstractions. Seventeenth-century England endowed English people with gender identities as men and as women; beginning with these ready-made identities, and drawing on a host of ideas about sex, gender, and social life, the urban men who created the Molly culture of London—which is one ancestor of modern Western European gay identities—shaped a new identity as a Molly, which interpreted sexual desire for men in a man as evidence that he was, in certain respects, a kind of woman.[13] This is, of course, much too simple-minded a story: what actually happened is that the Molly identity shaped a new gender option for people who were morphologically male, an option that led them to express their sexual desire for other men by feminizing themselves, cross-dressing, and giving each other women's names.

But, as this case should make absolutely clear, it is social life that endows us with the full richness of resources available for self-creation: for even when we are constructing new and counternormative identities, it is the old and the normative that provide the language and the background. A new identity is always post-some-old-identity (in the now familiar sense of *post* in which *postmodernism* is enabled by the very modernism it challenges).[14] If, like some of our fellow mammals, we lived with a parent only long enough to be *physically* independent, we would have a hugely impoverished range of such conceptual implements and institutional frameworks for exploring our autonomy.

These conceptual and institutional contributions are hugely important, but it would be a philosopher's mistake not to mention that it is social life, shaped (but not determined) by the state—particularly in the form of the modern market economy—that has provided the material conditions that

---

[13] See Rictor Norton, *Mother Clap's Molly House: The Gay Subculture in England, 1700–1830* (London, 1992).

[14] See my "Is the Post- in Postcolonial the Post- in Postmodern?", *Critical Inquiry* 17 (Winter 1991):336–57.

have enabled this exploration for a larger and larger proportion of people, especially in the industrialized world.

Among the resources thus made available in our contemporary form of social life is something that we can call a national identity, a form of identity that is central to the possibility of a modern patriotism. And I want to ask now how we are to understand national identity and more particularly what, for a cosmopolitan patriot, the role of a national culture might be in it.

Here is one model of the role of the national culture: we might call it the tribal fantasy. There is an ideal—which is to say imaginary—type of a small-scale, technologically uncomplicated, face-to-face society, where most interactions are with people whom you know, that we usually call traditional. In such a society almost every adult speaks the same language. All share a vocabulary and a grammar and an accent. While there will be some words in the language that are not known by everybody—the names of medicinal herbs, the language of some religious rituals—most are known to all. To share a language is to participate in a complex set of mutual expectations and understandings, but in such a society it is not only linguistic behavior that is coordinated through universally known expectations and understandings. People will share an understanding of many practices—marriages, funerals, other rites of passage—and will largely share their views about the general workings not only of the social but also of the natural world. Even those who are skeptical about particular elements of belief will nevertheless know what everyone is supposed to believe, and they will know it in enough detail to behave very often as if they believed it, too.

A similar point applies to many of the values of such societies. It may well be that some people, even some groups, do not share the values that are enunciated in public and taught to children. But, once more, the standard values are universally known, and even those who do not share them know what it would be to act in conformity with them and probably do so much of the time. In such a traditional society we may speak of its shared beliefs, values, signs and symbols as the *common culture*; not, to insist on a crucial point, in the sense that everyone in the group actually holds the beliefs and values, but in the sense that everybody knows what they are and everybody knows that they are widely held in the society.

There is a second crucial feature of the common culture in the tribal fantasy: it is that the common culture is, in a certain sense, at the *heart* of the culture of every individual and every family.[15] And by this I mean not just that, for each individual, the common culture encompasses a significant proportion of their culture—the socially transmitted beliefs, values, signs and symbols that populate their mental life and shape her behavior—but

---

[15] I should hasten to add that it would be preposterous to claim that most of the societies that have been called traditional fit anything like this pattern though we might suppose that, for example, congeries of related hunter-gatherer groups, speaking closely related dialects, might have fitted such a pattern.

that, whatever other socially transmitted skills or beliefs or values or understandings they have, the common culture provides a majority of those that
are most important to them.[16] Where the common culture of a group is also,
in this way, at the heart of an individual's culture, I shall say that that individual is centered on the common culture; being centered on a common culture means, in part, that those who are centered on it think of themselves as
a collectivity and think of the collectivity as consisting of people for whom a
common culture is central.[17]

Now the citizens of one of those large 'imagined communities' of
modernity we call nations are not likely to be centered on a common culture
of this sort. There is no single shared body of ideas and practices in India
that sits at the heart of the lives of most Hindus and most Moslems; that en-
gages all Sikhs and excites every Kashmiri; that animates every untouchable
in Delhi and organizes the ambitions of every Brahmin in Bombay. And I am
inclined to say that there is not now and there has never been a centering
common culture in the United States, either. The reason is simple: the
United States has always been multilingual and has always had minorities
who did not speak or understand English. It has always had a plurality of
religious traditions, beginning with American Indian religions, and Iberian
Catholics, and Jews, and British and Dutch Puritans, and including now
many varieties of Christianity, Judaism, Islam, Buddhism, Jainism, Taoism,
Bahai, and so on. Many of these religious traditions have been quite unknown to each other. More than this, Americans have also always differed
significantly even among those who do speak English, from north to south
and east to west, and from country to city, in customs of greeting, notions of
civility and a whole host of other ways. The notion that what has held the
United States together historically over its great geographical range is a citizenry centered on a common culture is—to put it politely—not sociologi-
cally plausible.

The observation that Americans are not centered on a national culture
does not answer the question whether there *is* an American national culture.
Comments about American culture, taken as a whole, are routine, and it
would be taking on a fairly substantial consensus to deny them all. American culture is, for example, held to be individualist, litigious, racially ob-
sessed. I think each of these claims is actually true because what I mean
when I say that Americans are not centered on a common culture of the
United States is not what is denied by someone who says that there is an

---

[16] My dictionary—*American Heritage Dictionary III for DOS* , 3d ed. (Novato, CA, 1993)—defines
culture (in part) as 'The totality of socially transmitted behavior patterns, arts, beliefs, institutions, and all other products of human work and thought'. The focus on social transmission in
defining *culture* is extremely important.

[17] I don't think we should require that people can't be mistaken about exactly who is in the
group or exactly what is in the common culture, but I think that the less they are right about
either of these things the less it makes sense to speak of the group as really centered on a common culture.

American culture; such a person is describing large-scale tendencies within American life that are not invariably participated in by—and are certainly not equally important to—all Americans. I do not mean to deny that these exist. But for such a tendency to be part of what I am calling the *common culture* it would have to derive from beliefs and values and practices (almost) universally shared and known to be so; and for it to center the lives of Americans, a common culture would then have to be at the core of the individual cultures of most Americans. I want to deny that there is any common culture that *centers* most Americans in this way.

At the same time, it was always true that there was a dominant culture in these United States. It was Protestant, it spoke English, and it identified with the high cultural traditions of Europe and, more particularly, of England. This dominant culture included much of the common culture that centered most members of the dominant classes—the government and business and cultural elites—but it was familiar to many others who were subordinate to them. And it was not merely an effect but also an instrument of their domination.

The United States of America, then, has always been a society in which people have been centered on a variety of common cultures. Recognizing that we in America are not centered on a national common culture is, as I have said, consistent with recognizing that (with, no doubt, a few exceptions) American citizens do have a common culture. What is interesting and important is that for many Americans that American core—and, in particular, the attachment to the constitutional order and the rights it conveys—is not what centers their lives. They support those institutions, they favor them. Many people have come here precisely because they exist; but still, these values are instrumental in their lives. What they desire centrally, what shapes their lives, is what the American freedoms make possible—your experience in a temple or mosque or church; my life with my family and the cultural riches of New York City or Boston; her search for philosophical understanding; their existence in a lesbian commune. They need America—they will defend it, especially, against foreigners who deplore its materialism or its vulgarity—but it is not at the heart of their dreams.

We have come to a crux: for if this is the situation, shouldn't the cosmopolitan who is an American patriot resent these fellow citizens for whom their country is a mere instrument, a means, not an end? My answer is no. For the French and American revolutions invented a form of patriotism that allows us to love our country as the embodiment of principles, as a means to the attainment of moral ends. It is true that the patriot always values more than what the state makes possible for me and mine, but if among the ideals we honor in America is that the enabling of a certain kind of human freedom, then we cannot, in consistency, enforce attachment either to the state or to the principles. In valuing the autonomous choices of free people, we value what they have chosen *because they have chosen it*: a forced attachment to a fine principle does not diminish the principle, but the force makes the attachment unworthy.

But if force is not the answer there is, of course, another possibility. Why not argue out democratically a common culture on which to center our national life? My first answer is that we do not have to do so. The question presupposes that what we *really* need is shared core values, a centering common culture. I think this is a mistake. What I think we really need is not citizens centered on a common culture but citizens committed to common institutions, to the conditions necessary for a common life. What is required to live together in a nation is a mutual commitment to the organization of the state—the institutions that provide the over-arching order of our common life. But this does not require that we have the *same* commitment to those institutions, in the sense that the institutions must carry the same meaning for all of us.

We live already with examples of this situation so familiar that they are easily forgotten. The First Amendment, for example, separates church and state. Some of us are committed to this because we are religious; we see it as the institutionalization of a Protestant insistence on freedom of conscience or because we are Catholics or Jews or Moslems, we do not want to be pressed into conformity by a Protestant majority. Some of us are atheists who want to be left alone. We can live together with this arrangement provided we all are committed to it for our different reasons.

There is a useful analogy here with much mass culture and other mass-produced goods. People in London and in Lagos, in New York and New Delhi, listen to Michael Jackson and drink Coca-Cola. They exist, in part, as an audience for his work, as consumers of that drink. But nobody thinks that what either of these products means in one place must be identical with what it means in every site of its consumption. Similarly, the institutions of democracy—elections, public debates, the protection of minority rights—have different meanings to different people and groups. Once more, there is no reason to require that we all value them in the same way, for the same reasons. All that is required is that everybody is willing to play the game.

A shared political life in a great modern nation is not like the life of the tribal fantasy. It can encompass a great diversity of meanings. When we teach children democratic habits we are creating a shared commitment to certain forms of social behavior. We can call this a political culture, if we like. But the meanings citizens give to their lives, and to the political within their lives, in particular, will be shaped not only (through the public school) by the state but also by family and church, reading and television, and in their professional and recreational associations. If American political culture is what Americans have in common, it is pretty thin gruel. And, so I am arguing, none the worse for that.

This sanguine conclusion will cause many patriots to object. 'In a world of changing challenges, shared institutions (shared laws, for example) need interpreting to fit new situations (new cases). And in thinking about these new cases, doesn't appeal have to be made to shared values, to substantial principles, even, in the end, to deep metaphysical convictions?[18] If we are to decide, say, whether to permit abortions, this argument suggests, we must decide first whether our shared commitment to the preservation of innocent human life—a commitment some derive from the thought that we are all children of a loving God—applies to the fetus in its first three months. For many—though certainly not for all—Americans, would oppose abortion if it was uncontroversially clear that it was the killing of an innocent human being.[19] Don't our difficulties in discussing this question flow, in part, from precisely the lack of shared values that I am arguing we must accept?

I am not sure that the answer to this last question is yes. I suspect that the difficulties about abortion have at least as much to do with the refusal of those who oppose it to acknowledge how large a part views about the control of women's sexuality—indeed, of sexuality in general—play in shaping the intensity of some of their responses. But this, too, may turn in the end on deep differences about metaphysical and moral questions; so, in the end, I agree that these will sometimes have to be faced.

It is here that the political values of the American republic must come to have some weight of their own: our democratic traditions require us to engage respectfully with our fellow citizens who disagree with us. In this sense, a political culture—the shared commitment to the political institutions of the republic, the content of a common citizenship—is more than an agreement to abide by the Constitution and the laws, by the judgements of courts, by the decisions of democratically elected lawmakers. It also involves a shared—and *evolving*—sense of the customary practices of political engagement in the public sphere.

Now I admit that there are circumstances in which such a sense of common citizenship is unavailable to some. While Jim Crow laws held in the American South, it is hard to see why African Americans should have felt a commitment to the customary practices of the American republic (even if they could and did feel attachment to most of the principles expressed in the Constitution precisely because they were at odds with the practice of Jim Crow.) It is, of course, just *because* citizens are entitled to participation in the political culture of their state that the effective exclusion of blacks from voting was inconsistent with democratic political morality. It follows, I concede, that if the state's actions so repudiate you and if, as a result, you are unable to accept and participate in the political culture in this sense, your fellow citizens cannot expect you to conform to the law.

---

[18] This is an objection Charles Taylor proposed to me in private conversation.

[19] *Innocent* here should presumably be understood, as it is in discussions of just killing in warfare, to mean 'posing no harm' and not 'guiltless'. It seems pretty clear that we can't blame the fetus even if its existence threatens the life or well-being of the woman who bears it.

Here then is a point where defenders of a centering national culture might find a new starting point. Why not admit, they might say, that you must guarantee at least this much: that citizens are trained in (and immigrants taught and required to assent to) the essentials of the political culture? And if that is desirable, will it not best be achieved by centering Americans on a broader common culture: by centering every American on shared values, shared literary references, shared narratives of the American nation?

Once more, to the first question, I answer yes, sure. And to the second I say no. If the political culture carries some weight for us, we will accept the laws and the terms of debate that it entails, and we will struggle within that framework for justice, as each of us understands it. If, as some claim is true of abortion, there are central debates that we cannot resolve within this framework, this is certainly a problem we would not face if every American was brought up with the same metaphysical convictions. But constraining a quarter of a billion American citizens into a life centered on a common culture—cultural Americanism, let us call it—would be too high a price to pay for the dissolution of this conflict. If, after all, the disputes about abortion seem contentious, think how bitter would be the argument if we insisted— as the Bill of Rights wisely insists we should not—on a single religion (or even, more modestly, a single view of family life) to teach all our children.

American citizenship, in other words, does require us to accept the political culture; and, as the case of African Americans shows, it is important that that culture has built into it the possibility of change. But if, as a result of the processes of democracy, laws are passed that are deeply repugnant to you— as is perfectly possible in a society not centered on a strong common culture—you may well reach the point where you consider that you have been, in the phrase I used earlier, repudiated by the state. The price of having no common culture to center our society is that possibility; but the cosmopolitan patriot believes that the creation of a common culture rich enough to exclude this possibility would exact a higher price. This is something that many in the world—Catholic bishops in Ireland, Buddhist politicians in Sri Lanka, ayatollahs in Iran, Communist party members in China—do not believe. They want to live in societies where everyone has a common cultural center, where every political dispute can be resolved because everyone has been constrained to accept a common sense of the meaning of life. The political culture of the American state excludes this vision because it is (in the understanding of the term long forgotten in our public debates) a liberal political culture, one that values individuals and celebrates, with cosmopolitanism, the great variety of what individuals will choose when given freedom.

There must be some who believe the rhetoric about the murder of infants that (in my judgement) pollutes the debate about abortion. For them, perhaps, religious duty transcends the demands of citizenship. But I do not see that one can resolve a disagreement with them by finding a common metaphysics of the person on which to center the next generation of Americans; it is precisely our disagreements about *that* which account for some of the intensity of the debate.

Surely, however, most of those who believe abortion should not be legal do not really think that the abortion of a first-trimester fetus is really *exactly the same* as the killing of a living child. If they did believe that, they would surely not even contemplate exemptions for rape and incest, for even those of us who favor laws allowing choice would not favor a rape-exception for infanticide. Like many who favor choice, I believe, as I say, that some of the intensity of the debate about abortion has to do with attitudes to sexuality and to women that the feminism of the last few decades and the practical successes of the women's movement have challenged. I think this is a fair thing to argue in the debates about choice. But I also think the political culture we have inherited in America requires us to take on their merits the arguments of those who oppose choice, and, where the disagreements flow from fundamentally different visions of the human good, I do not see that it profits us to deny or ignore this fact.

So, unlike many who favor the liberalism of our Constitution and the political culture that surrounds it, I do not favor silence in the public sphere about the religious views that underlie some of our deepest disagreements. Our laws and customs require us not to impose religious ideas on each other; but they also encourage us to debate among equals.

Finally, we should be skeptical, for historical reasons, about the creation of a national culture to center our lives; for us to center ourselves on a national culture, the state would have to take up the cudgels in defining both the content of that culture and the means of its dissemination. I have already argued that this would create deep schisms in our national life. But history suggests an even deeper difficulty. Collective identities have a tendency, if I may coin a phrase, to go imperial, dominating not only people of other identities but the other identities whose shape is exactly what makes each of us what we individually and distinctively are.

In policing this imperialism of identity—an imperialism as visible in national identities as anywhere else—it is crucial to remember always that we are not simply Americans or Ghanaians or Indians or Germans but that we are gay or straight or bisexual, Jewish, Christian, Moslem, Buddhist, Confucian—and also brothers and sisters; parents and children; liberals, conservatives and leftists; teachers and lawyers and auto-makers and gardeners; fans of the Padres and the Bruins; aficionados of grunge rock and amateurs of Wagner; movie-buffs; PBS-aholics, mystery readers; surfers and singers; poets and pet-lovers; students and teachers; friends and lovers. The state makes much possible for all of us and we owe it at least the consistent support to which it is entitled in virtue of those possibilities; it would be a grand irony if the price we paid for the freedom the state creates was to allow it to subject us to new tyrannies.

This is an especially powerful thought here in the United States. For so many have loved America, in part, exactly because it has enabled them to chose who they are and to decide, too, how central America is in their chosen identity. Those of us who are Americans not by birth but by election, and who love this country precisely for *that* freedom of self-invention, should not seek to compel others to an identity we ourselves celebrate because it was freely chosen.

I have been arguing, in essence, that you can be cosmopolitan—celebrating the variety of human cultures; rooted—loyal to one local society (or a few) that you count as home; liberal—convinced of the value of the individual; and patriotic—celebrating the institutions of the state (or states) within which you live. The cosmopolitanism flows from the same sources that nourish the liberalism, for it is the variety of human forms of life that provides the vocabulary of the language of individual choice. And the patriotism flows from the liberalism because the state carves out the space within which we explore the possibilities of freedom. For rooted cosmopolitans, all this is of a single piece.

But I have also been arguing that we do not need to insist that all of our fellow citizens be cosmopolitans, or patriots, or loyal to the nation; we need them only to share the political culture of the state. And sharing that political culture does not require you to be centered on it and certainly doesn't require you to be centered on a culture wider than the political.[20] What *is* essential is only—though this is, in fact, a great deal—that all of us share respect for the political culture of liberalism and the constitutional order it entails.

This formula courts misunderstanding: for the word *liberal* has been both divested of its original content and denied a solid new meaning. So let me remind you again that, for me, the essence of this liberal culture lies in respect for the dignity and autonomy of individual persons.[21] There is much to be said about the meaning of autonomy and of dignity; there is much to be said too, about how, in practice, individuals are to live with other values, political and not, that we cherish. This is not the place for that exploration.

---

[20] I think that in the United States that grasp of the political culture probably requires knowing (some) English. But since English, like the rest of the political culture, needn't center your life, speaking and even loving other languages is consistent with participating in the political culture.

[21] Despite recent communitarian arguments to the contrary, I do not think that the liberal respect for autonomy is inconsistent with recognizing the role of society in creating the options in respect to which free individuals exercise their freedom. As Taylor has argued so powerfully, it is in dialogue with other people's understandings of who I am that I develop a conception of my own identity; and my identity is crucially constituted through concepts and practices made available to me by religion, society, school, and state and mediated to varying degrees by the family. But all of this can, in my view, be accepted by someone who sees autonomy as a central value. See my "Identity, Authenticity, Survival: Multicultural Societies and Social Reproduction", in Amy Gutmann (ed.), *Multiculturalism: Examining 'The Politics of Recognition'* (Princeton, NJ, 1994) pp. 149–63.

But let me say one thing: since I believe that the state can be an instrument for autonomy I do not share the current distaste for the state that drives much of what in America is now called conservatism; and so I am often a liberal in the more colloquial sense as well.

The point, in sum, is this: it is important that citizens should share a political culture; it is not important (in America, without massive coercion, it is not even possible) that the political culture be important to all citizens, let alone that it matter to all of them in the same way. (Indeed, one of the great freedoms that a civilized society provides is the freedom *not* to preoccupy yourself with the political.) Only politicians and political theorists are likely to think the best state is one where every citizen is a politician (and when Western theorists think this, it may be because they are overinfluenced by the view of politics taken by some in the small self-governing town of Athens in the fifth century B.C.E.).

Not being political is not the same as being unsociable (though that is something we should be legally free to be also!). Many people express concern for their communities by acting through churches and charities, and, as observers of American since Tocqueville have pointed out, this is a distinctively American tradition. Part of what makes this tradition attractive is that it reflects elective affinities rather than state-imposed obligation.

You will notice, now, that I have been arguing for a form of state and of society that is pretty close to the model of a multicultural liberal democracy; and, you may ask, Where now is your much-vaunted cosmopolitanism? After all, the world is full of people—Chinese party leaders, Hindu nationalists, British Tories—who insist precisely on centering all citizens on a single culture that extends beyond the narrowly political. Do I not want to make allowances for this option, too?

When I first thought about this question, I was tempted to bite the bullet and say yes. But I didn't believe it; and I now understand why I must answer no. Cosmopolitanism values human variety for what it makes possible for free individuals, and some kinds of cultural variety constrain more than they enable. In other words, the cosmopolitan's high appraisal of variety flows from the human choices it enables, but variety is not something we value no matter what.[22] There are other values. You can have an enormous amount of diversity between societies, even if they are all, in some sense, democratic.[23] But the fundamental idea that every society should respect human dignity and personal autonomy is more basic than the cosmopolitan love of variety; indeed, as I say, it is the autonomy that variety enables that is the fundamental argument for cosmopolitanism.

---

[22] This is one reason why I think it is not helpful to see cosmopolitanism as expressing an aesthetic ideal.

[23] There is no reason to think that every society needs to implement the idea of popular choice in the same way; so different democratic institutions in different societies are consistent with the basic respect for autonomy, too.

A society could in theory come to be centered on a single set of values without coercion. I might be skeptical about the virtues of such a homogenized society as a place for myself to live (even if the culture it was centered on was in some sense mine). I would think it might risk many cultural and economic and moral perils, because it might require in the end a kind of closing oneself off from the rest of the world. But those in such a society would no doubt have things to say in response—or might refuse to discuss the matter with me at all—and, in the end, they might well find their considerations more weighty than mine. Freely chosen homogeneity, then, raises no problems for me; in the end, I would say, good luck to them. But what British Tories and Hindu chauvinists and Maoist party bosses want is not a society that chooses to be uniform, but the imposition of uniformity. That the cosmopolitan patriot must oppose.

One final corollary of the grounding of cosmopolitanism in individual freedom is worth insisting on. Cosmopolitans value cultural variety, but we do not ask other people to maintain the diversity of the species at the price of their individual autonomy. We can't require others to provide us with a cultural museum to tour through or to visit on satellite television's endless virtual safari; nor can we demand an assortment of Shangri-Las to enlarge the range of our own options for identity. The options we need in order for our choices to be substantial must be freely sustained, as must the human variety whose existence is, for the cosmopolitan, an endless source of insight and pleasure. But, as I said at the start, there is no ground for thinking that people are rushing toward homogeneity, and, in fact, in a world more respectful of human dignity and personal autonomy such movement towards homogeneity as there is would probably slow down.

Skepticism about the genuinely cosmopolitan character of the view I have been defending may flow in part from the thought that it seems so much a creature of Europe and its Enlightenment.[24] So it may be as well to insist in closing, as I did at the start, that my own attachment to these ideas comes, as much as anything, from my father, who grew up in Asante, at a time when the independence of its moral climate from that of European Enlightenment was extremely obvious. Of course, he also went on to live in London for many years and acquired there the training of an English lawyer; and, of course, the school he went to in Ghana was a Methodist school, a colonial variant of the English boys' public school, where he was taught to think morally through Cicero and Caesar as much as through the New Testament. It would be preposterous to claim, in short, that he came to

---

[24] I should explicitly record my opposition to the view that this origin in any way discredits these ideas, either for non-Europeans or, for that matter, for Europeans. The issues I want to explore have to do with the ways in which these views can be rooted in different traditions. I am not interested in the nativist project of arguing for these principles in the name of authentically Asante (or African) roots. The issues raised in the following paragraphs are thus historical, not normative.

his cosmopolitanism or his patriotism or his faith in human rights and the rule of law unaffected by European cultural traditions.

But it would be equally fatuous to deny that the view he arrived at had roots in Asante (indeed, as one travels the world, reviewing the liberal nationalisms of South Asia and Africa in the midcentury, one is struck not only by their similarities but also by their local inflections). Two things, in particular, strike me about the local character of the source of my father's increasing commitment to individual rights: first, that it grew out of experience of illiberal government; second, that it depended on a sense of his own dignity and the dignity of his fellow citizens that was almost entirely the product of Asante conceptions.

The first point—about experience—is crucial to the case for liberalism. It is the historical experience of the dangers of intolerance—religious intolerance in Europe in the seventeenth century, for example, for Locke; racial intolerance in the colonial context, for Gandhi (or for my father)—that often lies behind the skepticism about the state's interventions in the lives of individuals that itself underlies much liberal sentiment. My father saw the colonial state's abuses of his fellows and, in particular, the refusal to pay them the respect that was their due; he was imprisoned, later, by Kwame Nkrumah, without trial (and then released after a year and a half in detention with as little explanation as when he was arrested). As a lawyer and a member of the opposition, he travelled Ghana in the years after independence defending people whose rights were being abused by the postcolonial state.

The political tradition of liberalism is rooted in these experiences of illiberal government. That liberal restraint on government recommends itself to people rooted in so many different traditions is a reflection of its grasp of a truth about human beings and about modern politics.

Just as the centrality of murderous religious warfare in the period leading up to Locke's *Treatises* placed religious toleration at the core of Locke's understanding of the liberalism he defended, so the prime place of the persecution of political dissenters in the postcolonial experience of tyranny made protection of political dissent central to my father's liberalism.[25] (My father worried little about the state's entanglement with religion; once, I remember, as the national television came to the end of its broadcast day, my father sang along with the national hymn that they played some evenings, the religious twin of the more secular national anthem that they played on others. 'This would be a much better national anthem', he said to me. And I replied, ever the good liberal, 'But the anthem has the advantage that you

---

[25] Such historical context is important, I think, because, as Michael Oakeshott once observed, political education should instil in us 'a knowledge as profound as we can make it, of our tradition of political behaviour' (Michael Oakeshott, "Political Education", in *'Rationalism in Politics' and Other Essays* [New York, 1962], p. 128). We might say: liberal institutions are to be recommended, in part, as a practical response to the circumstances of modern political life.

don't have to believe in God to sing it sincerely'. 'No one in Ghana is silly enough not to believe in God', my father replied.[26] And, now, I think he was right not to be worried about the entanglement; there is no history of religious intolerance in Ghana of the sort that makes necessary the separation of church and state; a genial ecumenism had been the norm at least until the arrival of American TV evangelism.)

But more important yet, I think, to my father's concern with individual human dignity was its roots in the preoccupation of free Asante citizens— both men and women with notions of personal dignity, with respect and self-respect. Treating others with the respect that is their due is a central preoccupation of Asante social life, as is a reciprocal anxiety about loss of respect, shame, disgrace.[27] Just as European liberalism—and democratic sentiment—grew by extending to every man and (then) woman, the dignity that feudal society offered only to the aristocracy, and thus presupposes, in some sense, aspects of that feudal understanding of dignity, so Ghanaian liberalism—at least in my father's form—depends on the prior grasp of concepts such as *animuonyam* (respect). It is clear from well-known Akan proverbs that respect was precisely not something that belonged in the past to everybody: *Agya Kra ne Agya Kwakyer∈m∈, emu biara mu nni animuonyam* (Father Soul and Father Slave Kyer∈m∈, neither of them has any respect; that is, whatever you call him, a slave is still a slave.) But just as *dignitas*, which was once, by definition, the property of an elite, has grown into human dignity, which is the property of every man and woman, so *animuonyam* can be the basis of the respect for all others that lies at the heart of liberalism.[28] Indeed, *dignitas* and *animuonyam* have a great deal in common. *Dignitas*, as understood by Cicero, reflects much that was similar between republican Roman ideology and the views of the nineteenth-century Asante elite: it was, I think, as an Asante that my father recognized and admired Cicero, not as a British subject.

'In the course of my life I have seen Frenchmen, Italians, Russians etc.; I even know, thanks to Montesquieu, that one can be Persian; but *man* I have never met'.[29] So wrote Joseph de Maistre—no friend to liberalism—in his

---

[26] My father's thought clearly wasn't so much that there aren't any atheists in Ghana but that their views don't matter. Locke, of course, agreed: 'Those are not at all to be tolerated who deny the being of a God. Promises, covenants, and oaths, which are the bonds of human society, can have no hold upon an atheist. The taking away of God, though but even in thought, dissolves all.' (John Locke, "A Letter Concerning Toleration", *Political Writings of John Locke* , ed. David Wootton [New York, 1993], p. 426).

[27] There are scores of proverbs on this theme in *Bu Me B∈: The Proverbs of the Akan*, the more than seven thousand Akan proverbs that Peggy Appiah, my mother, will be publishing with my assistance, in 2000.

[28] The European history is taken up in Taylor, *Sources of the Self: the Making of the Modern Identity* (Cambridge, Mass, 1989).

[29] Joseph de Maistre, *Considérations sur la France*, 3d ed. (1797; Paris, 1821), pp. 102–3: 'J'ai vu, dans ma vie, des François, des Italiens, des Russes, etc.; je sais même, graces à Montesquieu, qu'on peut être Persan: mais quant à *l'homme*, je déclare ne l'avoir recontré de ma vie'.

Considérations sur la France. It is a thought that can, ironically, be made consistent with a liberal cosmopolitanism; a thought that may even lead us to the view that cosmopolitanism is, in certain ways, inconsistent with one form of humanism. For a certain sort of humanist says that nothing human is alien; and we could gloss this as saying that the humanist respects each human being *as* a human being. Maistre is suggesting that we never really come to terms with anybody as a human because each actual person we meet, we meet as a French person, or as a Persian; in short, as a person with an identity far more specific than fellow human.[30] Exactly, the cosmopolitan says. And a good thing too. But we do not have to deal decently with people from other cultures and traditions *in spite of* our differences; we can treat others decently, humanely, *through* our differences. The humanist requires us to put our differences aside; the cosmopolitan insists that sometimes it is the differences we bring to the table that make it rewarding to interact at all. That is, of course, to concede that what we share can be important, too; though the cosmopolitan will remind us that what we share with others is not always an ethnonational culture: sometimes it will just be that you and I—a Peruvian and a Slovak—both like to fish, or have read and admired Goethe in translation, or responded with the same sense of wonder to a postcard of the Parthenon, or believe, as lawyers with very different trainings, in the ideal of the rule of law.

That is, so to speak, the anglophone voice of cosmopolitanism. But, in the cosmopolitan spirit, let me end with a similar thought from my father's, no doubt less familiar, tradition: *Kuro korü mu nni nyansa*, our proverb says: In a single *polis* there is no wisdom. [31]

---

[30] If you communicate on the Internet, think about how difficult it is not to imagine your email correspondents (who present, after all, only strings of unspoken words) as having, for example, a specific race, gender, and age.

[31] *Kuro* is usually translated as *town*, but towns were relatively self-governing in the Asante past, so *polis* seems a translation that gets the right sense.

Contributors

J. 'Bayo Adekanye is a Professor and the Head of the Department of Political Science, the Director of the Strategic Studies Programme, and coordinator of the Centre for Peace and Conflict Studies, University of Ibadan, Nigeria. Previous appointments: Research Fellow and Programme Leader, Ethnic and Nationalist Conflicts Programme, the International Peace Research Institute, Oslo (PRIO), Norway, May 1994–September 1997. His most recent book is *The Retired Military As Emergent Power Factor in Nigeria*. Areas of current research interests are early-warning and conflict prevention, post-conflict peacebuilding in multi-ethnic societies.

Omar Ahmad was a practising physician from 1982 to1996. He obtained a doctoral degree from the Johns Hopkins School of Hygiene and Public Health, Baltimore, in 1993. Research coordinator for the Healthy Start Project, Baltimore City Health Department, 1993–1994. Research Fellow with the Demographic and Health Survey in Baltimore 1994–1996. Senior Lecturer in Biostatistics and Research Methods, University of Ghana, Legon, 1996–1999. Currently a Senior Global Health Leadership Fellow in the Division of Epidemiology and Burden of Disease, the World Health Organization, Geneva.

Kwame Anthony Appiah is Professor of Afro-American Studies and Philosophy at Harvard University and author of *In My Father's House: Africa in the Philosophy of Culture* (1992). *Color Conscious,* a pair of essays on race and public policy by Professor Appiah and Professor Amy Gutmann, has just been published by Princeton University Press. Professor Appiah is an editor of *Transition*.

Samantha Gibson will be completing her PhD in Social and Political Sciences at the University of Cambridge in 1999. She will then serve as a human rights and social development adviser in Zambia with the UK Department for International Development.

Mary Kaldor is Director of the Global Civil Society Programme, Centre for the Study of Global Governance at the London School of Economics and author of New and Old Wars: Organised Violence in a Global Era (Polity Press 1999).

Stephan Klasen is Professor of Economics at the University of Munich. His research focuses on development economics, with particular emphasis on southern Africa. Previously, he was a Fellow of King's College and Associate Director of the Centre for History and Economics. He holds a PhD in economics from Harvard University and worked for the World Bank in South Africa from 1994 to 1996.

Rama Mani is currently the Doris Woodall Scholar at Girton College, University of Cambridge. She will complete her PhD thesis on post-conflict peacebuilding in 1999. From 1992 to 1995 she served as the Senior External Relations Officer for the Commission on Global Governance in Geneva, working closely in this capacity with leaders around the world in the NGO community, the UN system, governments and academia. As a Thomas J. Watson Fellow in 1989–90, she worked in Algeria and France on immigration issues in collaboration with government, quasi/non-governmental and academic agencies.

Thandika Mkandawire is the Director of the United Nations Institute of Social Development (UNRISD) based in Geneva. He is former Executive Secretary of the Council for the Development of Social Science in Africa (CODESRIA), Dakar, Senegal. More recently he was visiting Research Fellow at the Centre for Development Research in

Copenhagen, Denmark. In 1996 he was awarded the distinguished 50th Anniversary Fulbright Fellowship. He has published extensively on the political economy of adjustment and is currently working on problems of economic policy-making and democratisation in Africa. He studied at Ohio State University and Stockholm University. He has taught at Stockholm University and the University of Zimbabwe.

Patrick Molutsi is currently the Dean of the Faculty of Social Sciences at the University of Botswana. He was formerly the Co-ordinator of the University of Botswana based Democracy Research Project from 1989 to 1993 and was actively involved in the writing of the SADC Governance and Human Development in Southern Africa in 1998. Molutsi who obtained his academic qualifications from the universities of Botswana and Swaziland, Legon, Ghana and Oxford has published widely in the area of democracy and governance, democratisation, the state, civil society, human development and trade unionism in Botswana and Southern Africa.

William Pick is a Professor and the Head of the Department of Community Health at the University of the Witwatersrand, South Africa, a Fellow of the Royal Society of Medicine, a Fellow of the Royal Society of Tropical Medicine and Hygiene, a Chairman of the National Committee on Human Resources for Health Care in South Africa, a Member of the Board of the Medical Research Council of South Africa and a Member of the Health Professions Council of South Africa.

Emma Rothschild is Director of the Centre for History and Economics at King's College, Cambridge, England, and a Distinguished Fellow at the Center for Population and Development Studies at Harvard University. From 1978 to 1988, she was Associate Professor of Humanities, and of Science, Technology and Society at MIT. From 1981 to 1982, she was Directeur de Recherches Invité at the Ecole des Hautes Etudes en Sciences Sociales, Paris. She is Chairman of the United Nations Research Institute for Social Development, a member of the United Kingdom government's Council on Science and Technology, and a member of the Board of the United Nations Foundation. She has written extensively on economic history and the history of economic thought, in the *Economic History Review*, the *Economic Journal*, the *Historical Journal*, *Population and Development Review* and other journals.

Siemon Wezeman studied Contemporary History at the State University in Groningen, finishing his MA in 1989. He has worked with the SIPRI Arms Transfers Project since 1992 as research assistant and since 1998 as researcher. His main work at SIPRI includes updating the database on arms transfers, his main areas of expertise are the use of weapons in conflicts, Asia and transparency in arms transfers (UN Register, etc). Among his publications are the regular chapters on arms trade and transfers in the SIPRI Yearbook, as well as other books and articles on arms transfers and the UN Register.

Lennart Wohlgemuth has been the director of the Nordic Africa Institute since 1993. Prior to this he worked for many years for Sida, most recently as Assistant Director General and Head of the Sector Department. Between 1981 and 1987 he headed Sida's educational division and since 1989 he has been a board member and from 1993 Chairman of the International Institute for Educational Planning (IIEP).

Fani Zulu is the Director for Communications of the South African Revenue Service. Previously, he worked for the World Bank Resident Mission in South Africa. He held several positions at the World Bank, including working as NGO liaison, media liaison, librarian, and information officer.

Authors' contact details

Bayo Adekanye
Department of Political Science
University of Ibadan, Nigeria
Tel/fax: +234 2 810 1618 (home)
Tel: +234 2 810 1526 (work)
E-mail: adekanye@ibadan.skannet.com.ng

Omar Ahmad
Epidemiology & Burden of Disease Unit
(Evidence & Information for Health Policy
Global Program on Evidence for Health Policy)
World Health Organization
20 Avenue Appia
CH-1211 Geneva 27, Switzerland
Voice: +41 22 791 3256
Fax: +41 22 791 4328
E-mail: ahmado@who.ch

Kwame Anthony Appiah
Afro-American Studies
Harvard University
Barker Center, 2nd Floor
12 Quincy Street
Cambridge, MA 02138, USA
Tel: +1 617 495 4113
Fax: +1 617 496 2871
E-mail: appiah@fas.harvard.edu

Samantha Gibson
Faculty of Social and Political Sciences
University of Cambridge
Free School Lane
Cambridge CB2 3RQ, UK
Tel: +44 1223 334535
Fax: +44 1223 334550
E-mail: sfg1001@cus.cam.ac.uk

Mary Kaldor
Centre for Study of Global Governance
London School of Economics
Houghton Street
London WC2A 2AE, UK
Tel: +44 171 955 6643
Fax: +44 171 955 7591
E-mail: m.h.kaldor@lse.ac.uk

Stephan Klasen
Department of Economics
University of Munich
Ludwigstrasse 28
80539 Munich, Germany
Tel: +49 89 2180 2459
Fax: +49 89 2180 3954
E-mail: klasen@lrz.uni-muenchen.de

Rama Mani
Faculty of Social and Political Sciences
University of Cambridge
8-9 Jesus Lane
Cambridge CB5 8BA, UK
Tel: +44 1223 312809
Tel: +44 1223 740071
Fax: +44 1223 740079
E-mail: rm237@hermes.cam.ac.uk

Thandika Mkandawire
United Nations Research Institute
for Social Development (UNRISD)
Palais des Nations
CH-1211 Geneva 10, Switzerland
Tel: +41 22 917 2927
Fax: +41 22 917 0650
E-mail: mkandawire@unrisd.org

Patrick Molutsi
Department of Sociology
University of Botswana
Private Bag 0022
Gaborone, Botswana
Tel: +267 355 0000
Fax: +267 355 2543
E-mail: molutsip@noka.ub.bw

William Pick
Department of Community Health
Medical School
University of the Witwatersrand
7 York Road
Parktown 2193, South Africa
Tel: +27 11 647 2051
Fax: +27 11 649 2084
E-mail: 081pick@chiron.wits.ac.za
pickwm@icon.co.za

Emma Rothschild
Centre for History and Economics
King's College
Cambridge CB2 1ST
Tel: +44 1223 331197
Fax: +44 1223 331198
E-mail: amp32@hermes.cam.ac.uk

Siemon Wezeman
Arms Transfer Project
SIPRI
Signalistgatan 9
SE – 169 70 Solna, Sweden
Tel: +46 8 655 9750
Fax: +46 8 655 9733
E-mail: swezeman@sipri.se

Lennart Wohlgemuth
Nordiska Afrikainstitutet
(The Nordic Africa Institute)
P O Box 1703
S-751 47 Uppsala, Sweden
Tel: +46 18 56 22 00
Fax: +46 18 56 22 90
E-mail: lennart.wohlgemuth@nai.uu.se

Fani Zulu
South African Revenue Service
299 Bronkhorst Street
Nieuw Muckleneuk
Pretoria 0181, South Africa
Tel: +27 12 422 4000
Fax: +27 12 422 5180
E-mail: fzulu@sars.gov.za

of participants

Geert Andersen
Ministry for Foreign Affairs
2 Asiatisk Plads
DK-1448 Copenhagen, Denmark

J. Bayo Adekanye
Department of Social Science
Faculty of Social Sciences
University of Ibadan
Ibadan, Nigeria

Omar Ahmad
Epidemiology & Burden of DiseaSE-Unit
World Health Organization
20 Avenue Appia
CH-1211 Geneva 27, Switzerland

Gun-Britt Andersson
Ministry for Foreign Affairs
Box 16121
SE-103 23 Stockholm, Sweden

K. Anthony Appiah
Afro-American Studies
Harvard University
Barker Center, 2nd Floor
12 Quincy Street
Cambridge MA 02138, USA

Tendai Biti
Honey and Blackenberg
5th Floor, Throgmorton House
51 Samora Machel
Harare, Zimbabwe

Anders Bjurner
Ministry for Foreign Affairs
Box 16121
SE-l03 23 Stockholm, Sweden

Jan Cedergren
Ministry for Foreign Affairs
Box 16121
SE-103 23 Stockholm, Sweden

Lincoln Chen
Rockefeller Foundation
420 Fifth Avenue
New York NY 10018-2702, USA

Catherine Cissé
War Crimes Tribunal
PO Box 13888
NL-2501, EW The Hague, Netherlands

Jean A.P. Clement
International Monetary Fund
700 19th Street NW
Washington DC 20431, USA

Nii Ayite Coleman
Health Research Unit,
Ministry of Health
PO Box M332
Accra, Ghana

Yusuke Dan
SPIRIT,Tokai University
2-28-4 Tomigaya, Shibuya-ku
Tokyo 151, Japan

Tom Eriksen
Ministry for Foreign Affairs
Postboks 8114 Pet
NO-0032 Oslo, Norway

Samantha Gibson
Faculty of Social and Political Sciences
Free School Lane
Cambridge CB2 3RQ, UK

John Grimond
The Economist
25 St. James's Street
London SW1A 1HG, UK

Aslaug Haga
Ministry for Foreign Affairs
Postboks 8114 Pet
NO-0032 Oslo, Norway

Karin Höglund
Ministry for Foreign Affairs
Box 16121
SE-103 23 Stockholm, Sweden

Uwe Holtz
Department of Political Science
University of Bonn
In der Wehrhecke 23
DE-53125 Bonn, Germany

Eboe Hutchful
Department of African Studies
Wayne State University
Detroit, Michigan, USA

Ruth Iyob
Department of Political Science
University of Missouri in St. Louis
St. Louis, Missouri, USA

Ruth Jacoby
Ministry for Foreign Affairs
Box 16121
SE-103 23 Stockholm, Sweden

Mary Kaldor
Centre for the Study of Global Governance
London School of Economics
Houghton Street
London WC2A 2AE, UK

Mats Karlsson
Ministry for Foreign Affairs
International Development Cooperation
SE-103 39 Stockholm, Sweden

Stephan Klasen
University of Munich
Ludwigstrafle 28
DE-80539 Munich, Germany

Melissa Lane
King's College
Cambridge CB21ST, UK

Anthony Lewis
The New York Times
2 Faneuil Hall
Market Place
Boston MA 02109, USA

Kirsti Lintonen
Finnish Ministry for Foreign Affairs
PL 176
FI-00161 Helsinki, Finland

Callisto Madavo
The World Bank
Washington DC 20433, USA

Rama Mani
OXFAM
PO Box 2333
Addis Ababa, Ethiopia

Reginald Matchaba-Hove
Department of Community Medicine
Medical School
University of Zimbabwe
PO Box A 178, Avondale
Harare, Zimbabwe

Thandika Mkandawire
United Nations Research Institute for
Social Development (UNRISD)
Palais des Nations
CH-1211 Geneva 10, Switzerland

Patrick Molutsi
Department of Sociology
University of Botswana
Private Bag 0022
Gaborone, Botswana

Eeva-Liisa Myllymäki
Ministry for Foreign Affairs
PO Box 176
FI-00161 Helsinki, Finland

Alastair Newton
Economic Relations
Foreign and Commonwealth Office
King Charles Street
London SW1A 2AH, UK

Thandeka Nkiwane
School of Advanced International Studies
Johns Hopkins University
1740 Massachusetts Avenue, N.W.
Washington DC 20036-1984, USA

Carin Norberg
Swedish International Development
Agency
SE-105 25 Stockholm, Sweden

Adebayo Olukoshi
Nordic Africa Institute
PO Box 1703
SE-751 47 Uppsala, Sweden

Olara Otunnu
Secretary Generalís Special Representative on
Children and Armed Conflict
UN Headquarters
New York NY 10017, USA

Alassane Ouattara
International Monetary Fund
700 19th Street N.W
Washington DC 20431, USA

Ahmedou Ould-Abdallah
Global Coalition for Africa
1750 Pennsylvania Avenue, NW
Suite 1204
Washington DC 20006, USA

Joakim Palme
Swedish Institute for Social Research
SE-106 91 Stockholm, Sweden

Lisbet Palme
Swedish Committee for Unicef
Box 222 23
SE-104 22 Stockholm, Sweden

Asha Patel
17 Crumpsall Street
Abbeywood
London SE2 0LP, UK

William Pick
Department of Community Health
University of Witwatersrand
7 York Road
Parktown 2193, South Africa

Daniel Rotfeld
SIPRI
Frösunda
SE-169 70 Solna, Sweden

Emma Rothschild
Centre for History and Economics
King's College
Cambridge CB2 1ST, UK

Sten Rylander
Swedish International Development Agency
SE-105 25 Stockholm, Sweden

Bengt Säve-Söderbergh
International IDEA
Strömsborg
SE-103 34 Stockholm, Sweden

Pierre Schori
Ministry for Foreign Affairs
Box 161 21
SE-103 23 Stockholm, Sweden

Sandro Scocco
Ministry of Education
SE-103 33 Stockholm, Sweden

Leni Silverstein
The MacArthur Foundation
140 South Dearborn Street
Suite 1100
Chicago IL 606-3-5285, USA

ιvιeena Singh
Centre for History and Economics
King's College
Cambridge CB2 1ST, UK

Noala Skinner
UNICEF Regional Office for Europe
Palais des Nations
CH-1211-Geneva 10, Switzerland

Filomena Steady
922 University Bay Drive
Madison WI 53705, USA

Carl Tham
The Ministry of Education
SE-103 33 Stockholm, Sweden

Peter Wallensteen
Department of Peace and Conflict Research
Box 514
SE-751 20 Uppsala, Sweden

Peter Weiderud
Ministry for Foreign Affairs
Box 16121
SE-103 23 Stockholm, Sweden

Siemon Wezeman
SIPRI
Signalistgatan 9
SE-169 70 Solna, Sweden

Michaela Wilhelmsson
Ministry for Foreign Affairs
Box 16121
SE-103 23 Stockholm, Sweden

Lennart Wohlgemuth
Nordic Africa Institute
PO Box 1703
SE-751 47 Uppsala, Sweden

Kiyoshi Yamada
Tokai Pacific Center
Honolulu
Hawaii, USA

Fani Zulu
South African Revenue Service
299 Bronkhorst Street
Nieuw Muckleneuk
Pretoria 0181, South Africa

Kajsa Övergaard
Nordic Africa Institute
PO Box 1703
SE-751 47 Uppsala, Sweden